Quod scriptura, non iubet vetat

The Latin translates, "What is not commanded in scripture, is forbidden:'

On the Cover: Baptists rejoice to hold in common with other evangelicals the main principles of the orthodox Christian faith. However, there are points of difference and these differences are significant. In fact, because these differences arise out of God's revealed will, they are of vital importance. Hence, the barriers of separation between Baptists and others can hardly be considered a trifling matter. To suppose that Baptists are kept apart solely by their views on Baptism or the Lord's Supper is a regrettable misunderstanding. Baptists hold views which distinguish them from Catholics, Congregationalists, Episcopalians, Lutherans, Methodists, Pentecostals, and Presbyterians, and the differences are so great as not only to justify, but to demand, the separate denominational existence of Baptists. Some people think Baptists ought not teach and emphasize their differences but as E.J. Forrester stated in 1893, "Any denomination that has views which justify its separate existence, is bound to promulgate those views. If those views are of sufficient importance to justify a separate existence, they are important enough to create a duty for their promulgation ... the very same reasons which justify the separate existence of any denomination make it the duty of that denomination to teach the distinctive doctrines upon which its separate existence rests." If Baptists have a right to a separate denominational life, it is their duty to propagate their distinctive principles, without which their separate life cannot be justified or maintained.

Many among today's professing Baptists have an agenda to revise the Baptist distinctives and redefine what it means to be a Baptist. Others don't understand why it even matters. The books being reproduced in the *Baptist Distinctives Series* are republished in order that Baptists from the past may state, explain and defend the primary Baptist distinctives as they understood them. It is hoped that this Series will provide a more thorough historical perspective on what it means to be distinctively Baptist.

The Lord Jesus Christ asked, *"And why call ye me, Lord, Lord, and do not the things which I say?"* (Luke 6:46). The immediate context surrounding this question explains what it means to be a true disciple of Christ. Addressing the same issue, Christ's question is meant to show that a confession of discipleship to the Lord Jesus Christ is inconsistent and untrue if it is not accompanied with a corresponding submission to His authoritative commands. Christ's question teaches us that a true recognition of His authority as Lord inevitably includes a submission to the authority of His Word. Hence, with this question Christ has made it forever impossible to separate His authority as King from the authority of His Word. These two principles—the authority of Christ as King and the authority of His Word—are the two most fundamental Baptist distinctives. The first gives rise to the second and out of these two all the other Baptist distinctives emanate. As F.M. lams wrote in 1894, "Loyalty to Christ as King, manifesting itself in a constant and unswerving obedience to His will as revealed in His written Word, is the real source of all the Baptist distinctives:' In the search for the *primary* Baptist distinctive many have settled on the Lordship of Christ as the most basic distinctive. Strangely, in doing this, some have attempted to separate Christ's Lordship from the authority of Scripture, as if you could embrace Christ's authority without submitting to what He commanded. However, while Christ's Lordship and Kingly authority can be isolated and considered essentially for discussion's sake, we see from Christ's own words in Luke 6:46 that His Lordship is really inseparable from His Word and, with regard to real Christian discipleship, there can be no practical submission to the one without a practical submission to the other.

In the symbol above the Kingly Crown and the Open Bible represent the inseparable truths of Christ's Kingly and Biblical authority. The Crown and Bible graphics are supplemented by three Bible verses (Ecclesiastes 8:4, Matthew 28:18-20, and Luke 6:46) that reiterate and reinforce the inextricable connection between the authority of Christ as King and the authority of His Word. The truths symbolized by these components are further emphasized by the Latin quotation - *quod scriptura, non iubet vetat*— i.e., "What is not commanded in scripture, is forbidden:' This Latin quote has been considered historically as a summary statement of the regulative principle of Scripture. Together these various symbolic components converge to exhibit the two most foundational Baptist Distinctives out of which all the other Baptist Distinctives arise. Consequently, we have chosen this composite symbol as a logo to represent the primary truths set forth in the *Baptist Distinctives Series*.

THE
TERMS OF COMMUNION
AT
THE LORD'S TABLE

R. B. C. HOWELL
(ROBERT BOYTE CRAWFORD)
1801-1868

THE
TERMS OF COMMUNION
AT
THE LORD'S TABLE

by

R. B. C. HOWELL

With a Biographical Sketch of the Author by John Franklin Jones

"Now I praise you, brethren, that ye remember me in all things, and keep the ordinances as I delivered them unto you." (I Corinthians 11:2)

Philadelphia, PA
The American Baptist Publication Society
1846

he Baptist Standard Bearer, Inc.
NUMBER ONE IRON OAKS DRIVE • PARIS, ARKANSAS 72855

Thou hast given a *standard* to them that fear thee;
that it may be displayed because of the truth.
— Psalm 60:4

Reprinted 2006

by

THE BAPTIST STANDARD BEARER, INC.
No. 1 Iron Oaks Drive
Paris, Arkansas 72855
(479) 963-3831

THE WALDENSIAN EMBLEM
lux lucet in tenebris
"The Light Shineth in the Darkness"

ISBN# 1579785050

TO THE

BAPTIST CONVENTION

OF THE

STATE OF TENNESSEE

By whose solicitation the work was undertaken, this little volume is most respectfully inscribed. If the efforts of the writer to illustrate the law of God, and the duty of Christians, in regard to SACRAMENTAL COMMUNION, shall be so fortunate as to merit the regard, and receive the approbation, of a body so learned in the Scriptures, and so well qualified to determine "what is truth," the recollection of his success will ever prove a rich reward to

Their fellow labourer in the Gospel,

And devoted brother in Christ,

THE AUTHOR.

PREFACE TO THE SECOND EDITION.

This little work has attained a popularity unanticipated by the author. Its wide circulation in this country, and its republication in England, he regards as the best testimonials of its usefulness. He has attempted some improvements in this edition, which he flatters himself will be acceptable to his readers. What they are, will be seen by those who may look over its pages. He again sends it forth, with his sincere prayer to God for his blessing upon this effort to defend and sustain the truth.

Nashville, Tennessee

February 3, 1846

CONTENTS.

Sacramental Communion has not been sufficiently considered—Who has written, and what—Why I write—We deplore the controversy—What part of the subject I have discussed—The internal controversy—Why the Church has always been unpopular—Misrepresentations—The argumentum ad hominum—Communion now the strong point of attack upon us—Spirit in which I shall conduct the discussion—We ask only to be candidly heard in our own defence.

CHAPTER I.

ARE WE AT LIBERTY TO ADOPT ANY TERMS OF COMMUNION NOT ESTABLISHED BY JESUS CHRIST? - - 21

Definition of Communion—General object—Several opinions on this question—Our own position defined—Nature of positive laws—Scripture proofs of our doctrines—Conclusions—Their general application—Their particular application—Powers of a Church—Church representatives—Rights of individuals—Error of New Test men—Consequences of violating the principles advocated—Conclusion.

CHAPTER II.

THE SCRIPTURAL TERMS OF COMMUNION AT THE LORD'S TABLE STATED AND PROVED, - - 35

Repentance, faith, and baptism are terms of communion—English authors—Hudson River Association Circular—The apostolic commission is the law of communion—The order of the sacraments—Their order in the primitive Churches—Emblematical representations—Inspired injunctions regarding the perpetuity of primitive order—By whom the sacraments are to be administered—How received—Conclusion.

CHAPTER III.

THE HISTORY OF OPINION REGARDING THE TERMS OF COMMUNION SHOWS THAT OUR DOCTRINE HAS BEEN UNIVERSALLY EMBRACED ON THE SUBJECT, - - 51

Baptism has been held in all ages, and by all denominations, to be a divinely prescribed preliminary to the Lord's supper—Dr. Priestley's opinions—Testimonies in proof, Justin Martyr, Jerome, Austin, Bede, Theophylact, Bonaventure, Frid. Spanheim, Lord Chancellor King, Austin's rule—Modern divines—Wall, Doddridge, Manton, Dwight, all the Catechisms and Confessions of Faith—Robert Hall.

CHAPTER IV.

REPLY TO SUCH OBJECTIONS TO OUR DOCTRINES ON THIS SUBJECT AS ARE DERIVED FROM THE PRESUMED NATURE OF JOHN'S BAPTISM, - - - 58

Opinions of Mr. Hall, that John's was not Christian baptism, and therefore that the original communicants had never been baptized—His own reasons refute his conclusions—Contrast of John's with Christ's baptism—Their respective formularies—Christ's desire to conceal his own character—If, on account of the objects designed to be represented, John's was not Christian baptism, for the same reasons the first administration of the Lord's supper was not Christian—The same correspondence in spiritual import—Difference in the ordinances before and after the death of Christ—Arguments as to time—Mistake in regard to the source of John's commission—Comparison between the baptism of John, and of the disciples of Christ.

CHAPTER V.

REPLY TO THE ARGUMENTS AGAINST OUR DOCTRINE ON SACRAMENTAL COMMUNION FOUNDED ON THE INSPIRED PRINCIPLES OF CHRISTIAN TOLERATION, - 77

The proposition examined, that a change of circumstances justifies a change of practice with regard to the ordinances—Inspired canons of Christian toleration recited—They require forbearance with things indifferent, but do not permit us to extend our fellowship to errors which are subversive of the divine law.

CONTENTS.

CHAPTER VI.

REPLY TO SUCH OBJECTIONS TO OUR DOCTRINE ON SACRAMENTAL COMMUNION AS ARE FOUNDED ON THE SPIRITUALITY OF THE GOSPEL, AND DRAWN FROM OTHER AND MISCELLANEOUS SOURCES, - - - 91

The spiritual nature of the Gospel not inconsistent with its outward forms—The promptings of Christian feeling—The duty of recognizing as such, all that we believe to be truly converted—Pedobaptists sincerely believe themselves right—We associate with them in other departments of worship—As every man is responsible for himself to God, we are bound to respect their faith, and in receiving them do not violate our own.

CHAPTER VII.

WE ARE NOT AT LIBERTY TO ADMINISTER THE LORD'S SUPPER FOR ANY PURPOSES OTHER THAN THOSE DESIGNATED BY OUR LORD JESUS CHRIST, - - - 103

The design of the Lord's Supper not a test of Christian love—Reciprocal confidence, or religious fellowship—Pedobaptists and Quakers—Communion administered to secure popularity—Withheld as a punishment—Verbal nonsense—Open communion not an act of faith, obedience, or worship

CHAPTER VIII.

WE CANNOT UNITE WITH PEDOBAPTISTS IN SACRAMENTAL COMMUNION WITHOUT AN ACTUAL ABANDONMENT, OR PRACTICAL FALSIFICATION OF ALL OUR PRINCIPLES ON BOTH BAPTISM AND THE LORD'S SUPPER, - - 118

Forced confessions—Anabaptism—Change of public feeling in regard to us—Former persecutions—Parliament of Charles I.—Assembly of divines at Westminster—Henry VIII.—Episcopal Convocation—Consequences—Queen Elizabeth and the Aldgate Church—Burning of Baptist women—American persecutions—Danger of popularity—Influence of open communion.

CHAPTER IX.

WE CANNOT ENGAGE IN COMMUNION WITH OUR PEDOBAPTIST BRETHREN, BECAUSE THEY ARE NOT BAPTIZED, HAVING RECEIVED THE RITE IN THEIR INFANCY,   -   131

There is no law for infant baptism—The commission does not authorize it—The teachings of the Apostles—Their practice—The object for which baptism is received—The actions of those baptized by the Apostles—Infant baptism is an evil—It is prohibited in the word of God.

CHAPTER X.

WE CANNOT COMMUNE WITH PEDOBAPTISTS BECAUSE, NOT HAVING BEEN IMMERSED, THEY ARE NOT BAPTIZED, 152

Immersion only is baptism, proved by the sense of the word—its philology—Its sense confessed by critics—By theologians—Ancient Confessions of Faith—The English Liturgy—Use of the word in our common translation—Ancient version of the New Testament—reasons why it received its present rendering—Translations into Hebrew—Conclusions.

CHAPTER XI.

WE CANNOT COMMUNE WITH PEDOBAPTISTS, BECAUSE, NOT HAVING BEEN IMMERSED, THEY ARE NOT BAPTIZED, 166

Objections to our conclusions founded on the New Testament refuted—Facts considered—Passages of Scripture—Metaphorical allusions to baptism—The design of baptism requires immersion—The places where baptism was administered—Concurrence in our views by scholars—Reasons of their agreement with us in sentiment, and different practice—Conclusion.

CHAPTER XII.

BAPTISTS CANNOT COMMUNE WITH PEDOBAPTISTS, BECAUSE THEY ADMINISTER BAPTISM FOR ILLEGAL PURPOSES, AND ATTACH TO IT AN UNREASONABLE AND UNSCRIPTURAL DEGREE OF EFFICACY AND IMPORTANCE, - 180

Pedobaptist doctrines of baptism—Baptismal regeneration held by the fathers—This originated infant baptism, pouring and sprinkling—The Catechism and Canons of the Council of Trent—All Pedobaptist Churches believe in baptismal regeneration—Book of Common Prayer —Confession of Faith—Discipline—Disciples of Christ—Conservative influence of Baptist principles.

CHAPTER XIII.

BAPTISTS CANNOT UNITE WITH PEDOBAPTISTS IN SACRAMENTAL COMMUNION, BECAUSE THEY ATTACH TO THE LORD'S SUPPER AN UNREASONABLE AND UNSCRIPTURAL IMPORTANCE AND EFFICACY, - - - 202

Early superstition—Roman Catholics—Infant communion—Came into the church with infant baptism and accompanied it for a thousand years—Its abrogation—When and why—Opinions of the Episcopal church—Of the Presbyterian—Of the Methodist—Communion with them is an assent to their doctrines on communion which we cannot give—Open communion is impracticable—It is subversive of all discipline—The law of God the only safe rule—Close of this part of the argument.

CHAPTER XIV.

THE POLICY OF FREE COMMUNION CONSIDERED, AND SHOWN TO BE DISASTROUS TO THE CHURCH, - - 215

Close communion is odious—the Church would be more prosperous were it abandoned—Argument from reason—from facts—Principles of free communion Baptists—Results of the practice—Bunyan's church—Foster's—Hall's—Giles' instances—Open communion abandoned by its advocates—Close communion most consistent with prosperity and harmony.

CHAPTER XV.

BAPTISTS, AFTER ALL, ARE MORE FREE AND LIBERAL IN THEIR COMMUNION THAN ANY CLASS OF PEDOBAPTISTS WHATEVER, - - - - 228

Baptists are not the only close communionists—Between Pedobaptists of different sects there is no more love or union than between them and ourselves—All Pedobaptists exclude from the Lord's Table two thirds of their own members—Episcopacy—Episcopal and Protestant Methodists—New and Old School Presbyterians—Present controversy on that subject in the Pedobaptist churches, Acts of Synods, &c.—The tone of the religious press—Inconsistency.

CHAPTER XVI.

CAN THE BAPTIST CHURCH, IN MAINTAINING CLOSE COMMUNION, BE JUSTLY CHARGED WITH THE SIN OF SCHISM? 245

That schism exists somewhere is evident—We have not produced it, and are therefore not responsible—We have adhered to original principles—Baptists are identical with primitive Christians—When the disciples became Pedobaptists they severed themselves from us—We have maintained ever since a separate existence on original ground not connected with Papists or Protestants—Historical proofs—Confessions of Faith—Our name—Duty of Pedobaptists, having produced the schism, is obvious—they are required to heal it—It is not difficult to determine how it may be done—Its consequences.

CHAPTER XVII.

RECAPITULATION AND CONCLUSION, - - 265

Contents of the several chapters—Summary of the whole—Exhortation—Union—Liberality—Prosperity—Firm adherence to original principles—Our ultimate triumph.

INTRODUCTION

The terms of intercourse at the Lord's table, have not been adequately discussed. Numerous fugitive productions have, at different times, appeared, mostly in the form of pamphlets, tracts, circulars of associations, and articles in the religious journals of the day. A few reprints of transatlantic works have been made. Booth and Fuller have been issued by our own denomination; and by our Pedobaptist brethren, Bunyan and Hall. But none of these, well written and useful, as many of them are admitted to be, are considered exactly of the character demanded. They are either too superficial and brief, or too elaborate and profound. They deal in generals, on the one hand, discuss arguments, and controvert doctrines, that do not obtain among us; or, on the other, they array the investigation in a deep and metaphysical process of literary and logical acumen, which render it of little worth, except to the few who are thoroughly educated. My object has been to pursue the medium between these extremes. I have written, not for scholars and divines, but for the mass of the people. I have sought, therefore, to avoid equally the ambiguity attendant upon studied sententiousness, the confusion of tortuous and protracted reasoning, and the tedium of a weary prolixity.

To the several works of Robert Hall, in favor of Mixed Communion, is devoted, as will be seen, rather special attention. If any apology is necessary for replying, as much at large as our limits would permit, to the imposing theories of which he was the advocate, it may be found, not only in his great abilities as a writer, joined to the fascination of his glowing and brilliant style,—characteristics which must ever invest them with no small degree of popularity,—but in the additional consideration that, in all parts of our country, they have been procured in great numbers, and circulated with the utmost industry, as the strongest weapons that can be employed against us. It was thought necessary that the charm of his authority should be dispelled; the sophistry of his principal arguments exposed; and that our brethren who cannot find time, or facilities, for extensive reading, should have at command, in a small compass, the information requisite to meet and refute those who may employ his reasoning. How far this object is accomplished, the event only can determine.

The sacred table should be surrounded only by purity and brotherly love. The many melting recollections with which it is associated, render a single discordant note there, painfully repulsive. It is connected with every consideration calculated to elicit the holiest feelings of the renewed soul, the most entire consecration to God, and the most unfeigned love to his people. We therefore expect to see every communicant fully imbued with the spirit of Christ, and conscious of no other feelings than those which prompted the great sacrifice, of which this is the established memorial. We recoil from the thought that censure, or reproach, should ever reach so pure a circle, or that the principles of their intercourse should become matter of invective and controversy. But upon earth, alas! we are not permitted to realize perfection. Yet corrupt, and his passions still unsubdued, man's nature characterizes every act in which he is engaged. Feelings of worldliness find their way into the midst of his holiest devotions. As a consequence, the Lord's supper has, of late, become the arena upon which the fierce spirit of conflict battles for the mastery in sectarian strife. While our Pedobaptist brethren have planted their artillery on these holy ramparts, as upon the very citadel of Zion, that they may pour into our ranks a more destructive fire; a disposition appears to be growing among our own people, to employ it as a means of dispensing rewards, and inflicting punishments. These agitations ought, by every means in our power, to be resisted. While permitted to prevail, they must be productive of incalculable injury to the advancement of truth and righteousness, as well as to the cultivation of brotherly love, and Christian union.

Disappointment may, by some, possibly, be felt, when it is found that I have not even alluded to several of the most prominent topics which belong to the subject of Sacramental Communion. To divest the rite of those mists in which it has so long been enshrouded, by the Popish expositions which represent it as an expiatory sacrifice, and teach the transubstantiation, or, the no less irrational, though protestant notion, the consubstantiation, of its elements, on the one hand; and, on the other, to refute the modern doctrine which assumes it as an "effectual means and seal of grace," would be a work of undoubted importance. Unless "the signs of the times" are deceptive, a full discussion, in our country, of all these dogmas will very soon be demanded. The task would be equally profitable and delightful to illustrate the metaphorical character of the eucharist, the various vital doctrines, and amazing facts, it exhibits to our view, connected immediately with our redemption, sanctification, and salvation; the nature of the spiritual measures by which its reception should be preceded and accompanied; the advantages arising from its regular observance; and numerous other considerations having direct and collateral bearings upon the subject. But were all these topics introduced, they would require more of both time and space than I have at present at command. Nor is it particularly necessary, since several works, embracing these topics, are accessible to our people, in some of which they are discussed with candor, and in a few, the general style and argument partake but little of the party prejudices which so frequently disfigure the productions of all the sects in relation to Christian fellowship and communion.

The internal controversy in relation to strict and free communion, the American churches have, thus far, almost entirely, escaped. I cannot but congratulate them on an event so fortunate. Agitations of this character are always productive of consequences the most lamentable. On the other side of the Atlantic they have prevailed for more than a century, and are now shaking the English church to its very foundation. Individuals have been found in our country, who express doubt as to the propriety of strict communion. A few isolated instances exist of communities who practise upon the opposite principles. But no association, nor even a single church, respectable for either numbers or intelligence, has, within the compass of my information, seceded from the great body of the denomination upon this ground. Our whole mighty army, bearing the banner of undeviating obedience to the word of God, the *whole* word of God, and *nothing but* the word of God, upon the ample folds of which is inscribed—"ONE LORD, ONE FAITH, ONE BAPTISM," presents an unbroken front. The internal controversy, therefore, need be considered, only in so far as may be necessary to guard our churches against its evils, and to maintain ourselves in opposition to the arguments drawn from that source by Pedobaptists.

The doctrine and worship of the true church of Christ, have never been popular with the world. Sometimes, and in some countries, one portion, and in other ages and nations, another, has been, during the whole Christian period, made the occasion of bitter reproach, and pleaded in justification of every persecution. It is still emphatically true, that "as concerning this sect, we know that everywhere it is spoken against." Our ecclesiastical polity has sometimes rendered us peculiarly obnoxious. Uniformly, in all countries, modeled upon the plan of the New Testament, it has ever necessarily been strictly *republican*. Such a government has an invariable tendency to exalt the intellectual powers, and to inspire an irrepressible love for political freedom. The inalienable right of all Christians to full liberty of conscience, free from any control whatever from the civil magistrate, and their accountability in matters of faith to God only, is another doctrine we have cherished, with enthusiasm, from the days of the apostles, until now. And, under all governments, we have constantly protested against the unholy alliance of church and state—the blending of the spiritual with the civil power. These and other similar characteristics, so offensive to a venal priesthood, so odious to the minions of political authority, and which the populace have been taught to loathe and abhor, could impress none but philosophers, and truly enlightened Christians. The multitudes have ever been ready to take the yoke, and move as they were directed by their leaders. In our own country, since the adoption of the present form of national government, these tenets, which, if history speaks truly, had no small influence in fixing its character, have been sufficiently popular. All parties *now*, tacitly or avowedly, accord their approbation. Until that time, however, as at the present moment, in every government in continental Europe, and in all the American states south of the Rio del Norte, they had called down upon the head of the church, the vengeance of every petty ruler, and ambitious despot. Political favorites have ever delighted to kindle the fires by which we were consumed, and left no efforts unattempted to exterminate us from the face of the earth.

All the principles of the church of Christ, however, have

not yet been adopted. Even Protestant denominations, and in our own free land, imagining that they still have reason to resist us, do so, in a manner evincive that they have not lost entirely the spirit of their ancestors. Their swords and chains are broken, their prisons are demolished, and their fires extinguished; still they have the means of annoyance. It is confidently alleged that our distinguishing doctrines had their origin with "the madmen of Munster," that they yet remain the same with theirs, and are, therefore, essentially revolutionary, and fanatical; our baptism is pronounced, in high quarters, indecent, revolting, and dangerous; and our *communion* is derided as, in principle, the very essence of bigotry, and, in practice, selfish, intolerant, and proscriptive.

To all this, were we so disposed, we might very successfully reply with the argumentum ad hominum. Were there Baptists among the men of Munster, and is our church therefore responsible for all the excesses of the mass in that scene? Then the Huguenots of France, are responsible for all the extravagancies and impostures of the Camisards, and the French Prophets; the Presbyterians are responsible for all the ravings of Irvingism; the Episcopalians for the fanaticism and fooleries of the followers of Joanna Southcote; the Methodists for those of Anna Lee; and the Pedobaptists generally for the Fifth Monarchy Men of London, who rose for KING JESUS, and threw that metropolis into consternation. But no sensible man will brand a whole denomination with shame, for the follies, or the crimes, of a few individuals who may chance to be ecclesiastically connected with it. We glory in our whole spiritual ancestry, among whom we number the Apostles of Christ, and the saints and martyrs of all ages.

The baptismal controversy is believed to be drawing near its close. A century of conflict is about terminating the victory in favor of apostolic forms. The noise of the tumult in that region is evidently subsiding. As the light of science has grown more and more bright, and candor has mingled with the piety of christians, truth has gradually gained ground. That infants should not be subjected to a rite which can do them no good whatever, and which, so far as they are concerned, is without authority in the word of God, is an impression which is rapidly advancing; and immersion, in the name of the Holy Trinity, is so evidently the only scriptural baptism, that on these points our opponents feel themselves driven to the wall. The growing popularity of the primitive mode and subjects of baptism, is sufficiently illustrated by the fact that, after the most poignant and ingenious ridicule that can be heaped upon them, all denominations are, even now, forced frequently to employ them, or lose many of their most estimable members.

One point of attack—Sacramental Communion—remains. Here the popular breeze appears, for the moment, to favor our assailants, and the onset is universal in all quarters. The more grave of our neighbors read us solemn lectures on christian liberality, humility, brotherly affection, and the importance of spirituality above mere form in religion. The pedantic and flippant catch the theme of detraction, and shower around us the shafts of their ridicule. The vulgar crowd follow, with coarse epithets, and boisterous denunciations! All these it becomes necessary for us to meet, in the best spirit and manner we can command. In attempting to do this, I would not be considered as laying claim to any knowledge on the subject not possessed by thousands of my brethren, but simply as manifesting a disposition, which I certainly deeply feel, to contribute my feeble aid to the triumph of " the truth, as it is in Jesus."

It is my purpose to conduct this controversy in the true spirit of our holy religion; it is true, we differ with christians of other denominations, yet, for them all, we can, with the utmost sincerity, aver, that we cherish the most hearty good will. We assail no one, we challenge no one, and trust that to none we shall give offence. We confess ourselves not indifferent to the good opinion of the virtuous, and intelligent, of every order in society. Nor is any thing further from our intention than a design, by any thing that we may say, to foster a sectarian spirit. We will not, if it can be avoided, " widen the branch, already too capacious, between christians of different denominations." We do not imagine that every excellence is confined to our own ranks, nor are we reluctant to acknowledge the children of God wherever they may be found. On the other hand, we deprecate, with equal earnestness, that spirit of *liberalism* which hesitates not to sacrifice the commandments of God to the courtesies of religious intercourse. If the pious tenor of a consistent christian life, which embodies our own principles, with unconcealed freedom, candor, and affection to all, will do so, we shall secure the favorable regard of our brethren of every class. But if their kind consideration demands a departure from the inspired law, we must not, we dare not, pay the price. Jehovah alone is legislator in his own kingdom. He has formed unalterably its government, and institutions. It is ours, not to repeal, change his laws, or add to their number, but humbly, and faithfully, to obey him in all things.

We have one, and only one, favor to ask, on this, or on any other subject in relation to either our doctrine or practice; it is that we may be patiently heard in our own defence, and have awarded to us a candid and impartial verdict. If, when so judged by the law of God, we are fairly convicted of material error, we will not shrink from, nor seek to avert the sentence of condemnation. On the other hand, if we are clearly sustained, we shall confidently expect to receive the ingenuous approval of the wise and the good, of every denomination.

TERMS OF COMMUNION.

CHAPTER I.

WE ARE AT LIBERTY TO ADOPT NO TERMS OF COMMUNION NOT ESTABLISHED BY JESUS CHRIST.

Definitions—General object—Several opinions—Our own doctrines defined—Nature of positive laws—Scripture proofs—Their general application—Their particular application—Powers of a Church—Church representatives—Rights of individuals—Error of new tests of fellowship—Consequences of violating the principles advocated.

COMMUNION is friendly intercourse. Its existence does not necessarily imply the presence of religion. The word is not the less applicable, whatever may be the character of the parties, the objects they pursue, or the motives which bind them together. All familiar converse, and consultation, is communion.

CHRISTIAN COMMUNION is christian intercourse. This is fully developed when those who love the Redeemer, are associated in consultation, in prayer, in conversation, in co-operation for the benefit of each other, for the advancement of the knowledge of Christ, and the salvation of sinners. A late learned writer bears testimony to the correctness of this exposition when he says—" Every expression of fraternal regard, every participation in the enjoyment of social worship, every instance of the unity of the spirit exerted in prayer and supplication, or in acts of christian sympathy and friendship," truly belongs to the communion of saints. "It extends to all the modes by which believers recognize each other as members of a common head."

SACRAMENTAL COMMUNION is a joint participation in the Lord's Supper. Those who unite at the sacred table, and together receive the eucharist, have, with each other, sacramental communion.

This solemn act of divine worship is called a *sacrament*, not on account of any *mystery* now supposed to be attached to it, either in its nature or effects, but because it is a public declaration of allegiance to our Lord Jesus Christ. We also denominate it the *eucharist*, because it is an act of personal adoration and thanksgiving to God. It is the united social reception of the appointed emblems of the *body* and *blood* of the Redeemer, offered as a sacrifice for our salvation, in the benefits of which we become interested through faith.

If in these expositions we do not materially err, it will be clearly seen that communion is of *three kinds*—general, christian, and sacramental. With the first we have, at present, nothing to do. The second we should not now consider, but because it is so universally and improperly confounded with the third. Christian communion and sacramental communion are two distinct things. Either may be in full and perfect exercise without the existence of the other. A gentleman, for example, is eminently religious; I am delightfully associated with him in the service of the Redeemer; we "take sweet counsel together, and walk to the house of God in company;" but he has never been baptized, and, therefore, cannot, without a violation of the law of Christ, go with me to the Lord's table. Another comes to the holy supper. I have, personally, no confidence in him as a christian, and never associate with him as such.

This, however is only my own private opinion. He is in fellowship in the church. He comes according to the law. I cannot debar him. With him I sit down to the eucharist. It will be seen by these facts, that, without any inconsistency, indeed, as a matter of necessity, I have christian communion with those with whom I have no sacramental communion, and sacramental communion with those with whom I have no christian communion.

Between Baptists and the members of all the surrounding evangelical denominations, I trust, and believe, that, in all respects, the most free and perfect christian communion exists, and will continue to be sedulously cultivated. We cherish for them, as the people of God, the sincerest affection; we preach, pray, and labor together; consult and co-operate for the spread of the Gospel; and take pleasure in being associated with them "in every good word and work." Nothing would be more pleasing to us than to go with them to the Lord's table, but we are repelled by the fact that a preliminary duty is essential, and with this they have not complied. We decline sacramental communion, not alone with those who can offer no satisfactory testimony of their soundness in the faith, or their purity of moral character, but, yielding unqualified obedience to inspired rules, and not without, in some degree, the concurrence of the several Pedobaptist churches in our interpretation of them, also with christians, however endeared, who have not been baptized. Let us, then, in defence, and explanation, of our course in this particular, proceed to consider *the laws of the Lord's Supper; the preliminary preparation for its reception; our reasons for declining a participation with those who violate the principles upon which, in our opinion, it is based; the policy of a strict adherence to divine laws; and our claims, in doing so, to be considered as consult-*

ing, by the only effectual means, the union and harmony of the body of Christ.

Jesus Christ has established in his Church terms of communion. In the general truth of this proposition, I believe, all denominations concur. Beyond this point agreement ceases. The several varieties of sentiment prevailing may, perhaps, with sufficient distinctness, be arranged under three general heads.

Those of the first class hold that it is very difficult to decide what Christ has appointed as terms of communion. They teach us that the whole matter is involved in so much darkness, and ambiguity, that it is impossible to arrive at any certainty in relation to it. On this view of the case, it is necessary to offer, in this place, but a single remark. If it is just, our condition is precisely the same that it would have been had no terms of communion been designated. The whole investigation is of no consequence, nor can our conclusions involve any practical obligations. It is evidently preposterous to imagine that we can be responsible for our obedience to a law, the import of which no ordinary mind is able to discover.

The second class profess to have embraced the more reasonable and consistent doctrine, that the terms of communion, as appointed by the Redeemer, are sufficiently plain and definite to be readily comprehended and exactly observed by every Christian. They have, however, added the unsupported and injurious notion that authority is granted to the Church to vary them, at least in some particulars, to dispense with them, or to adopt others of a different character, when she may think such a course necessary, for purposes of discipline, or of conciliation, to preserve her purity, or to extend her power and influence.

The third class maintain that Jesus Christ has established

all the terms of communion we are at liberty, under any circumstances, to recognize; that in his word they are so perfectly obvious as readily to be understood by every inquirer; that his church is obliged faithfully to conform to them in every respect; and that we are not permitted to change, or dispense with any of them, or to add to their number. These are the sentiments we have ourselves embraced, and shall now attempt to sustain their correctness. We shall be aided in our efforts in this particular, if we consider, for a moment, the nature of the laws by which this sacred institution is governed.

The Lord's Supper, like baptism, is established by *positive law*. The obligations of obedience to this code differ from those enjoined by *moral law* in several important particulars. For our purpose, at present, it is sufficient to observe, that the duties imposed by moral law are right in themselves; they are founded in the nature of things; and proceed upon the unchanging principles of justice between man and man, and between man and his Maker. Those commanded by positive law are right for no other reason than because they are commanded. They are based solely upon the authority of the Lawgiver, and are designed to test our disposition to bow to his requirements. The difference between them is plain. The former or *moral* code, is commanded because it is right; the latter or *positive* code, is right because it is commanded.

In these distinctions and observations I advance no novel or peculiar sentiment. The pious and learned of all ages and denominations fully concur with us. In proof of this statement I might refer to numerous authorities, but I will satisfy myself with two only. Dr. Owen says:—" That principle that the church hath power to institute and appoint any thing, or ceremony, belonging to the worship of God, either as to matter, or to manner, beyond the orderly observance of such circumstances as necessarily attend such ordinances as Christ himself has instituted, lies at the bottom of all the horrible superstition and wars, that have for so long a season spread themselves over the face of the Christian world; and it is the design of a great part of the Revelation of John—to make a discovery of this truth."*

Bishop Hoadly is still more in point. He says:—" The partaking of the Lord's Supper is not a duty of itself, or a duty apparent to us from the nature of things, but a duty made such to Christians by the *positive* institution of Jesus Christ. All *positive* duties, or duties made such by institution alone, depend entirely on the will and declaration of the person who institutes or ordains them with respect to the real design and end of them, and consequently to the due manner of performing them. For there being no other foundation for them with regard to us, but the will of the institutor, this will must, of necessity, be our sole direction, both as to our understanding their true intent, and practising them accordingly; because we can have no other direction in this sort of duties, unless we will have recourse to mere invention, which makes them our own institutions, and not the institutions of those who first appointed them. It is plain, therefore, that the nature, the design, and the due manner of the Lord's Supper, must, of necessity, depend on what Jesus Christ, who instituted it, has said about it."†

As an institution brought into existence by positive law, the observance of which is enjoined as a proof of our love, the words of the statute which exacts the communion are the only rule of obedience. This is a sufficient rule; and if it were otherwise, we could not arrive at any knowledge of our

* Commun. with God, part 2, ch. 5, p. 169.
† Works, vol. 3, p. 845, &c.

duty respecting it by abstract or analogical reasoning, because such reasoning does not apply to this class of laws. If any thing is deducted from it, or added to it, this at once makes it, in the language of Bishop Hoadly, our own, and not the institution of Jesus Christ.

These views of the question before us are not without the amplest support from the word of God. Respecting the ritual as well as other services of the Old Testament, Jehovah has said:—" Ye shall not add unto the word which I command you, neither shall ye diminish aught from it; that ye may keep the commandments of the Lord your God, which I command you."* This law is frequently, and in various forms, repeated to the children of Israel; and by the prophets they are often upbraided for their want of conscientious and literal compliance. By Malachi the Lord says to them :—" Even from the days of your fathers ye are gone away from mine ordinances, and have not kept them. Return unto me, and I will return unto you, saith the Lord of hosts. But ye said— Wherein shall we return?"† That equal stress is laid by Jehovah on a similar conformity to the ritual commands in the New Testament is abundantly evident. To John the Baptist Christ said—" Thus it becometh us to fulfil all righteousness ;"‡ and to his disciples—" If ye love me, keep my commandments."§ The apostle, referring to the same subject, thus addresses the Corinthians—" Now I praise you, brethren, that ye remember me in all things, and keep the ordinances as I delivered them to you."‖ At the close of the inspired canon, as if, by his parting words, solemnly to impress every heart with the importance of the admonition, Christ emphatically says—" If any man shall add unto these things, God shall add unto him the plagues that are written in this book."

* Deut. iv. 8.   † Mal. iii. 7.   ‡ Matt. iii. 15.
§ John xiv. 15.   ‖ 1 Cor. xi. 2.

These passages selected, almost at random, from the multitude with which the holy word abounds, together with the admitted nature and obligations of positive laws, most amply establish the great truth, that to his commandments we, as Christians, are under the most solemn obligations to conform, without addition, diminution or change. Let us now apply the deductions at which we have arrived, to the subject generally, and particularly to our duty with regard to the divinely appointed terms of communion.

They are obviously susceptible of a general application. A church, for example, is a voluntary association.* No one enters it, on Baptist principles, but by the free and unbiassed consent of his own will. When he has done so, or in the act itself, he is not at liberty to give influence to any motive, or to be guided by any laws other than those revealed and approbated by Jehovah. The same remarks are true even of civil society in all its forms. Men are at liberty to choose whether they will live in solitude or in company with others. If they determine upon the latter alternative, as God has prescribed the principles upon which the association shall be formed, they dare not enter it in contravention of his enactments. They may not do so, for instance, on the principle that a majority may control the consciences of the minority, or interfere with the rights and duties of parents and children, or of husbands and wives. For these facts, besides the law of God on the subject, there are most substantial reasons. The former would despoil men of their character as moral agents; and the latter would remove the responsibility from the only persons who will feel its weight, and who, therefore, are likely, with fidelity, to perform the duties involved in these relations.

* See Dr. Wayland's Extent of Human Responsibility, pp. 128, &c., some of whose sentiments I have copied.

The right of admission to membership in the church is established, in any specified case, by the proof that the candidate is conformed in heart and in life to the requirements of the Gospel. Such a man cannot be withheld from all the ordinances and privileges of the church, provided he receive them as they are enjoined. And while he continues to observe the divine rule, he is entitled to enjoy them. He is under law to God, no other is obligatory, or admissible. When we form, with our fellow Christians, the ecclesiastical tie, we promise merely to obey Christ, and while we do this, as we have never pledged ourselves to obey the commands of each other, every man is as free of his brother, as his brother is of him. We are bound to obey Christ, and no one else. Such is the only rational exposition of true christian liberty. The church has no authority as a body to make laws for us, nor can she enforce any, but the laws of Christ. We have never surrendered to her such right. An attempt to exercise it, therefore, to say nothing of its despotism, would be a violation of the spirit of religion, and a manifest infraction of the statutes of Jesus Christ already recited. No man, whatever may be the dignity of his office; nor company of men, however large, or wise, or sincerely desirous to do good, can change any thing which Jesus Christ has appointed, absolve our obligations to the least of his commandments, or make binding any thing he has not required. The church has no such power, and consequently can neither exercise it her self, nor delegate it to others.

These inductions apply to all ecclesiastical bodies of every description, district associations, general associations, councils, state and church conventions, and every other. Each of these, like a single church, is a society of which Christ is in fact, if not confessedly, the head, and sole Legislator. None of them have, consequently, any more authority in this character than they would have in the separate churches of which they are composed. The powers not bestowed by Jesus Christ are withheld for wise and benevolent purposes, their exercise is, therefore, prohibited. No legislative powers are granted by him to any church, or combination of churches, or individual, or body of ministers, or any other association whatever. If not, they are clearly prohibited. God has, indeed, in his word, nowhere more emphatically enjoined obedience to his laws, than he has interdicted the exercise by us in any conceivable capacity of all such powers for any purpose imaginable. It is treason against high Heaven to presume that any object the Gospel proposes to accomplish, cannot best be secured by the means which Christ has himself appointed. We may be asked what power then is granted, and whether we would fetter the church, and leave her fast bound in inextricable trammels? I answer, executive only; and this is sufficient for all desirable purposes. Our duty is to obey, not to command, and only when we are found in conformity to this principle are we happy and useful.

We regard a knowledge and belief of these doctrines the more important, because there is really no stable medium between them and all the absurdities of popery. Suppose we surrender these fundamental truths, and allow that the church, or the ministry, either in person, or by their representatives, or in any other manner, may make laws, binding on the consciences of men, or modify, change, or dispense with any established by Messiah, where do we find ourselves? All the horrors of popery are at once in view. The whole hideous superstructure of that corrupt church finds a license and support in the assumption that she has the power to rule men by her enactments as a legislative body, in faith and practice. Grant this, and all the requisite ability is conveyed, and if it is not now, it may soon, with impunity, be exercised

The principle is the same, whether adopted by Papists or Protestants. "If my conscience is to be bound by my fellow-men," says Dr. Wayland, "it matters not whether these men be a conclave of bishops and cardinals, or whether they be my brethren whom I meet every day, and with whom I sit down around the same communion table. My brethren will, I doubt not, use their usurped authority more mildly, but this alters not the fact that the authority is usurped, nor does it offer any guarantee that it may not, in the end, be as oppressive as the other."

I designed, however, to make of the doctrine under consideration, more especially, a particular application to the case in hand.

If the obligations of the divine law are imperative, and the declarations of the word of God are what we have represented them to be, and it is hardly possible we can be mistaken, it follows that no exigencies or circumstances can exist, which will authorize us to dispense with any qualifications to membership in the church which Christ has required; to adopt any terms of communion he has not established; or to demand of a candidate any thing which he has not demanded. I am aware that numerous and most specious reasons are often pleaded for a violation of these principles. It is contended that in this manner the church may be defended from encroachments, her doctrines be preserved pure, and many important and useful designs be greatly facilitated. But is it possible that such can be the case? The opinion is dishonorable to Christ, and essentially popish. When its practice has been attempted, as it often has, although for a time the results have appeared to favor the accomplishment of the objects proposed, they have ultimately proved themselves to be evils a hundred fold more enormous than those they were intended to remedy. What has Christ himself made the terms of communion? This is the only inquiry permitted, and to it the Gospel affords a plain and definite reply. If what we wish to enjoin is not commanded by him, we dare not require it; if it is, we dispense with it at our peril. "What thing soever I command you," says Jehovah, "observe to do it. Thou shalt not add thereto, nor diminish from it." Christ is the sole Legislator. No one may make laws but himself. It is his church, not ours. Our designs may be benevolent, our purposes honest, and our objects good; but the powers of which we speak are his alone, and we have no more right to assume them for a good object, than we have to accomplish purposes known to be evil.

The department of the Gospel, however, in which even intelligent and sincere Christians are most liable to infringe upon the doctrines now established, is that wherein the great Lawgiver has enjoined upon his people only a particular temper of mind, the motives to excite which he has suggested, but has not specified the outward manner of its manifestation. It may be asked whether, in such cases, the church may not adopt RULES for the guidance of her members, such as she may think wise and salutary? I answer, unhesitatingly, in the negative. Where Christ has made no laws, we are at liberty to allow none. He, for example, has ordered me to be temperate, to love the souls of my fellow sinners, and to do good to all men. These the church may and ought to require. If I violate the laws of temperance she is under obligations to debar my approach to the holy table. But she has no authority, by way of enforcing more effectually the duty in question, or on any other pretence, to oblige me to join a temperance society; nor, if I think proper to adopt this method of manifesting my sense of obligation, dare she prohibit me from exercising my inherent right to act in the case according to my convictions of duty. The church **may** assure me that if I do not love the souls of men I cannot enjoy her fellowship, because it is impossible that he who does not cherish this spirit can be a disciple of the Redeemer. But she is not permitted to prescribe to me, as the manner of evincing the required disposition, that I shall join a benevolent society—Missionary, Education, Bible, or any other. Nor, if I think proper to select this method of manifesting my love, has she any right, such as is exercised by the New Test churches of the South-west, to enact a prohibition, and make obedience to her order a condition of my approach to the Lord's table. Such a transaction is, as we have seen, essentially popish, and cannot, if persisted in, but be attended with the most disastrous consequences. It is a departure from the plain path in which Christ has commanded us to walk, and may lead we know not whither. As a precedent it will justify all the enormities which have been exercised by the Roman see, and with which the world has been cursed for a thousand years. It is, in fact, the same thing in narrow circumstances, and upon a small scale, and nothing is wanting but the secular sword for its enforcement, to enstamp upon it the same character of atrocity and blood. If, by sordid selfishness, I show myself destitute of love to God and the souls of men, the church ought to withdraw from me her fellowship. But to do so because I choose to exercise my discretion as to the mode of manifesting my christian spirit, while I evince that I do possess the required temper of heart, is to dispense with the laws of Christ, and assume the right to institute other terms of communion than those which he has appointed, a usurpation of authority, and a violation of the divine injunctions, against which it is the duty of every sincere Christian to enter his immediate and most solemn protest.

The truth of the proposition is, I trust, rendered without

further argument sufficiently apparent, that we are not at liberty to admit any terms of communion but those established by Jesus Christ himself, the only Lawgiver of his people. We have now considered briefly, the definition of communion, stated our object, and seen the various opinions which have prevailed, in regard to it, defined our own position, illustrated the nature of positive laws, which is the code that governs the sacrament, recited inspired commands, precepts and admonitions, requiring undeviating obedience on the part of the people of God, shown that Christ has established all the laws we are at liberty, under any circumstances, to recognize, that, in his word, they are so plain and obvious as readily to be understood by every inquirer, that his church is obliged faithfully to conform to them in every respect, and that we are not permitted to change, or dispense with any of them, or to add to their number. Of these conclusions we have made a general and a particular application, illustrated the awful consequences of departing from the principles we advocate, and have seen that they bear with all their force upon the terms of communion as established by Christ, requiring us to receive those enjoined by him, and to repudiate all others, from whatever quarter, or authority, they may have been derived. From these conclusions no Baptist, who deserves the name, will, I am assured, dissent. And to admit their correctness, what Christian of any church can hesitate, who has adopted the immortal maxim of Chillingworth, so often avowed in theory and violated in practice, and which deserves to be written in letters of gold upon every sanctuary in which man bows in the worship of his Maker:—" The Bible, the Bible alone, is the religion of Protestants."

CHAPTER II.

THE SCRIPTURAL TERMS OF COMMUNION AT THE LORD'S TABLE DESIGNATED AND PROVED.

Repentance, faith, and baptism are terms of communion—English authors—Hudson River Association circular—The apostolic commission is the law of communion—The order of the sacraments—Their order in the primitive Churches—Emblematical representations—Inspired injunctions regarding the perpetuity of primitive order—By whom the sacraments are to be administered—How received—Conclusion.

WHAT are the Scriptural terms of communion? To this inquiry it is not, I think, difficult to furnish a satisfactory reply. I answer, and to sustain this proposition is the object of the present chapter, that they are repentance, faith, and baptism. Between our own and the several Protestant Pedobaptist denominations, there is, except, perhaps, our Methodist brethren, who admit "seekers" to the Lord's table, as "a means of grace," in some sort, an agreement on this subject. I say in some sort, because, it may be, we totally disagree as to what faith, repentance, and baptism are, yet they require exercises and acts to which they give these names. With these explanations I remark, that however it may have formerly been, when infant communion was practised, we all now concur in maintaining that the candidate, to qualify him for the sacred supper, must, at least, be a sincere penitent, must believe himself regenerated, that he must not have forfeited his claims by immorality since his profession, nor by falling into heresy, and that he must have been baptized.

The principal works on both sides of the question, whether baptism is required as a preliminary to the Lord's Supper, beginning with that of the pious John Bunyan, entitled, "Water baptism not a term of communion," and extending down to our own times, have been carefully re-examined, and their arguments will be reviewed in the proper place, as much at length as the brevity of this volume will permit. After comparing the deductions of them all with the word of God on the subject, I am, if possible, still more fully convinced that my original conclusions are correct. The Hudson River Association, in a circular written by Rev. Dr. Cone, of New York, has presented the true exposition of the doctrine in question. "'The children of God," says that Association, "are bound to give thanks always to their heavenly Father, because he hath chosen them, from the beginning, to salvation, through sanctification of the Spirit and belief of the truth, whereunto they are called by the Gospel; and THEN, as lively stones, are built up a spiritual house, a holy priesthood, to offer up spiritual sacrifices, acceptable to God by Jesus Christ; and to manifest their attachment to the laws, doctrines, and ordinances once delivered unto the saints. If the primitive churches received only such as professed to be born of God, and gave evidence that they were begotten again unto a lively hope by the resurrection of Jesus Christ from the dead, we should imitate their example; and if there come unto us any, and bring not this doctrine, we are commanded not to receive them into our houses, neither to bid them God speed; for he that biddeth them God speed is partaker of their evil deeds: and how can we more fully do this than to receive them to our communion? All candidates, therefore, for communion or membership, must give evidence that they are born again. This is the first Scriptural term of communion;" and the second is, that they shall have entered the church by baptism. "Should this fundamental principle ever be abandoned, I hesitate not to believe the fine gold will become dim, the glory will depart from us, and the vengeance of him who walketh in the midst of the golden candlesticks may be fearfully apprehended."

The inspired law regulating the preliminaries of the communion, is the commission of the apostles. On this point the lamented Judd, in his truly learned and triumphant Review of Stuart,* justly remarks: "The Saviour," in this statute, requires "his ministers to go into all nations, and preach the Gospel, baptizing those who believe, with the promise that he will be with them, to aid and bless them, till the end of the world. As long, then, as it is the duty of ministers to preach, and of sinners to believe, so long it will be the duty of believers to be baptized. In other words, while the economy of grace is continued, that is, to the end of the world, baptism must be the appropriate badge of the Christian profession. So likewise the communion is enjoined on the church till the second coming of Christ." In relation to the divine injunction instituting the sacrament itself, Paul gives us the following account: "I have received of the Lord that which I also delivered unto you, that the Lord Jesus, the same night in which he was betrayed, took bread, and when he had given thanks, he brake it, and said—Take; eat; this is my body which is broken for you. This do in remembrance of me. After the same manner, also, he took the cup, when he had supped, saying—This cup is the New Testament in my blood. This do ye, as oft as ye drink it, in remembrance of me. For as often as ye eat this bread, and drink this cup, ye do show the Lord's death *till he come.*"†

---

* P. 120. To whom I gladly acknowledge my indebtedness on this part of the subject, and whose language I shall frequently employ.

† 1 Cor. xi. 23—26.

The whole inquiry to be decided in this argument is, whether the several duties commanded in the apostolic commission are, as we have intimated, to be observed in the order in which they were enjoined by Christ—first, to hear the Gospel, then to believe, afterwards to be baptized, and finally to partake of the Lord's supper; or are they left to be regulated by the convenience or inclination of the disciples. The former conclusion is maintained by us, and in which we have, substantially, the concurrence of most of the Pedobaptist world; the latter is defended by our opponents, consisting principally of open communion Baptists. Of this class of polemical writers, incomparably the most learned and vigorous is the late Rev. Robert Hall, of England. He remarks— "It has been inferred, too hastily, in my opinion, that we are bound to abstain from their communion"—that of unbaptized persons—"whatever judgment we may form of their sincerity and piety. Baptism, it is alleged, is, under all possible circumstances, an indispensable term of communion; and, however highly we may esteem many of our Pedobaptist brethren, yet, as we cannot but deem them unbaptized, we must, of necessity, consider them as unqualified for an approach to the Lord's table. It is evident that this reasoning rests entirely on the assumption that baptism is, invariably, a necessary condition of communion—an opinion which it is not surprising the Baptists should have embraced, since it has long passed current in the Christian world, and been received by nearly all denominations of Christians."* His own conclusions he states in another place—in the following terms: "It remains to be considered whether there is any *peculiar connection* between the two ordinances of baptism and the Lord's supper, either in the nature of things, or by divine appointment, so as to render it improper to administer the

* Works, vol. ii. p. 212.

one without the other. That there is no *natural* connection is obvious. They were instituted at different times, and for different purposes; baptism is a mode of professing our faith in the blessed Trinity; the Lord's supper is a commemoration of the dying love of the Redeemer; the former is the act of an individual, the latter of a society. The words which contain our warrant for the celebration of the eucharist, convey no allusion to baptism whatever; those which prescribe baptism carry no anticipative reference to the eucharist. To all appearance the rites in question rest upon independent grounds. But perhaps there is a *special* connection between the two, arising from *divine appointment.* If this be the case, it will be easy to point it out. Rarely, if ever, are they mentioned together, and on no occasion is it asserted, or insinuated, that the validity of the sacrament depends on the previous observance of the baptismal ceremony."*

I pause not now to consider the discrepancies of these opinions of the learned gentleman, such as that baptism is *a* mode, and not *the* mode of professing our faith; that the Lord's supper is an ordinance, not of an individual, but of a church, and therefore baptism is not a condition of its reception, as if persons could be lawfully in the church without baptism; and several others. These and many more of a similar character we shall examine when we come to reply to the objections which have been made to our deductions. The exposition of Mr. Baxter, is much more Christian-like, natural, and evidently correct: " This paramount law of the great Institutor, the commission, is not like some occasional historical mention of baptism, but is the very command of Christ, and purposely expresseth their several works, in their several places and order. Their first task is, by teaching, to make disciples, which Mark calls believers. The second

* Vol. ii. pp. 218, 219.

work is to baptize them. The third work is to teach them all other things which are, afterwards, to be learned in the school of Christ. To contemn this order, continues Mr. Baxter, "is to renounce all rules of order, for where," he asks, "can we expect to find it, if not here?"* *That this order is divinely prescribed we propose now to prove, by the apostolic commission itself, by the example of the apostles, and by the design of the two institutions.*

That the order indicated is divinely prescribed, is proved, in the first place, by the tenor of the apostolic commission itself.

"Go ye, therefore," said Messiah, "and teach all nations, baptizing them in the name of the Father, and of the Son, and of the Holy Ghost; teaching them to observe all things, whatsoever I have commanded you; and, lo, I am with you alway, even unto the end of the world."† This is "THE STATUTE, emphatically, OF THE CHRISTIAN CHURCH." It is one complete whole, of which the distinct laws commanding the propagation of the gospel, the exercise of faith, the duty of baptism, and visible church fellowship, form so many separate sections; each occupying its appointed, and therefore, *unchangeable* place. The disposition with regard to time in which these duties were first brought into being, and which is here preserved, although not wholly irrelevant to the argument, is still of comparatively inferior importance; but the arrangement in which they are commanded to be *observed*, is that in which they must be obeyed. A disregard of this divinely ordained series is most clearly a violation of the law. The order of the duties is as imperative as the duties themselves. The command requires us, in the first place, to preach the gospel, and, in the second place, to bap-

---

* Disp. of Right to Sacra. pp. 91, 149, 150.
† Mark xvi. 15, 16: Mat. xxviii. 19, 20.

tize those who believe. Now, instead of conforming in this respect, suppose we baptize men first, and afterwards preach to them the gospel, in expectation that they will believe, is not the law violated? Unquestionably. But in what does the infraction consist? Simply in reversing the order of our obedience. It is just as obvious, therefore, that we are restricted in the administration of baptism to a certain definite class of subjects, as that we are authorized to baptize at all; for on no rational principle of interpretation can the commission be supposed to warrant the baptism of any, but disciples, or such as are taught and believe the gospel. If this exposition is correct, and I presume all Baptists will admit it, since if it is not, baptism may be administered to any one, although not a believer, it is equally clear, for precisely the same reason, that baptism is an indispensable preliminary to that part of church fellowship of which the Lord's supper is considered as an expression. If the former part of our Lord's commission is authoritative in the order of its successive injunctions as well as in the injunctions themselves, and this is fully conceded, the latter part of it certainly cannot be less so. Is it possible the order of it can be binding in one part, and discretionary in another! If baptism is not necessary to communion, faith, for the same reason, is not necessary to baptism; for it may certainly be as conclusively maintained that the second duty must precede the third as that the first must precede the second. We cannot but believe that teaching and faith are intentionally enjoined as the first duty. Baptism, therefore, is intentionally enjoined as the second, and visible church fellowship as the third duty; and we are no more at liberty to invert the order in the latter case than we are in the former. We maintain, then, with exactly the same authority and conclusiveness that baptism should precede communion, as that faith should precede baptism. The two positions must stand or fall together. If we abandon the one it is impossible for us to adhere to the other. The same arguments, consequently, which make us open communionists make us at the same time Pedobaptists. But if we persevere in our principles, and baptize believers only, then it follows that to administer the Lord's supper to unbaptized persons, even if they are undoubtedly converted, is a manifest violation of the rule by which Christ governs his churches. Without obedience to the law we have no right to expect the fulfilment of the promise. Christ *may* bless, with his presence and favor, those who disregard his injunctions, but he has not covenanted to do so. The statute has not been abrogated, or changed. He designed that it should be obligatory as long as the promise attached to it remains in force— till he shall come the second time, without sin, unto salvation. That the order in which the several duties are enjoined in the commission is divinely prescribed, is thus conclusively established by the commission itself. The same fact is, in the second place, plainly confirmed by the example of the apostles.

These holy men were instructed to go, *ultimately*, into all the world, and preach the Gospel to every creature, but, *for the present*, they were required to wait at Jersusalem until they should receive power from on high—the requisite endowments by the Spirit of God—to qualify them for the great work of organizing among our fallen race the kingdom of the Redeemer. Fifty days from the resurrection of Christ had elapsed. The day of Pentecost was fully come. It was the glorious Christian sabbath. The followers of Messiah were assembled together " with one accord." Thus in expectation of the fulfilment of the Father's promise, they were associated. " Suddenly there came a sound from heaven, as of a rushing mighty wind, and it filled all the place where they were sitting. And there appeared unto them cloven tongues, like as of fire, and it sat upon each of them. And they were all filled with the Holy Ghost, and began to speak with other tongues as the Spirit gave them utterance." A flood of light now burst upon their minds. No longer were they in darkness in relation to any christian duty. The prophetic Scriptures, as well as the doctrines they had received from the lips of the Saviour himself, shone forth in all their transparent brilliancy, and they, for the first time, fully and correctly, conceived the spiritual and heavenly nature of the kingdom of Jesus Christ. The fame of these occurrences went out, and a numerous crowd were soon attracted to the place of the apostolic assembly. The apostles now proceeded in their great work by an address to the multitude, in relation to the mission, the character, death, resurrection, and ascension of Christ; the reasonableness and necessity of faith in him for salvation; and the awful consequences of despising and rejecting his Gospel. "The "word of truth and soberness," simple indeed in its arrangement and enunciation, but mighty in power, was carried with overwhelming conviction to the consciences of the auditors. They at once perceived their danger, the enormity of their guilt, and cried out, in the anguish of their hearts:—" Men and brethren, what shall we do?" To this anxious inquiry Peter responded —" Repent, and be baptized, every one of you, in the name of Jesus Christ, for the remission of sins, and ye shall receive the gift of the Holy Ghost; for the promise is unto you, and to your children, and to all that are afar off, even as many as the Lord our God shall call."[*] The number of the penitents became exceedingly great. They received the divine declaration of mercy with joy, came forward unhesitatingly, and boldly avowed themselves converts to the Christian faith.

[* Acts ii. 38, &c.]

The apostles were now called upon to give a practical exposition of their sense of the duties confided to them by the supreme Legislator. Examine their procedure, and it will be found to accord precisely with the order in which they are prescribed in the commission—" Then they that gladly received his word were baptized." They first, preached; secondly, the people believed; thirdly, they that believed were baptized; and, fourthly, they that gladly received the word and were baptized, " continued steadfastly in the apostles' doctrine and fellowship, and *in breaking of bread, and in prayers*"—these acts expressive, generally, of church-fellowship, and, particularly, of sacramental communion.

Thus was formed and ordered, upon the model drawn by Christ himself, the first Gospel church. The apostles who executed his commands were under the special inspiration and guidance of the Holy Spirit. That the organization of this church was faultless, all will admit. Nor will any one hesitate to concede that it was designed as "a pattern" for all succeeding churches, to the end of time. Its essential features were, accordingly, preserved, uniformly, in all the churches gathered by the apostles, at subsequent periods, and in different countries. Not to admit this fact would involve an absurdity too glaring for any man of judgment to tolerate, besides a direct contradiction of several positive declarations contained in the Gospel history. "For this cause," says Paul to the Corinthians, "I have sent unto you Timotheus, who is my beloved son, and faithful in the Lord, who shall bring you into remembrance of my *ways* which be in Christ, *as I teach every where in all the churches.*"* All the apostles spoke and taught the same things. They never countermanded in one church what they had ordered and taught in another. At Jerusalem they required faith as a

* 1 Cor. iv. 17.

preliminary to baptism, and baptism as a condition to the Lord's supper, or "breaking of bread." The order they established in one church was the order of every church; therefore, faith and baptism were, in primitive times, invariably, terms of communion. No instance can be found in which any person was received into the church, and admitted to enjoy its privileges, without them.

After having heard, and believed the inspired message, baptism was, without an exception, required as the very first act of obedience, and the Lord's supper was always subsequent. This was the course pursued, as we have seen, at Pentecost. When the people of Samaria believed Philip preaching the things concerning the kingdom of God, they were not received immediately to the communion, but were first *baptized*. When Paul, being opposed by the Jews at Corinth, turned to the Gentiles, we are told:—"Many of the Corinthians, hearing believed, and were baptized." And when the Holy Spirit fell on the Gentile converts at Cesarea, evincing to the apostles that God had accepted them, "he commanded them to be baptized." In no instance, until they had submitted to baptism, were the disciples ever permitted to approach the holy table. We could multiply examples, but it is unnecessary. Search the New Testament in every part; scrutinize the history of individuals, and of churches; and as far as the events of the times have been written, the series of the commission, without a doubt, governed all their acts. Faith is uniformly antecedent to baptism, and baptism is as constantly required as a preparation for the communion. In the constitution and discipline of all the apostolic churches, this rule is never violated. Can we see all these facts, and fail to be convinced as to the interpretation of the commission received by the first, and inspired teachers of religion? Their recorded example proves that they conducted all their administrations with scrupulous regard to the order of its several requirements. Faith and baptism, therefore, are ordained by Jehovah, unchangeably, as terms of communion, and their position, with respect to each other distinctly fixed, cannot be changed without a flagrant violation of the law of God.

That the order in which the several christian duties are enjoined in the apostolic commission is divinely prescribed is, in the third place, proved by the design of the two institutions.

The sacraments of the Gospel are emblematical representations of great and glorious facts. It may be said of them that they constantly hold up to our view the torch of truth, that we may avoid error in our knowledge and practice of the word of life. It will be our wisdom not to permit " the light that is in them to become darkness !" If we do, " how great," perplexing, and melancholy " will be that darkness !" " The true doctrine of the Trinity," says Dr. Waterland, " and the atonement of Christ, have been kept up in the Christian church by the institutions of baptism and the Lord's supper, more than by any other means whatever." Dr. Ryland observes —" These last legacies of a dying Saviour, these pledges of his eternal and immutable love, ought to be received with the greatest reverence, and the warmest gratitude. And as they relate directly to the death of the great Redeemer, which is an event the most interesting, an action the most grand and noble, that ever appeared in the world, they ought to be held in the highest esteem, and performed with the utmost solemnity. Of these institutions baptism calls for our first regard, as it is appointed to be first performed."* The venerable Booth speaks more directly with reference to their metaphorical bearings :—" In submitting to baptism we have an emblem of our union and communion with Jesus Christ, as our great repre-

* Beauty of Social Religion, p. 10.

sentative, in his death, burial and resurrection, at the same time declaring that we 'reckon ourselves to be dead indeed unto sin, but alive unto God,' and that it is our desire as well as our duty to live devoted to him. And as in baptism we profess to have received spiritual life, so in communicating at the Lord's table we have the emblems of that heavenly food by which we *live,* by which we *grow,* and in virtue of which we hope to *live for ever.* And as we are born of God but once, so we are baptized but once; but as our spiritual life is maintained by the continued agency of divine grace, and the comforts of it enjoyed by the habitual exercise of faith in a dying Redeemer, so it is our duty and privilege frequently to receive the holy supper."* Baptism, therefore, being the emblem of the reception of life, and the eucharist of the food by which we are sustained, the metaphorical representation requires that baptism should always be received as a condition of communion, since we must necessarily live before we are capable of receiving the food by which life is supported. "Baptism," says Mr. Judd, in his late able Review, "as an emblematical representation of death and resurrection, exhibits the believer as a new creature; as born again, and becoming a child of God, and a subject of Christ's kingdom. Of course the proper position of the initiating ordinance is at the commencement of this new relation. The nature and fitness of things seem to require that it should be the first public act after believing. On the other hand, the Lord's supper is a communion, or social commemoration of the Saviour's dying love, and, therefore, necessarily a church ordinance, and not obligatory on the Christian until he has entered by baptism into a church relation."

We are now, I trust, prepared to say confidently that the order of proceeding for which we contend agrees with the

* Booth's Vindication in Bap. Manual.

time in which the two institntions were appointed, with the words of the commission in which the observation of them was enjoined, with the invariable practice of the inspired apostles and primitive churches, and with the emblematical representations of the two ordinances. It is, therefore, the order of truth, the order of propriety, the order of duty, the order divinely prescribed, the desecration of which cannot take place without a palpable breach of the fundamental statute enacted by God for the government of his people until the end of the world. It was doubtless with respect to their relative positions as well as to the institutions themselves, and other duties, that the apostles were so particular as we find them to have been, in admonishing the churches. The ordinances delivered to them they were assured had been, by themselves, received, immediately, from the Lord Jesus. They insisted, therefore, that they should conform to them, they commanded their obedience in these particulars, they cautioned them of neglect, and exhorted them to perseverance. They had a right to do this, because they were ministers and stewards of the mysteries of God. Guided by the spirit of truth, they gave, also, in all these particulars, an infallible expression of the mind of Christ." "I have," say they, "received of the Lord Jesus that which also I delivered unto you."* "Be ye followers of me, even as I am of Christ. Now I praise you, brethren, that ye *remember*—μεμνησθε, follow—me in all things, and keep the ordinances as I delivered them to you."† "I beseech you, be ye followers of me. For this cause I have sent unto you Timotheus, my beloved son, and faithful in the Lord, who shall bring you into remembrance of my ways, which be in Christ, as I teach every where, in every church."‡ "Brethren, be ye followers of me, and mark them which walk so, as ye have us for an

* 1 Cor. xi. 23. † Cor. xi. 1, 2. ‡ 1 Cor. iv. 16, 17.

ensample."* "Though I be absent in the flesh, yet am I with you in the spirit, joying, and beholding your order, and the steadfastness of your faith in Christ. As ye have therefore received Christ Jesus the Lord, so walk ye him; rooted, and built up in him, and established in the faith as ye have been taught, abounding therein, with thanksgiving. Beware, lest any man spoil you through philosophy and vain deceit, after the traditions of men, after the rudiments of the world, and not after Christ."† "Therefore, my brethren, stand fast, and hold the traditions which ye have been taught, whether by word, or our epistle."‡ Such are the inspired exhortations and instructions addressed to us regarding our undeviating observance, in its primitive form, and with all its preliminaries and concomitants, of this sacred institution.

That the eucharist ought to be administered by a regularly authorized minister of the Gospel, I take it for granted, is admitted by all, for the same reasons that apply in the administration of baptism.

I have several times alluded to the fact that this ordinance is to be received by us in a social capacity. I shall not stop now to elaborate this proposition. If any one is disposed to assume the opposite, he will, of course, feel himself obliged to sustain his hypothesis by the requisite testimony.

It is now sufficiently evident that the subject before us is not an exception to the general rule, that whatever is important either in doctrinal truth, or practical religion, is plainly taught in the word of God. The law, particularly, by which the constitution of the Christian church is fixed, the qualifications of its members defined, and the order of its sacraments, and worship, established, is written as with a sunbeam in letters of light, and therefore so plain and unequivocal that it

* Phil. iii. 17. † Col. ii. 5—8. ‡ 2 Thess. ii. 15.

is difficult to conceive how it could, by an honest mind, be overlooked, or misinterpreted.

I have thus placed, as I believe, beyond the reach of successful controversy, the facts I proposed to establish, respecting the terms of communion, as prescribed by Jesus Christ. If the Christian commission be authoritative; if apostolic administration and example are to be regarded; if the nature and design of the two ordinances are worthy of notice in settling their relative positions; if the positive and repeated injunctions, and exhortations of the apostles to the churches, to keep the ordinances as they delivered them from the hands of Christ to the care and observance of his people, be obligatory—and if all these may be unheeded by us, what can be presented with sufficient force to claim our attention?—then must it be admitted that repentance, faith, and baptism, are indispensable qualifications for the admission of a candidate to the fellowship of the church, and that they are the divinely ordained, and unchangeable terms of *Sacramental Communion*.

CHAPTER III.

THE HISTORY OF OPINIONS REGARDING THE TERMS OF COMMUNION SHOWS THAT OUR DOCTRINES HAVE BEEN UNIVERSALLY EMBRACED ON THE SUBJECT.

Baptism has been held in all ages, and by all denominations, to be a divinely prescribed preliminary to the Lord's Supper—Dr. Priestley's opinions—Testimonies in proof, Justin Martyr, Jerome, Austin, Bede, Theophylact, Bonaventure, Frid. Spanheim, Lord Chancellor King, Austin's rule—Modern divines—Wall, Doddridge, Manton, Dwight, all the Catechisms and Confessions of Faith—Robert Hall.

THE history of opinions regarding the divinely ordained terms of communion at the Lord's table, affords the amplest testimony that the conclusions to which we have been conducted on the subject are not wholly novel, nor peculiar to our church. Baptism especially, and in purer communities and later times, repentance and faith also, have been held as indispensable prerequisites, the first, certainly, by all sects and denominations in all ages and in every country, from the days of the apostles, until within the last two hundred years, during which period some of our own people have seceded; and their opinions, set forth so ably and eloquently by Bunyan and Hall, have been embraced, probably, by a few individuals of Pedobaptist churches. "Before the grand Romish apostacy," says Mr. Booth, "in the very depths of that apostacy, and since the Reformation, both at home and abroad, the general practice has been to receive none but baptized persons to communion at the Lord's table." I may add that, during a thousand years, as I shall hereafter take occasion fully to demonstrate, the practice was as invariable to admit, and *require* to come to the communion, all, whether infants or others, who had received the baptismal rite. And, indeed, many of those who have the sagacity to perceive the inconsistency of abandoning Pedo-communion, while they adhere to Pedo-baptism, still insist that as baptism is required as a preliminary to communion, so all those who receive it are entitled and should be immediately brought to the eucharist. Dr. Priestley may be referred to as an example of this class of writers. "No objections," says he, "can be made to this custom"—of giving the Lord's supper to infants—"but what may, with equal force, be made to the custom of baptizing infants." He adds, "Infant communion is, to this day, the practice of the Greek churches, of the Russians, the Armenians, the Maronites, the Copts, the Assyrians, and, probably, all other Oriental churches."*

In regard, however, to the object especially before us, I shall sustain the proposition that baptism has ever been regarded as an essential preparation for the Lord's Supper by competent proof. I begin with the earliest Christian fathers, and shall quote at least one accredited writer in every century, or in every two or three centuries, down to our times, and thus make the truth of the statement I have submitted no longer a matter of doubt.†

Justin Martyr wrote about A. D. 150, not more than fifty years after the death of the apostle John. On the subject before us, he says: "This food is called by us the eucharist, of which it is not lawful for any to partake, but such as believe the things that are taught by us to be true, and have been baptized."‡

* Address to Protest. Dissent., pp. 28, 31.
† Vide Booth's Vindication, Part first.
‡ Apol. 2, p. 162, apud Suicerus.

Jerome, confessedly one among the most learned and candid of the fathers, wrote about A. D. 400. He says, "Catechumeni communicare non possunt, etc.—Catechumens cannot communicate at the Lord's table, being unbaptized."*

Austin, who wrote about A. D. 500, maintaining the absolute necessity of administering the Lord's supper to infants, remarks: "Quod nisi baptizati, etc.—Of which certainly they cannot partake unless they are baptized."†

Bede, who flourished about A. D. 700, narrates the following incident: "Three young men, princes of the Eastern Saxons, seeing a bishop administer the sacred supper, desired to partake of it as their royal father had done. To whom the bishop replied—If you will be baptized in the salutary fountain as your father was, you may also partake of the Lord's supper as he did; but if you despise the former, ye cannot, in any wise, receive the latter."‡

Theophylact, in a work, published about A. D. 1100, remarks: "No unbaptized person partakes of the Lord's supper."§

Bonaventure, who wrote about 1200, observes, "Faith, indeed, is necessary to all the sacraments, but especially to the reception of baptism, because baptism is the first among the sacraments, and the door to the sacraments."‖

Frid. Spanheim, who flourished about A. D. 1600, on the point before us asserts—"Subjecta ad eucharistiam, etc.—None but baptized persons are admitted to the Lord's table."¶

Lord Chancellor King wrote about A. D. 1700. He says —"Baptism was always precedent to the Lord's supper; and none (ever) were admitted to receive the eucharist till

---

* In cap. 6, Epist. 2 ad Corinth. † Epist. ad Bonaf. Epist. 106.
‡ Hist. Eccl. Lib. 2, cap. 5, p. 63. § Cap. 4, Mat. p. 83.
‖ Apud Forbesium, Instruct. Historic. Theol. lib. 10, cap. 4, sect. 9.
¶ Hist. Christian Col. 623.

they were baptized. This is so obvious to every man that it needs no proof."*

These authorities, which I have selected from hundreds in my possession, all of which speak invariably the same language, sufficiently demonstrate what has been the doctrine of the church in every age. They are quoted simply as witnesses of a matter of fact, in which capacity they are undoubtedly competent. I am not unapprised that there were people of several classes, who, in the second and third centuries, made profession of the name of Christ, and who wholly *rejected* baptism. They, however, generally treated the Lord's supper in the same manner. A learned writer says of them all, that, generally, they entirely renounced the Scriptures as the word of God.† Nor am I ignorant of the fact, that in the latter end of the sixteenth century, Socinus, and his followers, considered the reception of baptism as indifferent, except in reference to such as are converted from judaism, paganism, or mahommedanism.‡ But none of the denominations which prevail in our country, and it is evident that all the respectable writers we have quoted, and others of all evangelical churches concur with them, would admit that either these ancient corruptors of christianity, or the more modern Socinians, are worthy to be called churches of Christ.

Let us now apply to the decision of this matter the celebrated rule of Austin,§ and surely if any doctrine or practice can, by this means, be proved apostolical, that now under consideration has claims to the distinction not inferior to any other, however firmly established. Dr. Wall translates it thus:—" What the whole church, through all the world, does

* Enquiry, part 2, p. 44.
† Suicerus Thesaurus, sub. voce $Βαπτισμα$.
‡ Wall's Hist. &c. part 2. ch. 5.
§ De baptismo contra Dona. Lib. 4, cap. 23.

practice, and yet it has not been instituted by councils, but has been always been in use, is, with very good reason, supposed to have been settled by authority of the apostles." That it is necessary to receive baptism prior to the Lord's supper is "what the whole church, through all the world," has ever "practised;" it "never was instituted by councils;" it has, also, "been always in use." "With very good reason," therefore, is it "supposed to have been settled by authority of the apostles."

It is now determined that we have the concurrence of all Christians in every age and country in the conclusion that baptism, at least, must always be received before the eucharist. To prove the other part of our proposition—that we have, in this doctrine, at the present day, the unanimous suffrage as such, of all the prevailing denominations—I will briefly refer to a few of their most popular writers of recent date.

Dr. Wall avers—" No church ever gave the communion to any persons before they were baptized. Among all the absurdities that ever were held, none ever maintained that any person should partake of the communion before they were baptized."*

Dr. Manton observes—" None but baptized persons have a right to the Lord's table."†

Dr. Doddridge says—"It is certain that Christians in general, have always been spoken of, by the most ancient fathers, as baptized persons. And it is also certain that, as far as our knowledge of primitive antiquity extends, no unbaptized person received the Lord's supper."‡

To these decisive testimonies, we will only add that of Dr. Dwight, who thus expresses his opinion—"It is an

---

* Hist. Inf. Bap. part 2. ch. 9.
† Supp. to Morn. Exer. p. 199.
‡ Lectures, p. 510.

indispensable qualification for this ordinance, that the candidate for communion be a member of the visible church of Christ, in full standing. By this I intend, that he should be a person of piety; that he should have made a public profession of religion; and that he should have been baptized."*

Perfectly conformable to these views of the subject are the catechisms, and confessions of faith, that have been published at any time, or by any denomination of Christians. If the mention of the positive institutions of Christ is not wholly omitted, baptism is not only always spoken of first, but generally in such a way, if that fact is not declared in so many words, as intimates that it is regarded as a prerequisite to the Lord's table.

To both these solemn appointments our Pedobaptist brethren attach an importance which we can by no means admit, and administer them for purposes we cannot approbate. To these considerations we shall pay our respects in due time. Still we do not derive the less pleasure from the fact that they agree with us, and ever have done so, in holding baptism as one of the terms of communion, and, as we have before remarked, in purer communities, and later times, that they generally also require both repentance and faith. So Christ ordered in the commission; so the apostles administered the discipline of the gospel, and admonished all subsequent churches to follow their example; and so have Christians conducted the house of God in all ages. What more need we say firmly to settle the principles of our faith? In relation to so plain a truth it is difficult involuntarily to err.

The influence of these facts and considerations, when they come to be understood, which must be the case at no distant day, for the people cannot always be kept in ignorance of them, will be felt by the denominations around us. "The

* Syst. Theol. Serm. 160.

wide circulation," says Mr. Hall, "of the doctrine," that baptism must, agreeably to the law of Christ, be received anterior to the Lord's supper, "ought, undoubtedly, to have the effect of softening the severity of censure on that conduct which is its necessary result; such is that of the great majority of the Baptists in confining their communion to those whom they deem baptized: wherein they act precisely on the same principle with all other Christians, who assume it for granted that baptism is an essential preliminary to the reception of the sacrament. The point on which they differ is the nature of that institution, which we place in immersion, and of which we suppose rational and accountable agents the only fit subjects; this opinion, combined with the other generally received one, that none are entitled to receive the eucharist but such as have been baptized, leads inevitably to the practice which seems so singular, and gives so much offence—the restricting of communion to our own denomination. Let it be admitted that baptism is, under all circumstances, a necessary condition of church-fellowship, and it is impossible for the Baptists to act otherwise. The recollection of this may suffice to rebut the ridicule and silence the clamor of those who loudly condemn the Baptists for a proceeding which, were they but to change their opinion on the subject of baptism, *their own principles* would *compel* them to adopt. They both"—Baptists and Pedobaptists—" concur in a common principle, from which the practice deemed so offensive is the necessary result. Considered as an *argumentum ad hominem*, or an appeal to the avowed principles of our opponents, this reasoning may be sufficient to shield us from that severity of reproach to which we are often exposed, nor ought we to be censured for acting upon a system, which is sanctioned by our accusers."*

* Works, vol. 2. pp. 212, 213.

CHAPTER IV.

REPLY TO SUCH OBJECTIONS TO OUR DOCTRINES ON THIS SUBJECT AS ARE DERIVED FROM THE PRESUMED NATURE OF JOHN'S BAPTISM.

Opinions of Mr. Hall, that John's was not Christian baptism, and therefore that the original communicants had never been baptized—His own reasons refute his conclusions—Contrast of John's with Christ's baptism—Their respective formularies—Christ's desire to conceal his own character—If, on account of the objects designed to be represented, John's was not Christian baptism, for the same reasons the first administration of the Lord's Supper was not Christian—The same correspondence in spiritual import—Difference in the ordinances before and after the death of Christ—Arguments as to time—Mistake in regard to the source of John's commission—Comparison between the baptism of John, and of the disciples of Christ.

The principles we have established in the two preceding chapters, venerable, and almost universally received, as we have seen that they are; enjoined by divine law, of which there has been, and can be no repeal, do not appear, to two classes of logicians, to be satisfactorily sustained. Open communion Baptists, and some individuals among Pedobaptists, who have been persuaded to adopt their opinions, dissent. Their reasons it is proper for us now to examine, and dispassionately determine whether they are sufficient to invalidate in any respect, or even to weaken the force of our conclusions. All the objections worthy of our attention may be arranged under three general heads; the presumed character of the dispensation of John the Baptist; the inspired principles of christian toleration; and the spiritual nature of the Gospel of Christ. Besides these it will be necessary to notice only a few of a miscellaneous description. A consideration of the first I have mentioned will occupy the present chapter.

By far the most able and successful individual, as a writer and divine, who has ever employed his pen in opposition to restricted communion, is, as I have before remarked, the late Rev. Robert Hall, of Bristol. His work on the subject is ample, and elaborate. Enjoying the unlimited confidence of all parties, he may be considered as speaking by authority. As such we shall regard him. And as we shall have occasion to scrutinize his opinions somewhat at large, and may sometimes be tempted to do so with severity, I owe it to myself to say of him, in advance, as he does,* of the excellent Booth: " I trust the free strictures which it will be necessary to make on his performance, will not be deemed inconsistent with sincere veneration for his character, which I should be sorry to see treated with any disrespect." This learned and eloquent man presents his proposition on the question now to be decided in the following terms—" It is demonstrable that John's baptism was a separate institution from that which was enacted after our Lord's resurrection," therefore, " the Lord's supper is evidently *anterior* to baptism, and the original communicants consisted, entirely, of such as had not received that ordinance."†

The apostles were not baptized, in the Christian sense of that term, at the time the Lord's supper was instituted! Indeed, as they unquestionably did not afterwards perform that duty, they never did receive christian baptism at all! The great mass of the first Christians, all, in truth, baptized by John and the disciples, were in the same predicament!

---

* Works, vol. i. p. 295.
† Works, vol. ii. pp. 218, 219.

These are certainly strange opinions. They appear to us palpably preposterous. But for the respectability of their origin they would not be thought worthy of notice, or to need a single word of refutation. What, we would ask, are the reasons which induced Mr. Hall, and weigh with his admirers, on account of which they imagine that " John's baptism was a separate institution from that enacted after our Lord's resurrection?" He explains himself *—" The rite performed by John is rarely, if ever, introduced without some explanatory phrase or epithet. It is sometimes denominated the baptism of John; on other occasions, baptism in water, and the baptism of repentance; but it is never expressed in the absolute form in which the mention of Christian baptism invariably occurs."†

These are the first reasons. We have considered them carefully, and find ourselves utterly incapable of perceiving their applicability or force. Let all the facts enumerated be admitted, and what then? Do they prove any thing? They only show that John's baptism was a *new* rite, introduced by him. That such a new institution should be designated by certain descriptive phrases and epithets, is perfectly natural. It could not be otherwise. But we go further than this. The suggestion places in our hands the means of additional confirmation of our own conclusions, and enables us to turn the arguments of our opponents against themselves. The true inquiry is this—In speaking of baptism in water subsequent to the pentecost, do the inspired writers ever append to it any " explanatory phrase or epithet," by which to distinguish it from John's baptism? Had it been different, they would doubtless have so represented it; but if they do, I have never been able to make the discovery. The natural

---

* I quote the New York edition, 1835.
† Works, vol. i. p. 369.

inference, therefore, is, not that Christian baptism is "a distinct institution" from that of John, but, with whatever circumstantial differences, essentially the same baptism. The argument relied upon to prove it a different baptism, consequently, turns actually in our favor. It shows that if the baptism administered after the ascension of our Lord had been, in any important respect, dissimilar to that administered previously, some distinctive appellation would have been introduced in connection with it to apprise us of that fact. No such intimation is given. We cannot, therefore, avoid the conclusion, that John's baptism and Christian baptism are identical, and that they form but the "one baptism" of the gospel economy.*

A second reason for the conclusion that "John's baptism was a separate institution from that which was enacted after our Lord's resurrection," and that as a consequence the Lord's supper was anterior, and of which, when the first communicants partook, they had never received Christian baptism, is thus stated by the distinguished writer already quoted—"John himself contrasts his baptism with a superior one, which he directs his hearers to expect at the hands of the Messiah."†

Upon this matter but a single remark is necessary. John, it is true, does contrast his own with a superior baptism which he directs his hearers to expect at the hands of the Messiah. But who is so ignorant of the word of God as not to know, especially as John himself declares it, that this baptism to be expected from Christ was not of water but of the Holy Ghost—"I, indeed, baptize you with water, but he shall baptize you with the Holy Ghost." From this, therefore,

---

* In this chapter, and the two following, I am deeply indebted to the younger Fuller, the line of whose thought in his admirable Conversations on Communion is generally pursued, and whose words are often freely employed.

† Works, vol. i. p. 369.

Christian baptism, all will admit, is as distinct as that of John could possibly be. Where then is the applicability of the argument to the question at issue? It has evidently none whatever.

A third reason for the conclusion that John's was not Christian baptism, is expressed in these terms—"It is universally admitted that Christian baptism has been invariably administered in the name of Jesus, and that circumstance is essential to its validity; while it is evident, from the solicitude with which our Saviour avoided the avowal of himself as the Messiah, that, during his public ministry, his name was not publicly employed as the object of a religious rite.—The practice of baptizing in his name must have been equivalent, at least, to a public confession of his being the Messiah.— The historian informs us that, while John was baptizing,— all men were musing in their hearts whether *he* were the Christ, or not.—But how is it possible, let me ask, that such a question should arise among the people on the supposition that John baptized in his name?"*

This view of the matter is radically defective, primarily, because it misstates the matters of fact. That Christian baptism was invariably administered, *verbally*, in the name of *Jesus*, is not true. Its formulary was—" In the name of the Father, and of the Son, and of the Holy Ghost." Neither was John's baptism administered, *verbally*, in the name of *Jesus;* but in the name of *Messias*, or the Christ—him who was to come—ὁ ἐρχομενος. " John—says Paul—verily baptized with the baptism of repentance, saying unto the people, that they should believe on him who should come after him— that is, on Christ Jesus." These distinctions are vital to a just conception of the argument. As the name of Jesus of Nazareth did not occur in the form of words used by John

* Works, vol. i. p. 370.

in the rite he administered, ample room is furnished for the musings and inquiries of the people, whether the son of Zechariah was really the Christ, the expected deliverer. Thus also is fully exposed the fallacy of the objection founded on the supposed solicitude of the Redeemer to conceal, for the present, his character and office. These corrections as to the facts, remove instantly every difficulty. It is very evident that John, and after him the disciples of the Saviour, might have baptized the whole Jewish nation in the name of *Messias*, or the *Christ*, and had they not informed the people, at the same time, that Jesus was the person entitled to be so considered, they would not, in a single instance, have violated the caution he manifested to avoid an *indiscriminate* avowal of his claims to Messiahship.

Having noticed one so material an error, in these postulates of our opponents, we are naturally inclined to suspect the presence of others. To ascertain their existence let us inquire whether Mr. Hall does not lay too much stress on the desire of Christ for concealment. It will not be denied that, during his personal ministry, our Lord commissioned, not only the twelve apostles, but also the seventy disciples, to perform, and that too *in his name*, acts calculated to excite at least as much attention, and to give fully as much publicity to whatever the action revealed, as could have attended baptism in his name. They were authorized, and instructed, to heal the sick, to cast out devils, to preach the gospel, and to perform miracles, *in his name*. They went forth in obedience to the order of their appointment, and having fulfilled their mission, they returned exulting in their success. "Lord—exclaimed they—even the devils are subject to us *through thy name*." A public act of the nature of any of these, in the name of Jesus, was, undoubtedly, equivalent to a public confession that he was the Messiah.

These facts are inconsistent with the notion that he either felt or exercised all the caution which the objection now under consideration assumes. The secret which it is imagined he was so solicitous to conceal, was as fully exposed by these exorcisms, sermons, and miracles, as it could possibly have been by baptizing in his name. Why, then, should he command the former, while he prohibited the latter? The whole matter, therefore, amounts simply to this. Our Lord studiously avoided an *indiscriminate verbal* declaration that he was the Christ, because he did not wish his claims to rest on this ground. But he never shrunk from such an avowal of his Messiahship as might be inferred from his works. To these, indeed, he constantly appealed as testimony of his objects and character. And can the required proof be hence gathered that John's was not the Christian baptism? No more than it can be established by the same evidence that Peter had no right by which he could be recognized, as the apostle of the circumcision.

A fourth reason is offered which it is imagined invalidates the Christian character of John's baptism. It is the admitted fact that the events baptism was designed to commemorate had not yet occurred—the death, burial, resurrection, and ascension, of Jesus Christ. He, it is alleged, directed the minds of his hearers to the Messiah to come, or the Christ who is coming. And as an event cannot be commemorated until after it has transpired, the baptism, which is defective in this respect, cannot be Christian baptism.

Admit all this to be true—which, by the way, could not have been long so, for John soon pointed to him in person, and said to the listening multitude—" Behold the Lamb of God, who taketh away the sin of the world"—but admit it all to be true, and, therefore, that his baptism could not, like the Christian, have represented events which had yet occurred, or truths already fully delivered, and what advantage would our opponents thereby secure to their cause? We can perceive none whatever. The Lord's supper as administered previous to the death of Christ is involved in precisely the same predicament. If this kind of argument establishes an essential difference between that *baptism* which was administered before, and that which was administered after, the passion of our Lord, it must, by the same process, also establish a difference equally essential between the Lord's supper before and after the same event. When first administered, the transactions it was designed to celebrate had not taken place. Both the ordinances were alike prospective. So, then, if the baptism was not Christian, neither, for the same reason, was the eucharist Christian. If we must seek for the genuine Christian institutions in the administrations subsequent to the resurrection, baptism was received in every case before the Lord's supper, and no one approached the latter who had not submitted to the former. It follows, therefore, that so far as this objection is concerned, whatever may be considered true as to the facts involved, our conclusions remain equally firm and unshaken.

A fifth reason for the opinion that John's was not the Christian baptism is stated in the following language—" The spiritual import of Christian baptism, as asserted by Paul, transcends, incomparably, the measure of religious knowledge possessed during the ministry of John. 'Know ye not,' is his appeal to Christians, ' that so many of us as were baptized into Jesus Christ were baptized into his death?' What is the meaning of the words '*baptized into his death?*' Whatever e.se it may comprehend, it unquestionably means the being baptized into a belief of his death. But at the time that John was fulfilling his course, this belief was so far from possessing the minds of his converts, that even the apostles were not only ignorant of that event, but impatient of its mention. 'As many of us,' says Paul, 'as were baptized into Jesus Christ were baptized into his death;' which is surely equivalent to affirming that whoever were not baptized into his death, were not baptized into Christ. But the disciples of John were not baptized into the belief of his death. Therefore, they were not baptized into Christ."*

This argument, to perceive its want of conclusiveness, needs but a moment's examination. Were it valid, it would, like that we have just dismissed, recoil with a force equally fatal in its effects against the Lord's supper as administered before the death of Christ. To illustrate this remark let us briefly test its powers. To say that the apostles *commemorated* an event before it occurred, is plainly a contradiction in terms. But this is not all. The spiritual import of the Lord's supper, as asserted by the apostle Paul, exceeds the measure of religious apprehension which possessed the minds of its recipients at its first celebration. "As often," says Paul, "as ye eat this bread, and drink this cup, ye do show the Lord's death." What is meant by the phrase "*ye do show the Lord's death?*" Whatever else it comprehends, it unquestionably includes the belief of his death. But at the first celebration of the sacred supper this belief was so far from possessing the minds even of the apostles, that they were not only ignorant of that event, but impatient of its mention. When Jesus was about to be taken in the garden, we find Peter, the prince of their number, engaged in active *combat*, sword in hand, to prevent that identical tragedy. "As often," says Paul, "as ye eat this bread and drink this cup, ye do show the Lord's death;" which is surely equivalent to saying that those who did not thus show the Lord's death, did not partake of the Lord's supper. But the apostles at its first

---

* Works, vol. i. pp. 371, 372.

celebration did not thus show their belief of the Lord's death. Therefore, they did not partake of the Lord's supper. Thus have we demonstrated that the same argument that proved that the baptism of John and of the disciples, was not a Christian rite, and, therefore, that they were not baptized, establishes, with the same decisiveness, that the Lord's supper they received was not a Christian ordinance, and, therefore, that they did not, until after the resurrection of Messiah, receive any Christian sacrament whatever. If so, baptism still maintains its priority, and the state of the case continues unchanged.

The thought will readily occur to the mind of every one that both the ordinances in question, previous to the death of Christ were in some respects, though not essentially, different from what they were afterwards. This dissimilarity consisted, not in their spirit, object, or manner, but simply in the amount of information possessed by those who received them. The recipients of both were not aware of their full import, because the events they recognized were still in the future. But their knowledge was sufficient, for the time being, for all practical purposes, and, therefore, their deficiency in this respect was not such as to vitiate the validity of the divine appointments. The period of which we speak was the twilight, the early dawn of the Gospel day. The shadows of night had not yet departed. A dimness and mystery enshrouded every event intended ultimately to illustrate and endear the death of the Son of Man. Previously the church had been totally obscured and invisible. Baptism by John and the disciples of Christ, began to make ready a people prepared for the Lord, and thus to trace the great outlines of the kingdom. The Lord's supper completed the sacred work. The Church, when it was received, although it had not assumed all its destined beautiful proportions, was rendered fully visible. The imperfections assignable to one sacrament, are equally characteristic of both. The recipients of either could not realize the amazing transaction to which they pointed. This was a glory not yet revealed. Shall we, however, on this account, consign them to the darkness of a preceding dispensation? Rather shall we not recognize them, although in the incipient stages of being, as the impressive and affecting ordinances the full signification of which the clear shining of the Gospel was soon gloriously to discover. Whatever may be their destiny, the two sacraments, as administered before the death of Christ, must most evidently stand or fall together. But suppose we repudiate them, what will be the consequence. If these, as they existed during the personal ministry of our Lord, are taken away, how, as we have no others to which we may refer, in teaching men, as the commission prescribes, to observe all things, whatsoever he had commanded *them*, will any one be able to discover, and establish, a single duty peculiar to the fellowship of the church of Christ?

A sixth objection is introduced. "As the ministry of John," says Mr. Hall, "commenced previously to that of the Messiah, which succeeded his baptism, no rite celebrated at that time, is entitled to a place among Christian sacraments, since they did not commence with the Christian dispensation, nor issue from the authority of Christ, as head of the church."*

In this short sentence we have two distinct reasons for dissent. It is proper for us to notice them separately. The former is, that the ministry of John did not commence with the Gospel dispensation; and the latter is, that John's baptism did not proceed from the authority of Christ as head of the church. Upon both we join issue, and plead that neither is entitled to the consideration of a matter of fact.

* Works, vol. i. p. 372.

JOHN'S ADMINISTRATION NOT CHRISTIAN. 69

In relation to the former, is it true, allow me to ask, that the ministry of John did not commence with the Gospel dispensation? I know it is insisted,* that this is impossible, for the reason that—" During our Lord's residence on earth, until his resurrection, the kingdom of God is uniformly represented as future, though near at hand." This, also, is a mistake, as will be clearly seen, the moment we consult the Evangelists on the subject. "If I cast out devils," said our Lord on one occasion, and that too, long before his resurrection, "by the Spirit of God, then *the kingdom of God* IS COME *unto you.*" And when the Pharisees inquired of him *when* the kingdom of God should come, he replied in these terms: " The kingdom of God cometh not with observation. Neither shall men say, lo here! or lo there! for, behold, *the kingdom of God is within you.*" Nor is it possible to evade the force of the arguments thus furnished by distinguishing between our Lord's personal ministry, and the ministry of John; since Mark expressly assures us that his coming was " In the beginning of the Gospel of Jesus Christ the Son of God."†

---

* Ut supra.

† The commencement of the narrative of Mark i. 1, is thus translated by Michaelis in his German New Testament :—" The beginning of the Gospel of Jesus Christ, the Son of God, was made by John, who baptized in the wilderness, and preached the baptism of repentance for the remission of sins; as it is written, &c." He adds :—" If the first sentence—The beginning of the Gospel of, &c. was"—as some contend— " used as a title only to the rest of the book, then it would have begun with ὡς γέγραπται, which would be an unsuitable commence to any narrative." In the correctness of this exposition the following writers, as Biblical critics and scholars, were obliged to concur : Bishop Marsh —Notes to Michaelis, vol. iii. part 2, p. 5. Archbishop Newcome— Notes to the Harmony of the New Testament, p. 1. Lightfoot—Works, fol. ed. 1684, vol. ii. p. 331. Doddridge—Family Expositor, vol. i. p. 93, 8vo. 1810. Markland—apud Elsley in loc. Whitby—Comm. in loc. Grotius—Annotationes in V. et N. T. in Compendium deductæ a Sam.

That the ministry of John was within the Gospel dispensation is plainly declared by Jesus Christ himself, in such terms as to place the question beyond dispute. "From the days of John the Baptist until now," said he, speaking of his precursor during his imprisonment, "the kingdom of heaven suffereth violence." He doubtless had allusion in this remark to the eagerness with which the people received the doctrine, and pressed to join themselves to the disciples of John. But if his ministry had not been within, or as it really was, the commencement of "the kingdom of heaven," in the New Testament sense of that phrase, that is the Gospel, or Christian dispensation, how could this kingdom, this dispensation, this Gospel, which did not visibly exist, have been said to suffer violence? Evidently it could not. The figurative descriptions of the Gospel kingdom are also equally as much at war with the opinions of our opponents, as the plain representations just noticed. By the Great Teacher himself the kingdom of God is compared to "*leaven* hid in three measures of meal," which commences, and by slow, and, at first, almost imperceptible degrees, performs its work of fermentation until the whole mass is leavened. This accords with the facts as they are understood by us. Commencing with the preaching of John, and continuing through the personal ministry of the Saviour, the Gospel gradually insinuated itself into the minds of the people, until ultimately the most glorious results were achieved. It is also compared to "a grain of mustard seed." At first the Gospel grew in obscurity, and put forth its shoots imperceptibly to those who were expecting some sudden and splendid display of the

---

Moody, 4to 1727. Kuinoel—Comment. in lib. N. T. historicos, vol. ii. p. 11, and many others, who consider the passage but the first phrase of a long sentence, and, consequently, not to be separated from the context. Vide Townsend in loco.

power of Messiah. On the hypothesis that the kingdom of God, or the Gospel of Jesus Christ, commenced, agreeably to the declaration of Mark, with the ministry of John, there is a fitness in these resemblances—a thorough keeping between the comparisons and the reality. While, on the contrary, if we could suppose, with Mr. Hall, that the Christian dispensation commenced with the splendors of Pentecost, it must have burst upon the world, in a moment, with overwhelming majesty. Nothing in such a case would have been less appropriate to illustrate it than hidden leaven working its effect in secret, and the unobserved germination of the smallest of seeds.

To reply to us that during our Lord's personal ministry the kingdom of God is *always* represented as future, is to assume what, as we have already seen, is not true. That it is *occasionally* so represented is admitted. But this will not avail to turn aside our argument. It was in part future, because not yet fully revealed. But does it, therefore, follow that its *commencement* was in the future? Surely not. To affirm this for such reasons, as our opponents do, is as inconclusive as it would be to contend that we have not to this day witnessed its approach, because in our daily aspirations to God we are instructed to say—" Thy kingdom come." As the first rays of light which shoot forth from the east, and struggle with surrounding darkness, contain all the incipient elements of the perfect day, so the glimmering of the gospel which characterized the ministry of John, were the same elements which continued to increase in brightness during the ministry of our Lord, and contained all the essential properties which constituted the blazing splendor of the ministry of the Spirit. So far, therefore, is it from being true, that the ministry of John did not commence with the Gospel dispensation, it is rendered certain beyond a doubt, that it constituted of it a most important and interesting part—its auspicious commencement, the springing dawn of its visible existence.

The latter objection of the two now under consideration is that "John's baptism did not issue from the authority of Christ as head of the church." In reply, I remark, that the proposition, although it carries with it a semblance of truth, cannot be supported. That John received his commission from *Jesus, in person*, no one pretends. But if Christ is God, one with the Father, and inseparable from the Triune Deity, and from whom, as Jehovah, John certainly did receive his appointment, and by whom he was clothed with authority, how can it be said that he did not receive his commission from Christ as head of the church? It cannot, without either manifesting an obvious disposition to sophisticate by the aid of unmeaning distinctions, or palpably derogating from the character of Jesus Christ as the God of his people. And suppose it could, without an indignity to the Messiah, be proved that John was sent by the Father, independent of any concurrence of the Son, would this prove that his baptism was not a Christian institution? Apply the same argument in other cases, and it is, in any, equally appropriate, and the consequences would be most alarming. John's baptism, it is true, would, on this principle, be unchristianized, but the Gospel he preached would share the same fate. Nor could the desolating process of it be arrested here. The baptism of our Lord himself, the miracles which he wrought, and the Gospel which he preached, would all be found in the same unchristianized category, because he too as well as John received his commission from the Father. Christ was not self-commissioned—self-sent—self-authorized. Whence, then, did he receive his commission? By whom was he sent? By what authority did he preach, and act?

I abhor the idea of detracting in any way, even by implication, from the perfect, the essential divinity of Jesus Christ. We cannot be suspected of doing so if we maintain that, as the Messiah, his authority was received from the same source, and was of the same character, with that which appointed John to the office and duties which he fulfilled in the Christian kingdom.

Let us still further illustrate this topic. The chief priests and elders, as he was teaching in the temple, interrogated our Lord in this language, "By what authority doest thou these things? And who gave thee this authority?" Jesus answered them—"I will ask you one thing, which, if you tell me, I, also, will tell you by what authority I do these things—The baptism of John—whence was it?" This question evidently implies that the answer to his inquiry would be an appropriate response to that which they had propounded to him. If we need any additional testimony to place the correctness of our conclusions on this subject beyond a doubt, we have only to refer to our Lord's discourses themselves. "I am come," said he, "in my Father's name, and ye receive me not—I do nothing of myself; but as my Father hath taught me I speak these things—The works that I do in my Father's name, they bear witness of me—As my Father hath sent me so send I you." On the presumption that it is essential to a Christian ordinance that it should be instituted by Christ in person, in distinction from the Father, the works Jesus performed, as they confessedly have not that sanction, are at once divested of their Christian character. The Gospel which he preached was not, as we have seen, the Christian *doctrine;* the miracles he wrought were not *Christian* miracles; the commands which he issued were not *Christian* commands! Yet that the Gospel which our Saviour preached *was* the Christian doctrine; that the miracles which he performed *were* Christian miracles; and that the commands which he issued *were* Christian commands; who will, for a moment, pretend to deny? Why, then, deny that John's baptism was the *Christian* baptism, merely because it is imagined he received his commission, not from Jesus in person, but from the Father, who is one and the same with Christ! Nothing can be more supremely preposterous.

But numerous instances of baptism, other than those administered by John, occurred before the resurrection of Messiah. They were performed by the disciples—for Jesus, be it recollected, made and baptized *more* converts than John. These baptisms must have emanated from the *personal authority* of Jesus Christ, and they all occurred, undeniably, anterior to the institution of the sacred supper. The rite administered by the *twelve*, and by the *seventy*, under the direction of the great head of the church, was either John's baptism, or it was Christian baptism. If it was *not* John's, then it was certainly the Christian baptism; if it *was* John's baptism, then John's baptism issued from the *personal authority* of Christ. In either case Christian baptism was administered before the death of Christ, was an institution prior to the eucharist, and had been received by all who were admitted to the Lord's supper.

This argument need not, I think, be pursued further. Enough has been said to show that the proposition, " that John's baptism was a separate institution from that which was enacted after our Lord's resurrection, that the Lord's supper was *anterior* to baptism, and that the original communicants consisted entirely of such as had not received that ordinance," is an error, and cannot be supported. This we have demonstrated by examining and illustrating the fallacy of the reasoning by which the notion in question is attempted to be maintained. There are also, on the other hand, proofs, most ample and conclusive, that John's was in every essential particular the Christian baptism. To these we can, at present, but very briefly allude. John's baptism, and that of the disciples, were administered within the period of the Christian dispensation, by the authority of Christ, in the name of Christ, in the same mode, and to the same subject, with that of Christ, and no person who had received it, notwithstanding the imperative command to give Christian baptism to every believer, ever was, afterwards, rebaptized, either at Pentecost, or subsequently. In the absence of all proof to the contrary, and we have seen that no counter testimony can be produced, if these facts do not constitute John's baptism the Christian baptism, we have not now, and never have had, any ordinance that deserves the name, or that can claim to be regarded as Christian baptism. So palpably evident, indeed, is this truth, that on another occasion,* Mr. Hall himself acknowledges, perhaps by accident, when under the influence of his better judgment, that our conclusions are just and legitimate. "The baptisms," said he, "celebrated by Christ's disciples, during his personal ministry, in no respect, differed from John's either in the action itself, or in the import, but were merely a joint execution of the same work." We have already seen that the baptisms of the disciples did unquestionably emanate from "the authority of Christ as the head of the church." These baptisms, therefore, all belong to the Christian dispensation; and, having been performed in obedience to the Christian legislator, were undeniably Christian baptisms. But it is affirmed that "these baptisms, in no respect, differ from John's." Consequently, John's baptism and Christian baptism are identically the same baptism. This fact being now established,

* Terms of Com. Amer. ed. Works, vol. i. p. 362.

one of the most formidable objections against our doctrine is overthrown, and forever destroyed, and it remains true that repentance towards God, faith in our Lord Jesus Christ, and baptism, in the name of the Father, and of the Son, and of the Holy Ghost, are invariably and indispensably, preliminaries to sacramental communion.

CHAPTER V.

RLPLY TO THE ARGUMENTS AGAINST OUR DOCTRINE ON SACRAMENTAL COMMUNION FOUNDED ON THE INSPIRED PRINCIPLES OF CHRISTIAN TOLERATION.

The proposition examined, that a change of circumstances justifies a change of practice with regard to the ordinances—Inspired canons of Christian toleration recited—They require forbearance with things indifferent, but do not permit us to extend our fellowship to errors which are subversive of the divine law.

THE revealed principles which regulate sacramental communion, as explained and established by us, cannot, it is alleged, however strongly they may appear to be supported by the word of God, be always obligatory, because they are modified, to meet the different circumstances under which we may, at any time, be placed, by the inspired canons of Christian toleration. The general views illustrative of this hypothesis are set forth in the following terms: "The apostles, it is acknowledged," says Mr. Hall, "admitted none to the Lord's supper but such as were previously baptized; but under what circumstances did they maintain that course?"* *Circumstances* have now changed, and it is insisted our practice ought also to change! When the apostles required baptism as one of the terms of communion, we are told, "a mistake respecting the will of the supreme Legislator on the subject was impossible." At present, however, than such mistakes nothing is more common, or innocent; they have even become an "infirmity." "Con-

* Works, vol. ii. pp. 213, 214.

vince our Pedobaptist brethren," remarks this eloquent writer, "that it is their duty to be baptized in the method which we approve, and they stand ready, many of them at least, we cannot doubt, stand ready to perform it. Some of them"— who fail to be convinced, are "illustrious examples of piety."* That they are not baptized is rather their infirmity than their fault! "Shall we separate ourselves from the best of men" because of such mistakes? We might, perhaps, inquire, why Infinite Wisdom did not foresee this state of things, and provide for it by refraining to place baptism in the attitude of a qualification requisite to prepare us for an approach to the sacred table? It is replied, baptism was essential to communion in the apostles' days, not because there was or is "any possible connection between the two ordinances," but because baptism was then essential to salvation. Now it has ceased to be so. Only regeneration is essential to salvation; and that alone is necessary to communion which is required to fit us for salvation. "I assert, that baptism, in the apostolic age, *was* essential to salvation."† But in these degenerate "latter days, it is a mere rite,"‡ the reception or rejection of which is of so little moment that it cannot, in any way, affect even church fellowship, or be of the least consequence as respects our title to all the privileges and immunities of the kingdom of Messiah! "This reasoning," it is added, "proceeds not on the principles of the innocence of error in general, or of infant sprinkling in particular;"§ but,∥ "We may with great propriety allege the spirit of the times, the genius of the age," as a reason for overleaping all the ancient barriers.

* Works, vol. ii. pp. 214, 215.
† Reply to Kinghorn, Works, vol. i. p. 416.
‡ Ut Supra, Works, vol. i. p. 417.
§ Vol. i. p. 338. ∥ Vol. ii. pp. 229, 230.

Such are the reasons of Mr. Hall for free communion, and that, in these quotations I have not misrepresented him, all will at once perceive, who have ever carefully examined his works. Can it be necessary, before our enlightened churches and friends, seriously to argue such monstrous propositions? Are the practice and order of the apostles, established as they are upon unchanging principles, no longer examples for us to follow! Are we so differently associated from the primitive disciples that we must not be governed by the laws which directed their obedience, but resort to circumstances, the spirit of the times, the genius of the age, as more proper, and safer rules of action! The sprinkling of an infant by *mistake*, and the refusal to be *baptized*, commonly its consequence,— acts which, in the apostles' days, would have damned the perpetrator—are now innocent and familiar things, absolutely sanctioned by Jehovah; or at the worst, regarded only as *mistakes*, perhaps *infirmities*, because not particularly averse to "the spirit of the times, the genius of the age!" All is defended as at least harmless, and that too, not on the ground of "the innocence of error in general, or of infant sprinkling in particular," but of some imagined mysterious "canons of Christian toleration!" To such latitudinarianism as this—to such self-contradictions—what can we say? Had they been proposed by an ordinary man, or were they divested of their sparkling beauty of manner, brilliancy of metaphor, and glowing elegance of style, they would at once be condemned by every man of ordinary judgment, as a jumble of nonsense, indicative alike of weakness and insincerity.

Such are the general principles of open communion. The specific and particular arguments are more tangible. The inspired laws of Christian toleration, which, it is alleged, clearly include the subject of communion, and which are violated by excluding from the Lord's table pious unbaptized

Pedobaptists, are stated by Mr. Hall thus—" We are expressly commanded to tolerate in the church those diversities of opinion which are not inconsistent with salvation. We learn from the New Testament, that a diversity of views subsisted in the times of the apostles, betwixt the Jewish and Gentile converts especially, the former retaining an attachment to the ancient law, and conceiving the most essential parts of it to be in force, the latter from correcter views rejecting it altogether. Some declined the use of certain kinds of meat forbidden by Moses, which others partook of without scruple. 'One man esteemed one day above another,' conscientiously observing the principal Jewish solemnities; 'another esteemed every day alike.' Instead of attempting to silence these differences, by interposing his authority, St. Paul enjoins mutual toleration. ' Him that is weak in the faith receive ye, not to doubtful disputations. For one believeth that he may eat all things, another, who is weak, eateth herbs. Let not him that eateth despise him that eateth not; and let not him that eateth not, judge him that eateth; for God hath received him. Who art thou that judgest another man's servant? Unto his own master he standeth or falleth. Yea, he shall be holden up; for God is able to make him stand. One man esteemeth one *day* above another. Another esteemeth every day alike. Let every man be fully persuaded in his own mind.' Rom. xiv. 1—5. To the same purpose are the following injunctions in the next chapter: ' We, then, that are strong, ought to bear the infirmities of the weak, and not to please ourselves. Now the God of peace and consolation grant you to be like minded, one towards another, as Christ also hath received us to the glory of God.' Rom. xv. 1, 5, 7. It cannot be denied that these passages contain an apostolic canon for the regulation of the conduct of such Christians as agree in fundamentals, while they differ on points of subordinate importance; and by this canon they are commanded to exercise a reciprocal toleration and indulgence, and on no account to proceed to an open rupture. In order to determine how far these apostolic injunctions oblige us to tolerate the supposed error of our Pedobaptist brethren, we have merely to consider whether it excludes them from being of the number of those whom Christ has received to the glory of the Father."* In another place he adds: " Neither of the ancient nor of the modern error, is it pretended that they are fundamental, or that they endanger the salvation of those who hold them. Thus far they stand on the same footing, and the presumption is that they ought to be treated in the same manner."

This argument is ingenious in its construction. I doubt not Mr. Hall himself was deceived by it. But it is sophistical in its premises, erroneous in its form, deceptive in its language, inapplicable in its matter, and therefore inconclusive, and without effect on the subject in controversy. It is sophistical in its premises, because the argument is made to stand partly on grounds admitted to be true, and partly on grounds notoriously untenable and inadmissible. It is erroneous in its form, because the reasoning founded upon the apostolic instructions in regard to diversities of opinion and practice in the primitive churches respecting old Jewish rites and things indifferent, neither commanded nor prohibited in the Gospel, is made to apply to baptism, an ordinance enjoined by divine law, and regulated by an express statute of Messiah. It is deceptive in its language. Whether the "supposed errors" are "fundamental to salvation," is the form employed, when the only question at issue is, whether they are subversive of any divine law. No other reasons than these need be given for the assumption

* Works, vol. i. pp. 324, 325, et seq.

that it is inapplicable in its matter, inconclusive, and without effect on the subject in controversy.

I will not, however, despatch this topic quite so summarily. More extended remarks are to the sincere inquirer after truth desirable with reference to three particulars—our doctrine regarding Christian toleration in the aggregate; the violence inflicted on its principles in forcing their application to free communion; and a correct exposition of inspired teaching on the subject.

The duty, in the first place, of maintaining Christian toleration in the broadest and most liberal sense of the legitimate use of that term, we not only admit, but also strongly inculcate, and resolutely defend. The word of God teaches it; the spirit of the Gospel illustrates it; and I should feel myself unworthy the name of Christian if I did not reverently and gratefully appreciate it. For the generous, persevering, profound, and noble advocacy, by her sons, of Christian toleration, more than for any other distinction, has our venerable and beloved church been rendered illustrious through fifteen centuries. And shall we now change this honor into a weakness and make it a positive defect? In our enthusiasm to maintain our reputation as the friends of religious liberty shall we lose our discrimination, and cease to understand, or apply, the laws of Jesus Christ. "All men," says a recent distinguished writer, with whom we most heartily and fully concur, "are bound by the laws of God, and are responsible to him." Let that fact be distinctly recollected. "From this primary and supreme obligation the conscience cannot be freed. All human authority is subordinate to that which is divine, and is submitted to with the reservation of allegiance to the Universal Sovereign. That allegiance no man has a right to forego. God may prescribe, as supreme Ruler, the truths necessary to belief, and the modes of worship acceptable to him, and, *if he pleases*, enforce conformity by temporal, as well as eternal penalties. This he did once in the Hebrew commonwealth. He *there* authorized the civil magistrate to act in his name; and armed him with coercive power to maintain the revealed national religion. But this system was changed on the introduction of Christianity. The Son of God declined totally the use of the civil or coercive power in the propagation of the Gospel," to maintain its doctrines, or obedience to its commandments. "The obligation to love God, and obey the Gospel, binds the conscience of every man under this new dispensation as before; but he is now made responsible, not to the magistrate, but to God. Every thing is referred to the individual's own conscience, quickened by the view of the divine tribunal. His fellow men have no right to interfere. All human laws, therefore, which either prescribe or prohibit certain doctrines or rites, not inconsistent with the civil peace, are manifestly unauthorized by the Bible, and are obviously unjust. They invade the divine prerogative. They trespass on the most sacred right of the human soul, the right of seeking and serving God in the manner we are persuaded he requires. They are, therefore, null and void, and no man is bound to obey them."*

These principles, every particular of which, were this the place, I would sustain by the amplest testimony from the word of God, are applicable to the church. She is now the only lawful theocracy existing. Such a form of national government cannot, under the Gospel, take place. Those who enter the church must come as the laws of God prescribe, and to no other can obedience be required. In her fellowship these, and no other, are to be enforced. Should any man refuse compliance he is to be resisted, by moral means alone. If in disobedience he claims privileges and

* Encyc. Rel. Knowl. p. 1014.

immunities to which, by the divine rule, the submissive only are entitled, they are to be withheld. Does he persevere in his disregard of spiritual obligations? The inspired remedy is to be applied. This course alone Jehovah approves:— "Withdraw thyself from every brother that walketh disorderly." Beyond this no church dare go. The delinquent is not accountable to human authority, ecclesiastical or civil. God only is his judge, and "to his own master he standeth or falleth." So long as a man does not violate the civil peace and order by the exercise of his religion, he cannot, by the laws of the state, be disturbed. For his faith and practice he is accountable only to God. Such are our doctrines on the subject of religious toleration.

In applying these principles, we in the second place remark, that to maintain free communion, as that phrase is commonly understood, there is inflicted upon them the most palpable and injurious violence.

The scriptural canon, given in the passage quoted from Mr. Hall, furnishes an inspired precedent, which is accompanied by an application made by the apostle himself, fully illustrating what is required of us in its exercise. All matters in relation to which we have no inspired instructions, either contained in particular injunctions, or involved in general principles, and which are therefore indifferent, such as those especially named by Paul, the eating or not eating certain kinds of food, or the keeping or not keeping specified days as holy, are certainly embraced in the laws of toleration, and every man has a right to act without restraint, as he may "be fully persuaded in his own mind." But when he proceeds to embrace doctrines and indulge in practices plainly and necessarily subversive of the law of God, must we still conduct ourselves towards him in the same manner? Would it be faithful to God to do so? Ought such a man to expect the church, in such a case, to act upon the same principles as they would were his peculiarity only a matter of eating certain kinds of food, or of keeping a holy day? Pedobaptism is demonstrably a subversion of the law of Christ. Arguments based upon the apostolic rules regarding Jewish peculiarities, are wholly inapplicable here, and cannot, without great injury, be forced into such a service. Is the desecration of a precept which the Hebrew Christians supposed to be in force, but which all now admit was not so; and, whatever formerly might have been true, never was obligatory on the Gentiles, to be placed on the same level with the neglect of a Christian ordinance, which all confess is binding upon every believer? The indiscriminate participation of meat was not binding on the Jew or the Gentile, because it was not commanded. Nor was a scrupulous abstinence imperative, for the same reason. Each party might retain his peculiarity, and while he did not violate the law of love, practice as his discretion might suggest. Let our opponents prove that this is true of baptism, and I, for one, have no more to say on the subject. I will confess that to church fellowship it is a matter of no consequence, and that if we believe a man is a Christian, that he is born again of the Spirit, we are bound to receive him to communion without baptism. But who will venture to maintain that the substitute of a worldly ceremony, such, for example, as infant sprinkling, for an ordinance of God, is admissible under any circumstances? Who will suggest that Christian baptism is not enjoined on all believers? Until it can be established that infant baptism is allowable, and Christian baptism indifferent, the apostolic canon recited can have no application to the point in debate; and it remains true that our doctrine is yet untouched, which fixes repentance, faith, and baptism, as the terms of communion.

We are here met, however, with the declaration that neither a man's doctrine nor practice on the subject of baptism, can be of "fundamental importance." He may reject our opinions, and yet he may be eminently pious. It is insisted, therefore, that to tolerate every error not inconsistent with a state of salvation, and Pedobaptism among the number, is not only sanctioned by these rules, but is made an indispensable duty. Consequently that all such professors, of whatever denomination, as cannot be proved guilty of errors which would preclude the hope of their attaining to everlasting life, we are bound to invite, and admit to the Lord's table! But how is this hypothesis to be upheld? Not surely by any of the "canons" recited. Paul's principles of toleration are threefold. They require, first, that God shall have received the parties. Secondly, that they shall be conscientious. And, thirdly, that their peculiarities be not subversive of any divine law. All these were united in the case in question, decided by the apostle of the Gentiles. Is it so in the matter now before us? If this much can be made to appear, there is an end of the controversy. We must receive all candidates for communion without troubling ourselves to inquire whether they have been baptized. Mr. Hall selects a part of this threefold principle, reasons from it as if it were the whole, and thus arrives at a conclusion unwarranted by the premises. Reduced to a simple proposition, it amounts to this: Christian churches are to receive all whom God has received, who are conscientious, and whose peculiarities are not subversive of any existing divine law. Let us now see whether this rule enjoins the reception to church fellowship of pious Pedobaptists. Has God received them? We trust he has. Are they conscientious? We are willing to admit that they may be. Is this peculiarity subversive of any existing divine law? Most assuredly it is; nor is it admissible, as has been done to turn aside the argument, to substitute for the phrase "not subversive of any existing divine law," "not incompatible with a state of salvation." This is a logical finesse, makes a false issue, and cannot be allowed. Their reception by us would, on our part, amount to a conspiracy with them in their design to overthrow the law of God, and render us, not Christian communicants, but partners in their rebellion against the authority of the supreme Legislator.

We are authorized, therefore, to conclude, that the apostolic canons enjoining toleration, relate to things we have explained by the term indifferent, and cannot be forced into the service of open communionists. The fallacy which has led any sensible man to a different conclusion, has been, as we have now seen, induced by their confounding things which are essentially different, such as those we have just mentioned —the making principles subversive of a divine law, the same thing with principles incompatible with a state of salvation. Need I say a single word to demonstrate their palpable difference? Surely it is one thing to tolerate, in a Christian church, the eating or not eating certain food, and similar matters; yet another to tolerate a human invention which is brought in to take the place of a Christian ordinance; and still quite another to be in a state of salvation. If these are all the same, as the argument we are now controverting assumes, we may well exclaim, with the disciples, "Who then can be saved?" For in what direction do we cast our eyes, among the sects around us, in which we do not see human inventions substituted for divine institutions! It is one thing to dispense with that uniformity which *was not* required in the primitive churches, and quite another thing to dispense with that which *was, confessedly*, demanded. It is one thing to abstain from *new* terms of fellowship, and altogether another thing to deviate from *old* terms, which are of divine appointment; unchangeable in their nature; and of universal obligation; even though in both cases the parties may be Christians, and in a state of salvation. Repentance towards God, a profession of faith in Christ, and submission to baptism, *were*, it is acknowledged, in the primitive church, the terms of communion. Unless we are at liberty to nullify the laws of God by which they were made such, and to enact others, it is still true that the experience of whatever is essential to repentance for sin, the profession of whatever is essential to saving faith, and the submission to whatever is essential to Christian baptism, must continue to be the terms of communion. Let us never forget the inspired admonition, " There is *one* Lawgiver,"* and forbear any attempts to supplant him. His wisdom forbids us to imagine that by his general enactments, he destroys the authority and obligation of his special statutes, or that he will permit us to assume his prerogative, and place our own inventions superior to his laws in the government of his kingdom.

It remains for us, in the third place,—and in view of what has now been said, we can do so with much brevity,—to present a correct exposition of the word of God relating to this subject.

As if he had foreseen, and designed to counteract, the identical perversions now attempted to be made, Paul, in the very context of the passages recited, setting forth the inspired rules of toleration, expressly distinguishes the diversities then practised, in relation to which these rules were revealed, from the righteousness which pertains to the kingdom of God. " The kingdom of God," he asserts, " is not meat and drink, but righteousness, and peace, and joy in the Holy Ghost." And to the same purpose, in relation to observances which under a former dispensation, had been imperative, he said to the Corinthians:—" Circumcision is

* James iv. 12.

nothing, and uncircumcision is nothing, but keeping the commandments" of God is of great moment. Thus he carefully distinguishes between abrogated rites, ceremonies indifferent in themselves, and existing christian commands, obedience to which is requisite to "fulfil all righteousness." The apostle, in other words, says to the primitive churches:—Do not mistake the principle upon which toleration is enjoined. The points of disagreement between you, if subversive of no existing divine law, may be safely left to your own discretion. Each party is at liberty to eat meat or herbs, to observe days, or to disregard them, as his inclination may prompt. But beware of extending this rule too far. Remember, that though the kingdom of God consists not in meat and drink, it does consist in righteousness, and peace, and joy in the Holy Ghost. You are required to fulfil *all righteousness*, in the manner, and order, of the divine appointment. The keeping of the commandments of God is of perpetual obligation. The duties belonging to the Christian dispensation, consequently, although their neglect may not be considered destructive of the salvation of the soul, so far from being confounded with the peculiarities of the Jews or of the Gentiles, are exhibited by the apostle, in contrast with them. To treat them as similar then is preposterous, and diametrically in conflict with the true intent and design of the very canons so gratuitously pressed into service on the subject.

How, then, stands the case? Mr. Hall asserts that the ancient diversities respecting meats, holydays, and circumcision, and the modern diversities regarding the question whether we shall or shall not be baptized, are similar; Paul declares they are dissimilar. Mr. Hall insists they should be treated alike; Paul tells us they must be treated differently. I need not intimate which of the two is entitled to superior respect, nor suggest the direction in which our decision should incline. A diversity of opinions and practice regarding things indifferent, and abrogated Jewish rites, was, it is granted, no bar to Christian fellowship in primitive churches, nor is it so at present. To argue on this account, that a diversity of opinions and practice in relation to the subjects, the substance, and the benefits of Christian baptism is alike of no consequence in our churches, and that the only preliminary to sacramental intercourse now to be regarded is the hope that the candidate may be in a condition "not inconsistent with salvation," is to place a public profession of religion, in the form commanded by the blessed Redeemer, on the same level with the old abrogated Jewish rites, and things indifferent; to advocate principles opposed equally to sound reason, and plain Scripture truth; to plead in behalf of a theory which, if permitted to enter into our practice, must, in a variety of important respects, ultimately, render **wholly** inoperative the laws and authority of Jesus Christ.

CHAPTER VI.

REPLY TO SUCH OBJECTIONS TO OUR DOCTRINE ON SACRAMENTAL COMMUNION AS ARE FOUNDED ON THE SPIRITUALITY OF THE GOSPEL, AND DRAWN FROM OTHER AND MISCELLANEOUS SOURCES.

The spiritual nature of the Gospel not inconsistent with its outward forms—The promptings of Christian feeling—The duty of recognizing as such, all that we believe to be truly converted—Pedobaptists sincerely believe themselves right—We associate with them in other departments of worship—As every man is responsible for himself to God, we are bound to respect their faith, and in receiving them do not violate our own.

THE principles which we advocate for the regulation of Christian communion, which we have shown to be scriptural, and the only divinely appointed rules existing on the subject, cannot, it is alleged, be maintained for another reason. They are, it is affirmed, at war with the spirituality inculcated by the Gospel. "The genius of the Gospel, let it be remembered," says Mr. Hall, "is not ceremonial, but spiritual; consisting not in outward observances, but in the cultivation of such interior graces as compose the essence of virtue, perfect the character, and purify the heart. These form the soul of religion; all the rest are but her terrestrial attire, which she will lay aside when she passes the threshold of eternity. When, therefore, the obligations of humility and love come in competition with a punctual observance of external rites, the genius of religion will easily determine to which we should incline."*

* Complete Works, Amer. ed. vol. i. p. 360.

The dazzling beauty of style in which this argument is clothed, must not withdraw our attention from the fact, that it proceeds wholly upon the assumption, that obedience to the laws of the Gospel may be, and sometimes is, in conflict with the genius of the Gospel. Is it possible that this can ever be true? If so, by all means let these laws, so inimical to spirituality, be canceled. Let us banish the antiquated notion that external rites are still obligatory. These are the mere attire, the garments in which religion is dressed. They may be Roman or English, Lutheran or Reformed, Mahommedan or Christian. It is of no importance. Spirituality is all! But let us pause, and reflect. Is not obedience to the Christian commands, the very criterion, not only of love to the Saviour, but also of love to our brethren? Can we, without this testimony, give sufficient or satisfactory proof of our spirituality? Did not Christ require of his disciples this evidence of their affection? "If ye love me keep my commandments. Ye are my friends if ye do whatsoever I command you." Do you love me; are you my friends? How do you establish the affirmation of these inquiries? By cultivating exclusively the interior graces of spirituality? So thought not Jesus Christ—Keep my commandments, for by this means alone can you prove your claims to spirituality. John, the beloved, the affectionate, the spiritual disciple, never once imagined that "the obligations of humility and love" could possibly "come in competition with a punctual observance of external rites," and thus violate "the genius of religion." If he did he preached most strangely. "By this," said he, "we know that we love the children of God, when we love God, and keep his commandments. For this is the love of God, that we keep his commandments, and his commandments are not grievous." But I am reminded that all this was long since. At that time it was in perfect *harmony* with the genius of the Gospel. A change has since come over us. Years have passed, centuries have multiplied, hoary time has set his seal of condemnation upon these unfashionable notions. The order established by Christ, to govern the administration of Christian ordinances, is *now* in conflict with the genius of the Gospel! This, indeed, is giving us new light, for which, as in duty bound, we offer expressions of gratitude to the bold illuminator, whose hand has unlocked the hidden reservoir of so much effulgence. But let us analyze more closely its properties. Is it not merely a phosphoric glare which has its origin from buried putrescence?

By whom is the assertion authorized that "The genius of the Gospel is not ceremonial, but spiritual; consisting not in outward observances, but in the cultivation of such interior graces as compose the essence of virtue, perfect the character, and purify the heart?" Certainly the great Author of Revelation, in no part of his word, gives any countenance to such a dictation. That spirituality is an essential, and the most essential feature, in the religion of the cross, all well regulated minds firmly believe, and unwaveringly maintain; but that this is its only feature; that it has no other; in a word that religion is exclusively spiritual, no one, I had supposed, but a Quaker, would, for a moment, imagine. If religion is not still, partly at least, ceremonial, consisting in external observances, why this controversy about partaking of the symbols of the Lord's death; this hubbub to decide who shall, and who shall not, commune? The eucharist is nothing but an external rite, an outward observance merely. They ought to discard this also as well as baptism. Let them both go together. They should, to be consistent, adopt a communion that is wholly spiritual. These very sticklers for spirituality and against form, have, however, all received what they call baptism, they insist too upon coming to the Lord's table; and what are these, but ceremonies—the solemn, significant, and divinely appointed ceremonies of the Gospel dispensation? For a Baptist, or a Pedobaptist, who derives his nominal designation from his practice of ceremonies, to deny that the genius of the Gospel partakes in any degree of outward forms, is in one word to contradict and condemn himself.

It is in vain to tell us that "The interior graces form the soul of religion," and that "all the rest are but the terrestrial attire, which she will lay aside when she passes the threshold of eternity." It so happens that we are, at present, and all Christian communicants must necessarily continue, while this controversy shall remain of any importance, on this side the threshold of eternity. As Christians, therefore, whose dwelling place is still the earth, our duty is not to lay aside the terrestrial attire of religion, but to "put on the Lord Jesus." It would not be seemly to receive into our family, and entertain a man, destitute of garments. The decencies of society demand that he shall be clothed. But it is equally uncomely to introduce to the sacred table those who are not furnished with the vestments of the former ordinance. We have no right, until Christ shall call us hence, to lay aside the habiliments with which he has supplied us, and which he has commanded us to wear.

Punctilious attention to outward rites is unquestionably our duty. So is the cultivation of spirituality. The authority for both is the same. The graces of the Spirit were certainly never intended to supersede the forms of religion; nor is ritual obedience necessarily inimical to the cultivation of such interior endowments as compose the essence of virtue, perfect the character, and purify the heart. If a scrupulous regard of one of these involved a neglect of the other, then we would weigh them, select the more important, and abandon the rest. But as no such thing can be pretended, the inapplicability of the argument renders it utterly pointless. He who sent forth his Spirit to sanctify his disciples, and enjoined them to love one another, also commanded them to teach all nations, baptizing them in the name of the Father, and of the Son, and of the Holy Ghost. This they were to do, and subsequently admonish them to observe all other things enjoined by the Redeemer. Instead, therefore, of appealing to " the genius of religion," to determine " to which we shall incline," we should be attentive to the instructions of him who has said " These things ought ye to have done, and not to have left the other undone."

Can any thing be discovered, I now ask, in the spiritual nature of religion to change our conclusions regarding the scriptural doctrines respecting the sacrament. I fearlessly reply, it is impossible. It remains, for aught we have seen, still true, that repentance, faith, and baptism, are the inspired and indispensable terms of communion.

We shall close this branch of our discussion by replying briefly to some arguments of a miscellaneous character, which have been thought pertinent to the subject. The first of these is that the promptings of religious affection are inconsistent with close communion. It is alleged that it " sets the conduct and the feelings at variance, and erects into a duty the mortification of our best and holiest propensities."

Can this statement, let me ask, be true? I think it cannot. Are not our best and holiest propensities those which lead us to a strict adherence to all the laws of Christ? When forced to choose between a union with a particular class of Christians, and a violation of our duty to the Redeemer, which do our best and holiest feelings prompt us to select? I hold it to be evident, beyond question, that a refusal to unite, even with those whom we most love, in an infraction of the law of God, so far from being a mortification, is the most appropriate exercise of our best and holiest propensities. The Christian feelings which are incapable of such decision cannot be good or holy.

The second argument alluded to, maintains that we are bound in duty to recognize at the Lord's table all those we believe to be Christians. "The Bible," says Mr. Hall, "gives general rules of action, broad principles, leaving them to be applied under the guidance of sound discretion; and wherever it has decided a doubtful question, accompanied by an express statement of the principle on which the decision is founded, such explanation has all the force of an apostolic canon, by which we are bound to regulate our conduct in all the variety of cases to which it applies."

But Mr. Hall himself says, as we have before seen—"The *apostles*, it is acknowledged, admitted none to the Lord's supper, but such as were previously baptized." Why then, let me ask, should *we* do so? Our opponents talk of "General rules, broad principles to be applied under the guidance of sound discretion." Are the general rules of the Bible so framed that they subvert its especial laws? Are the "broad principles" of the Scriptures at variance with the commandments of Christ? Has our Lord given us rules of perpetual obligation to regulate Christian and sacramental intercourse, and then by a general arrangement, broad principles, authorized us to dispense with them? Baptism was, for a special purpose, enjoined on every believer, at the commencement of the Christian life; but general rules, broad principles, are furnished, which, "under the guidance of sound discretion," justify us in dispensing with the injunction! Does sound discretion teach us such a lesson? Assuredly not. We are to receive all he has received, and according to the laws, not which we imagine may govern him in bestowing upon them salvation, but which he has enacted for our intercourse; which are, as we have shown, ample in their extent, and obvious in their import. We have no authority from any laws, *general*, or *special*, nor are we permitted to receive any man, however undoubted may be his piety, in any other manner than as he has prescribed and commanded. When it was apparent to Peter that God had received those converts who were assembled in the house of Cornelius, he immediately inquired—" Can any man forbid water that these should not be baptized, who have received the Holy Ghost, as well as we? And he commanded them to be baptized." Our opponents propose to dispense with all such sectarian proceedings. They will ask, simply, whether the Lord has received them to commune with him. If this can be made probable, they must receive them to all ecclesiastical privileges without regard to any divine law on the subject. Can it be pleasing to God, or religious in men, in deference to a spurious catholicism, thus to withstand Jehovah, and set at naught his commandments? I presume not.

A third objection is proposed against confining sacramental intercourse to baptized believers. Pedobaptists, if they are in error, it is alleged, sincerely believe themselves right; their error, being " involuntary," is more an " infirmity" than a fault. " The only method," observes Mr. Hall, " of arriving at a satisfactory conclusion, is to consider how the apostles conducted themselves towards sincere but erring Christians, together with the temper they recommend us to cultivate towards such as labor under mistakes and misconceptions not inconsistent with piety."*

We undoubtedly ought to act towards such persons as the apostles themselves would have done. But how shall we judge of what their conduct would have been in relation to

* Works, vol. ii. p. 217.

such, had any appeared in their churches, afflicted with the malady of being in involuntary error, and of sincerity, and conscientiousness, in maintaining it? I answer, by what, under the influence of divine inspiration, they instructed others to do. We can be at no loss, whatever, on this part of our subject. Such a rule of judgment is not, I think, likely to lead us into material error in our decision. Had an unbaptized Christian presented himself to the apostles, claiming immunities on the score of his sincerity, or on any other score, they would certainly have treated him precisely as we do Pedobaptists, as nothing more nor less than as an unbaptized Christian. They would have recognized his Christianity, but they would not have deviated from the law of Christ in deference to his error, however sincere he might have been in embracing or maintaining it. This is precisely the course we pursue. We think our Pedobaptist brethren Christians, and we treat them as such. We believe them to be unbaptized Christians, and we treat them as such. We regulate our thoughts, and our actions, in both cases, by the laws of Christ. One of these laws requires us to judge of men by their fruits, and another obliges us to admit to the communion only baptized believers. By the former we decide that our Pedobaptist brethren are Christians, and we should rejoice to extend to them the fellowship of the church; but agreeably to the latter we can receive them in that way, and in no other, which Christ has prescribed. Thus we are perfectly certain we act towards all such, and treat them precisely as the apostles would have done, had they appeared in their assemblies.

Those Christians who sincerely and conscientiously exclude baptism from their system, may act in the matter to please themselves. It is no concern of ours. To their own master they stand or fall. They have, it may be, "conscientiously mistaken the mind of Christ." They govern themselves, individually and as churches, by their own convictions of obligation. But am I, because such is the state of the case, required, or if I felt inclined to do so, am I permitted to infringe inspired injunctions by recognizing their sincerity in error as a substitute for the practice of the truth, and that too for no other reason than to prove that I entertain for them a very high Christian regard? Am I told that I have nothing to do with the faith of another; that he is accountable alone to God? All this is true as long as he makes no pretensions to connect himself with me in church fellowship. But apply the doctrine to church discipline, that we have no right to inquire into the faith of our associates, and whom could you ever exclude for heresy. Unitarians, Mormons, Universalists, and all other defamers of evangelical piety, might fix themselves upon you like an incubus, and you would be destitute of any remedy whatever. No, when an individual enters the church he declares his union with the faith of the church. Does a Pedobaptist honestly believe, after an impartial examination of the best evidence to which he can gain access on the subject, that he has received Christian baptism, and that he has truly entered the congregation of Christ, in the way of the divine appointment. Let him prosecute the course he has adopted. But, certainly, he has no right to expect me, on that account, to abandon my own convictions and to unite with him in those practices which he may have thought proper to adopt. I am guided by my own faith, and not by the faith of any other man. Baptism without a profession of faith is justified as readily as the administration of the Lord's supper without baptism. They have no scriptural authority for either, but they do both. They act upon their own belief, and upon their own responsibility. But in neither case may the dictates of their consciences be the directory for my actions. It is no more a consequence that, because on their own principles, they are entitled to approach the Lord's table, that, therefore, it is my duty to unite with them in that ordinance, than that, because on their own principles they are obliged to baptize their infants, that, therefore, I am required to unite with them in that ceremony. Besides all this, it is to me evident that a deviation from the law of Christ in complaisance to the mistakes of Christians, however conscientiously entertained, would indicate a greater value for the erring servant, than for the infinitely wise and supreme Lord. Could we regard their neglect of divine ordinances as a deliberate contempt, this would invalidate, in our esteem, all their Christian pretensions, and we should govern our conduct towards them accordingly. We cannot, however, but admit that an error of this nature, sincerely entertained, though not entirely involuntary, is compatible with Christianity. If we cannot produce a conviction and practice of the truth, we have no alternative but to be guided by the apostolic instructions before recited to the church at Thessalonica, in the case of a member who walked not according to the commandment. They were directed to "withdraw themselves" from him, yet "not to count him as an enemy, but to admonish him as a brother."

It is suggested, as a fourth argument, that as we are associated with Pedobaptists in all other forms, it is inconsistent to withdraw from them in this department of Christian worship.

We have, I observe in reply, already fully conceded their general Christian character. As such we fraternize with them in every form not sacramental. We deem this a sufficient testimony of our good will, and desire for their prosperity, so far as they are engaged with us in the same common cause. We give them credit for sincerity, and for conscientiousness. What more can be required? The exercises in which we unite with them were duties before baptism was instituted, and would have remained duties to the end of time had no Christian churches existed. Since these facts are undoubted, can the course on our part indicated, be inconsistent with the opinions we entertain? Such a thing is impossible. It is our pleasure to pursue it, when we think proper; and still, in our judgment, infant sprinkling is not Christian baptism : Christain baptism is the only authorized mode of entrance into the visible church; the church of Christ must be constituted and governed agreeably to his laws; and, in no case, can even a consicentious performance of any ceremony not authorized by the supreme Legislator, be considered equivalent to Christian obedience.

Numerous other objections have been started against strict communion; but, as they are of very little importance, and will be alluded to, incidentally, hereafter, I shall not now pause to consider them. They assume that the practice is illiberal and harsh, that it is injurious, that it is odious, and that it is unpopular. It is sufficient to respond to them all by the single remark, that our blessed Redeemer is the best judge as to what is illiberal, harsh, injurious, odious, and unpopular. To him we cheerfully submit the decision.

We have now, briefly, but carefully, and impartially, reviewed, in this chapter and the two preceding, all the arguments acknowledged to be of any importance, employed to overthrow the principles we have established, and by which sacramental communion is divinely regulated; whether derived from the supposed nature of the administration of John the Baptist; the inspired canons of Christian toleration; the spiritual nature of the Gospel; the promptings of religious feeling; the obligations of brotherly love; the duty of exercising lenity towards erring brethren; and the supposed inconsistency of engaging with Pedobaptists in other departments of worship, and declining their intercourse at the Lord's table; and we have seen that so far from invalidating or even weakening in the slightest degree, they all combine to strengthen, and more fully confirm our conclusions. Here we rest this part of the discussion, under the fullest conviction that repentance towards God, faith in our Lord Jesus Christ, and baptism in the name of the holy Trinity, are incontrovertibly the terms of communion appointed and established by the King in Zion, and from which we are forbidden, by the most sacred obligations, at any time, for any purpose, or under any circumstances, to depart. "What thing soever I command you," saith the Lord Jehovah, "observe to do it. Thou shalt not add thereto, nor diminish from it."

CHAPTER VII.

WE ARE NOT AT LIBERTY TO ADMINISTER THE LORD'S SUPPER FOR ANY PURPOSES OTHER THAN THOSE DESIGNATED BY OUR LORD JESUS CHRIST.

The design of the Lord's Supper not a test of Christian love—Reciprocal confidence, or religious fellowship—Pedobaptists and Quakers—Communion administered to secure popularity—Withheld as a punishment—Verbal nonsense—Open communion not an act of faith, obedience, or worship.

THE inquiry is now suggested whether we are at liberty to administer the Lord's supper for any purposes other than those appointed by our Lord Jesus Christ. Let us determine what these purposes are. We will also designate some of the errors which have prevailed in relation to them, among ourselves and our brethren of other denominations. Let us inquire by what evils the errors in question have been attended. These considerations, if properly examined, and fully understood, will more deeply impress us with the duty of circumspection, and a firm and unyielding conformity in all things to the teachings of the divine law.

What are the specific purposes for which the sacrament of the Lord's supper was instituted? To determine what is the correct answer to this question we can have no difficulty. "Do this," said the Saviour, "in remembrance of me:" and, "as oft as ye eat this bread, and drink this cup, ye do show the Lord's death till he come." The observance of the institution is to be continued in the church until the second advent of Messiah, and it is to be invariably administered and received for these purposes, and for no other. In its participation, we profess our faith in the efficacy and vicariousness of the atonement of the Son of God, and declare our belief of a personal and saving interest in its benefits. The broken body and shed blood of our Lord, which characterized his sufferings and death, are thus continually held up to our view, and exhibited before the eyes of the world, forming a memorial of his grace, and to perpetuate our gratitude and love to him, more indestructible than monumental brass. If in these opinions we are not mistaken, the true inquiries to be made in relation to a candidate for the eucharist are not so properly, is he a Christian, and am I required by this means to express towards him my confidence and brotherly love? Much less may we ponder the questions, can I by receiving him advance my own, or the interests of religion, and can I secure a greater degree of popularity for a favorite doctrine, or specified system of theology? But, does he come according to the laws of Christ? Has he not, since his baptism, forfeited, by immorality or heresy, his Christian character? Does he propose to receive the eucharist with the views and purposes authorized by the word of God? These are the legitimate inquiries. If they are answered in the affirmative, the applicant must be admitted. If otherwise, it is at our peril that he is received. Mistakes upon this point lead to errors that deteriorate religion, perplex Christians, and agitate and divide those who ought to be united. Were this part of our subject studied and understood, we should never again be told that if we decide that our Pedobaptist brethren, or any others, are Christians, that God has received them into his favor, we dare not debar them, and we should no more be *warned* that the withholding this *test* of our confidence and regard, is a denial of their claims to the character of Christians.

Such a view of the matter can find no support in divine revelation.

The Lord's supper* was not appointed to be so much a test of our love and confidence in each other, as of our obedience to Christ. As it is a sacred feast, and an ordinance of divine worship, mutual Christian affection among communicants at the same table is very becoming, and highly necessary; but not more so than in any other branch of social worship. That sitting down with them at the Lord's table, however, should be considered as the criterion of our love to individuals, or to any Christian community, does not appear from the word of God. The supper of our Lord was intended to teach the most wonderful of all truths, and to exhibit the most glorious of all transactions. It is a memorial of God's love to us, and of Immanuel's death for us, in memory of whom it is received. But the proof, the scriptural proof, of love to the children of God, is not given at so cheap and easy a rate. Many do this who give indubitable evidence that they do not love the disciples for the truth's sake. The presence in our hearts of heavenly affections requires to be sustained by better testimony. Christian love involves the exercise of tempers, and the performance of actions, which embrace much of self-denial, and without which, no matter how promiscuous may be our communion, or how loudly we may talk of a liberal spirit, we shall remain destitute of that charity, without which we are nothing. The true test of mutual affection and confidence as Christians, is not found in a joint participation of the eucharist, but in sympathy with each other in affliction, in feeding the hungry, in clothing the naked, and in doing for the suffering and miserable of all classes, but especially of the household of faith, whatever good their necessities may require. For these facts

* See Booth's Vindication.

I have the authority of the final Judge, who, in the last day, will say to his people, "Come, ye blessed of my Father, inherit the kingdom prepared for you from the foundation of the world." But what are the claims on account of which you receive so unspeakable a boon? It is because you have manifested your love to the saints by holding free communion at the Lord's table with Christians of all denominations? Such an intimation nowhere exists. This is too small and easy a matter. The reasons are altogether of a different character. " I was an hungered," said our Lord, " and ye gave me meat; I was thirsty, and ye gave me drink ; a stranger, and ye took me in ; naked, and ye clothed me ; I was sick, and ye visited me ; I was in prison, and ye came unto me." If the inquiry is made, how all these things could have taken place, the reply of the Redeemer is, " For as much as ye did it unto one of these, my brethren, ye did unto me." The Lord's supper was not designed, therefore, to be a test of Christian love. For such a purpose it is incapacitated and inadequate.

What, however, it is asked, if the candidate for our communion be truly a man of God, for whose Christian experience we have entire fellowship, and he sincerely believes himself to be baptized? It is maintained that, in such a case, we ought to give him this evidence of our respect for the sincerity of his faith, and that as a genuine disciple of Christ, we dare not debar his approach to the holy table.

Were these, then, let me inquire, the objects for which the sacrament was instituted? Are we at liberty to administer, or receive it, for such purposes? But the proposition divides itself into two parts. We will notice each separately.

The former assumes that as the Pedobaptist sincerely, if such a thing be possible, believes himself baptized, he is to be received by us as baptized. But still the question occurs, is he baptized? With whom is the decision of this matter to be lodged? If *we* are to judge, he will inevitably be rejected, because it is impossible for us to believe any such fallacy. If *the candidate* is the sole arbiter in the case, then we adopt a rule the operation of which cannot be confined to baptism. It irresistibly extends itself to all matters both of faith and practice. To what results will such an interpretation lead us? It forces us into the dogma adopted only by shallow minds, which constitutes, to the Popish denial of the right of private judgment, the opposite extreme, and which meets and harmonizes with it in absurdity, that if a man sincerely thinks a thing is right, to him it is right. This doctrine, all must instantly perceive, dethrones the Bible, exalts sincerity in its place, and at once breaks down all distinctions between truth and error. A man's principles are of no consequence. We dare not in any case inquire into them. All we have to do is to determine whether he sincerely believes they are scriptural. If so, he is entitled to all the privileges and immunities of the church. Such extravagant vagaries cannot need from me a serious refutation.

The latter takes it for granted, that, as this is the Lord's table, and these are the Lord's children, they are entitled to it, and we dare not debar them. This is a claim of grave importance. Let us carefully consider it.

Yes, it *is* the Lord's table. All his children have an undoubted right to it, because whatever is his, is theirs. We are not permitted to preclude them. We make no such pretensions. But has the Lord established no laws for the government of the feast? If it should appear that he has not, we will admit of none. Were it our table, we would invite all our friends, and rejoice in their society. It is *not* ours; it is the Lord's table. All confess too, that he has enacted laws for its government, and that they are paramount. What these laws are we have already been sufficiently informed. We need not repeat them. Pedobaptists themselves fully concur with us in relation to some of them. Dr. E. D. Griffin, the late learned President of Williams College, in his well known Letter on Communion, embodies them in a small compass:—"I agree," says the erudite president, "with the advocates of close communion, in two points. First, that baptism is the initiating ordinance that introduces us into the visible church; and, secondly, that we ought not to commune with those who are not baptized, and, of course, not members of the church, even if we regard them as Christians." We appeal to their own principles. This is the Lord's table, and we are his children; and do these facts authorize us to violate his laws? Are we told that the parties sincerely believe they have complied with all the required rules? But we have seen that this plea is insufficient. Our Pedobaptist brethren themselves will not act upon this principle, when it is applied in the case of a candidate for *their* communion, and they thereby evince that *they* do not think that it is legitimate to administer the Lord's supper as a testimony of confidence in the gracious state of an individual, or to evince respect for the sincerity with which he entertains the belief of the correctness of *his* opinions, irrespective of their own convictions of what is required by the laws enacted to govern the ordinance.

To illustrate this remark, let us suppose a case. A good Quaker all charitably suppose to be a Christian. As such he is entitled to the confidence and affection of all other Christians. He is a child of God, and has a right to all the ordinances of the Gospel. He, having, as *he* supposes, received the baptism of the Holy Spirit, has complied with that baptism which alone, he believes, is now authorized by the New Testament. He sincerely believes himself to be baptized. This good Quaker, who is a Christian, one of the

Lord's children, whom God has accepted, and with whom they expect to commune in heaven, presents himself at a Pedobaptist communion table. Will they unite with him in the sacred ordinance? They respectfully decline. But why? His only deficiency is a want of baptism. In whose estimation, however, does this defect exist? Certainly not in his own. He is rejected. On what account? Not because he does not sincerely believe himself baptized; but because his Pedobaptist brethren do not believe that he is baptized. Thus it is seen that they refuse to practice upon **the principles** they recommend to us. The piety of the candidate for communion, and the evidence it affords that God has accepted him as one of his children, the sincerity and conscientiousness with which he believes himself conformed, in every respect, to the divine law, are no longer in their judgment arguments applicable to the case. If God has some secret code by which he saves those who habitually violate his revealed will, it is for his own government, not ours. Pedobaptists propose, in effect, that we shall repudiate God's written law, and guide our conduct in this matter, by what is conceived to be the law that will influence the acceptance of sinners in the last day. This course, however, they design for us, not for themselves. All classes of Protestant Pedobaptists, I think, except, probably, the Episcopalians, confess that we are unquestionably baptized. They can, therefore, if they think us orthodox and orderly, commune with us without any sacrifice of principle. We do not, we cannot, believe that Pedobaptists are baptized. And, as they teach us, by their example, to act, not upon their faith, but upon our own, they thus nullify all their arguments against us, and justify our course in refusing them, for the same reasons that they decline communion with the Quaker.

One of three things we are compelled to do. We must

violate the acknowledged law of Christ respecting both the qualifications of the candidates and objects of the ordinance, and receive unbaptized believers; profess that we believe the sprinkling they received in infancy true and lawful baptism; or we must decline the communion of Pedobaptists. Which shall we choose? The first would be an act of deliberate and known sin; the second would be the grossest hypocrisy; we have, therefore, chosen the third, which, though it may be a painful alternative, is an act candidly expressive of our faith, and of unwavering fidelity to the Redeemer.

The hypothesis is sometimes assumed, that we may administer the Lord's supper to secure our own interests, the interests of religion, a more ready acceptance of a favourite doctrine, the popularity of a specified system of divinity, or that it may be withheld as a punishment to compel our brethren to embrace our opinions, or to abstain from the exercise of their own. I consider myself justified in this statement by the numerous acts of nonfellowship with which the proceedings of our churches and associations in this country abound, and such passages as I will now quote from the works of Rev. Robert Hall. He remarks on this subject—
" The first effect necessarily resulting from strict communion is a powerful prejudice against the party which adopts it When all other denominations find themselves lying under an interdict, and treated as though they were heathens or publicans, they must be more than men not to resent it; or if they regard it with a considerable degree of apathy, it can only be ascribed to that contempt which impotent violence is so apt to inspire."* The same writer discusses the expediency and effect of " close communion considered as a punishment:" as the means of bringing a larger number within the circle of our influence; and of inducing men favorably

* Works, vol. ii. p. 226.

to consider, and to submit to, the ordinance of baptism.* He observes—"The hope of producing conviction by such an expedient is equally groundless and chimerical, since conviction is the result of evidence, and no light whatever can be pretended to be conveyed by interdicting their communion, unless it be that it manifests our intolerance. We propose to extirpate an error, and we plant a prejudice; and instead of attempting to soften and conciliate the minds of our opponents, we inflict a stigma. Professing serious concern that the ordinance of baptism, as it was practised in the first ages, is fallen into neglect, we attempt to revive an unpopular rite by a mode of procedure which, without the remotest tendency towards the removal of error, or the elucidation of truth, answers no other purpose than to make ourselves unpopular."†

If these arguments are used in seriousness, and I imagine we must so regard them, they certainly assume that the eucharist may be administered, not only, in commemoration of the death and sufferings of our Lord, and as a testimony of our united love and obedience to him, purposes alone sanctioned by the holy word, but also, to evince our liberality, to inflict punishment, to bring a larger number of persons under our influence, to produce conviction in favor of the correctness of our opinions, to extirpate error, to soften and conciliate our opponents, to revive the neglected use of baptism, in any way, and for almost any purpose, so as to avoid making ourselves unpopular! Need I say a single word to expose the fallacious character of such opinions as these? It is matter of no surprise that a man so great as Mr. Hall, with principles so loose and contradictory, should have been, at once, the glory and the shame, the boast and

* Works, vol. i. p. 337, et seq.
† Works, vol. ii. p. 227.

the blight of the Baptist church. The opinion prevails pretty extensively, in some quarters, that the Lord's supper is designed to be a pledge of Christian fellowship. I have already alluded briefly to a collateral topic, the question whether it is a test of Christian love, and, incidentally, to the view of the subject now introduced. It, however, in my judgment, demands a somewhat more extensive consideration. The New Testament must necessarily guide us in all our deductions, but neither in the Gospels, nor in the Epistles,* is there the least intimation that any such purpose was contemplated, nor is there any thing in the nature of the ordinance indicating that it should be so regarded. The true test of either individual or social Christian fellowship must be sought in something else besides sacramental intercourse. Nothing can be plainer than the exposition on this subject by Christ and his apostles. We are taught by them in the language already quoted, that the solemn and expressive use of the bread and the cup, with the forms of devotional exercise, is a symbol of his mangled body and shed blood, and of our spiritual interests in the great sacrifice thus offered. No evidence exists which warrants the conclusion that this sacrament is to be employed for any other purpose. Union and fellowship among Christians, it is true, are indispensable to church membership. For "how can two walk together except they be agreed?" These, however, are secured by the previous measures which connected them with the people of God in their ecclesiastical relations. In the act of the Lord's supper we are not to busy ourselves in scrutinizing those who are present, to determine whether we have fellowship with all who propose to participate. These solemn moments should be occupied in endeavours to direct our minds to Christ, and

* Vide an Essay, by Rev. John M. Peck, of Rock Spring, Ill. in the Banner and Pioneer, 1840.

to realize our "fellowship with the Father, and with his Son, Jesus Christ our Lord." If the communicants come according to the laws Jesus Christ has established for the government of the feast, and retain their places in the membership of his church, our private opinion of them has nothing to do with the performance of our duty.

If in these conclusions we are correct, it is apparent that several occasions of reproach from others, and difficulty among ourselves, are entirely obviated. We are not unfrequently told by unbaptized Christians—Christ communes with us, but you will not—You expect to commune with us in heaven, but you will not do it on earth! But a moment's thought, however, is necessary to show that all this, and much more of the same character, is the merest verbal nonsense. Do they mean to say that Jesus Christ comes literally to their table, and actually eats bread and drinks wine with them, when they celebrate the sacrament of the Lord's supper? They do not, surely, intend to convey such an idea. How, then, does he commune with them on earth? By sympathy with them, by bestowing his favor upon them, and by the blessings of his holy Spirit. Precisely the same kind of communion, as far as we are capable, we are willing to hold with them, and do hold with them all—not sacramental, but Christian communion. When, therefore, it is alleged that Christ communes with them, and that we will not, the statement is not entitled to the regard which is due to truth, since it is evident that, in all these respects, we commune with them to the full extent of their communion with Christ. The other postulate in the argument is of the same sophistical character, and appears to have weight merely by a deceptive play upon the word *communion,* which is assumed in one sense in the premises, and applied in another sense in the conclusion. We shall commune together, say they, in heaven. Why not, therefore, commune together on earth? Is it true, that we shall actually sit down at the communion table in heaven, and literally eat bread and drink wine in a sacramental sense? No one, I imagine, supposes that such will be the case. If not, should we happily reach that "better land," our communion will be wholly spiritual. We shall, therefore, assuredly, never commune with Pedobaptists in any manner in heaven, in which we do not now commune with them on earth. The charge, so frequently preferred, that, by refusing their communion, we declare nonfellowship with them, and deny their title to the Christian character, is, as every one will readily perceive, based upon the mistaken notion, the exploded dogma, that the Lord's supper is designed as a test of Christian fellowship, and that one purpose, at least, of its administration is to express mutual religious affection. All such reasoning as this, is indicative of singular obscurity of thought, and proceeds upon the deception which narrows the vast field of Christian communion to the limits of sacramental intercourse, a conception equally at war with philological accuracy, and religious truth. And what is even more melancholy, the declamations founded upon it, and they are in some parts of our land exceedingly exuberant, partake of the same attributes. They are passionate appeals, not to enlightened and scriptural views of the design of the ordinance, but to the strong prejudices and coarser feelings of the human heart, emotions so easily aroused, and so mischievous in their influence upon all the interests of religion, and the courtesies of brotherly love.

The testimony now submitted, in proof that sacramental intercourse at the Lord's table is not designed as a test of Christian fellowship, and that we are not at liberty to administer the eucharist for such a purpose, if regarded as conclusive, will also serve to remove another perplexity, often found to exist in our own churches. Not unfrequently does a member absent himself from the Lord's table on account of the presence of some other member who has offended him. He will not take his seat there, because he imagines that by doing so he will express a fellowship that does not really exist; and he chooses not to falsify by his act, the true convictions of his heart. Entire churches, similarly judging, sometimes suspend wholly the observance of this ordinance, for indefinite periods, on account of internal disagreement, guided by the unscriptural impressions we are now attempting to remove. Offences, and consequent unholy feelings, cannot always be avoided. They will, sometimes, find their way among the people of God. Every proper effort should be made to prevent them, and when they occur, to suppress them, with the least possible delay. If, however, they are found to have place, they afford no more reason for a suspension of the regular commemoration of the Lord's supper than of baptism, preaching, singing, prayer, or any other department of religious worship, all of which are no less forms of communion than the sacrament in question, and a united participation in them, equally expressive of *Christian* fellowship.

The conclusions to which we have been conducted will enable us properly to estimate the acts of our churches and associations, to which we have alluded, and by which they have employed the Lord's supper, not only as an expression of Christian fellowship, but also as an engine for the infliction of punishment. Movements such as these last by the Roman See do not surprise us, nor when even Protestants resort to them, are we much astonished, because, in other respects, they symbolize with Popery. But that Baptists, who profess to be guided, in all things, by the word of God, are not more intelligent and consistent, is matter of equal grief and amazement. The propensity to imitate others is one of the most prominent traits in the human character, nor has it failed to develope itself in this particular, as the numerous proceedings, in all parts of our land, abundantly testify. Every Baptist church, by the very articles of its constitution, is declared to be perfectly independent of every other, obliged to be governed by no standard but the word of God, and responsible only to her celestial Head for her faith and practice. Yet one church is found nonfellowshiping, or *excommunicating* another; and the churches in one region exscinding those in another region! Could such wounds as these be inflicted upon the body of Christ, did just conceptions prevail of the design for which the Lord's supper was instituted? What, under existing circumstances, can be gained by these proceedings? Nothing whatever, but the publication of our own errors and inconsistency, the exhibition of our intolerance, and the proof that Christian charity has not yet assumed the entire control of our hearts.

Having now seen that we are not at liberty to administer or receive the Lord's supper for any purposes other than those designated by the great Lawgiver; determined what those purposes are; noted the errors that prevail on this subject; and considered some of the evils, both among ourselves and others, which have been the consequences; it is unnecessary, probably, further to extend our discussions. I repeat the important truth that, like every other department of the divine service, communion has its laws by which it must in all respects be governed. To violate them in its observance, is a contempt of the authority from which they emanated, and in consequence of such dereliction, where it exists, this part of sacred devotion, and it would be true of any other under similar circumstances, ceases, at once, to be an act of either faith, obedience, or worship. "There can be no faith, because that requires a promise, or some divine declaration; there can be no obedience, because that supposes a precept, or something equivalent to it; and where there is no faith, nor obedience, it is evident, there can be no acceptable worship."

CHAPTER VIII.

WE CANNOT UNITE WITH PEDOBAPTISTS IN SACRAMENTAL COMMUNION WITHOUT AN ACTUAL ABANDONMENT, OR PRACTICAL FALSIFICATION OF ALL OUR PRINCIPLES ON BOTH BAPTISM AND THE LORD'S SUPPER.

Forced confessions—Anabaptism—Change of public feeling in regard to us—Former persecutions—Parliament of Charles I.—Assembly of divines at Westminster—Henry VIII.—Episcopal Convocation—Consequences—Queen Elizabeth and the Aldgate Church—Burning of Baptist women—American persecutions—Danger of popularity—Influence of open communion.

PREPARATORY to entering upon a more full and explicit exposition of the reasons why Baptists cannot unite with Pedobaptists in Sacramental Communion, let us briefly recapitulate the topics which have passed in review, and to which our conclusions must have immediate reference. We have seen, in the preceding chapters, that we are not at liberty to adopt any terms of communion not instituted and established by our Lord Jesus Christ; we have specified the terms which are prescribed by him, and shown them to be such; the extent to which the opinions entertained by us on this subject have been, and are, substantially, embraced by all other denominations; we have replied at large to the arguments by which our conclusions are impugned, employed particularly by open communion Baptists, and generally by Pedobaptists; and we have shown that we have no authority to administer, or to receive the Lord's supper, for any other purposes than those designated by the Christian Legislator. If we have thus far comprehended the subject in all its relations and bearings, it will not be difficult for us to specify satisfactorily the particular reasons why we decline communion with Pedobaptists. We proceed to this part of our task.

Three prominent considerations influence our conduct, into which all those of a subordinate character may be resolved. The first is, that we cannot mingle with them in sacramental intercourse without an actual abandonment, or practical falsification of all our principles on both baptism and the Lord's supper; the second is, because Pedobaptists are not baptized; and the third is, because they attach to both baptism and the Lord's supper an unscriptural and unreasonable degree of efficacy and importance, and therefore administer them for purposes not authorized by the word of God. The examination of the first of these reasons for strict communion will occupy the present chapter.

When we receive the Lord's supper with Pedobaptists, we either actually abandon, or practically falsify all our principles in relation to the sacraments of the Gospel. These consequences, one or the other, cannot be avoided. Do our brethren of the several churches designated desire us to commune with them without such an understanding, tacit or avowed? I cannot persuade myself that they do. Any other hypothesis would not express respect for their candor. We should violate equally our own tenets and theirs, and thus adopt a form of liberality which could in no wise increase their estimation for us, either as intelligent men or conscientious Christians. Dr. Worcester, a distinguished Pedobaptist of the present century, in his Letters to Dr. Baldwin, expresses on this subject the unanimous sense of all his brethren. He remarks: " If professed believers are the only proper subjects for baptism, and if immersion be not a mere circumstance or mode of baptism, but essential to the ordinance, so that he that is not immersed is not baptized, the sentiments of strict communion would be sufficiently established." Both these, they all know, we unwaveringly believe. They maintain, as will be perceived, that if they held as we do in relation to baptism, they would practice as we do in relation to the Lord's supper. Now, is it possible they can wish us to admit them to communion with us, or desire us to sit down with them, without acknowledging the validity of their baptism? The supposition is unreasonable. I will not do them the injustice to presume they would tolerate such a course, because they are fully assured that in adopting it, we must either violate their principles as well as our own, or incur, and justly, the charge of dissimulation, neither of which are they likely to regard as well befitting the solemn services of the holy table. Read all their books on this subject, and the conviction cannot be resisted that they esteem our communion with them as worth nothing except as an acknowledgment of their baptism, or a renunciation of our own—an humble confession that, after all, we are wrong and they are right. Who does not see that all who do this, actually renounce their own principles as Baptists, or practically falsify and dishonor them? Why, then, should any one claim to be still considered as a Baptist, when the mere profession is all he retains, and even this is contradicted and disproved by his whole life and conduct?

Were I, as a minister of Jesus Christ, to go to the Pedobaptist communion table, without hypocrisy, and in the exercise of a good conscience, I should, in that act, acknowledge, as we all agree that baptism is an indispensable preliminary to communion, that those who surround me, and who have only been sprinkled in infancy, have, in that ceremony, been truly baptized. I must, therefore, from that moment, either refuse to baptize such when they become believers, or if not, confess myself guilty of rebaptizing them. Thus I should become most certainly what I have ever disowned with abhorrence, an anabaptist, or re-baptizer. But I never did, I never shall, knowingly, baptize any person who had been previously baptized. I will therefore never take a position which will force me to confess that I have done so, or that, in other respects, will embarrass my obedience to any command of the divine law.

That we do not materially err in the view of the subject now submitted, I feel the utmost confidence. What, then, I ask, are we to think of all the railing and clamor in regard to it with which our ears are perpetually stunned? It is, beyond question, a mere "*coup de main*"—a stroke of policy, either to roll upon us such a tide of public obloquy as will overwhelm us by its force—a most brotherly and affectionate act—or to drive us from our principles, and by involving us in fatal contradictions, to break down our doctrines and destroy our churches. Do we need stronger testimony to evince that the artillery *professedly* leveled against the restrictive feature in our sacramental communion, is *in reality* designed to act against our mode and subjects of baptism? It cannot be concealed that the plain propriety and scriptural character of both of these is a perpetual rebuke, which they constantly feel, and from which, in this indirect and more popular way, they are evidently striving to be delivered. When translated into intelligible English, it all amounts to about this :—You Baptists are beyond measure stubborn and unaccommodating. Do acknowledge our infant sprinkling to be true and lawful baptism. When you baptize a person who has been sprinkled by us in infancy, admit that you re-baptize him. You can now make all these concessions in the easiest, in the most affectionate, kind and agreeable manner imaginable. Just sit down with us, or invite us to sit down with you, at the Lord's table. That will be amply sufficient. Come, now, we love you as Christians, and the affection and confidence are mutual.

Jesus Christ communes with us, and we shall all commune together in heaven. Why not upon earth? You will not—we have determined to give it such a direction that public opinion will not permit you to decline our solicitation. Thus you will accomplish all we desire.

To those who are familiar with the history of the Church, this condition of things cannot but appear in singular contrast with the tone and bearing formerly maintained towards us. Different, however, as it may seem, it is nevertheless, dictated by precisely the same spirit. Not two centuries have elapsed since Baptists and Roman Catholics were denounced by the Protestant world as equally abominable. If there was, in their estimation, any difference, the Baptists were regarded with the greater abhorrence. In proof of this remark, I refer to Dr. Wall,* who observes: " When the Protestants arose, the Papists, in scorn, called them Anabaptists,† but the Protestants disowned 'em, and wrote against 'em. And Sleidan gives several instances wherein Protestant princes and states declared against harboring 'em; and made answer to the reproaches of the Papists, that they took more care to rid their countries of 'em than they themselves did." The Assembly of Divines at Westminster was held during the Protectorate of Cromwell. From Dr. Lightfoot's Works,‡ we learn the temper of that body towards us. Woolsey on Baptism§ says, " While all, not Presbyterians, suffered on account of their sentiments, the Baptists especially were made to feel the weight of their power. Often did the Assembly, during its

---

* Hist. Inf. Bap. Lond. ed. 1705, vol. ii. p. 202.

† The Anabaptists of that day are, on all hands, confessed to be the Baptists of our times. Does not this fact prove that Baptists are older than Protestants?

‡ Vol. xiii. pp. 299, 302.—Journal of Proceedings, &c. from Jan. 1, 1643, to Dec. 31, 1644.

§ Appendix.

session, consult with the House of Commons, how they might suppress Baptists, or, as they were pleased to call them, Anabaptists. As strange as it may appear, yet it is no less true, that the Assembly of Divines attributed their Lord General's defeat in the west to ' Parliament not being active in suppressing Baptists.' "* The record for Friday, August the 9th, is in these words : " Then did Mr. Marshall report from the committee chosen to study a remedy against the Anabaptists, Brownists, &c. This business was also ordered to be sent to the House" of Parliament. When Charles II. was restored to the throne of England, all his offending subjects were pardoned, except such as had committed the crime of becoming Baptists. Wall says—" The Parliament assembled upon the restoration, expressed the dislike the nation had conceived against the tenets and behavior of these men"†—Baptists—" who"—in the language of Judge Hale, " pretended so highly to liberty of conscience.‡ An act (was passed at the same time) for the confirming all ministers in the possession of their benefices, how heterodox soever they had been, provided they would conform for the future, except such as had been of this way"—had committed the unpardonable crime of embracing Baptist principles.

As I have mentioned these instances, and it may not be considered entirely irrelevant to do so, I will, at the risk of being thought somewhat prolix, introduce one or two other facts of the same character. In a speech of Henry VIII., made at the proroguing of Parliament, December 24, 1545, complaining of the discord among his subjects on religious accounts, he exclaims—" What love and charity is there among you, when one calls another heretic and Anabaptist,

* Journal of the Assembly, Sept. 9, 10, A. D. 1644.
† History Infant Baptism, vol. ii. p. 215.
‡ Burnet's Life and Death of Sir Matthew Hale, p. 44.

and he calls him again Papist, hypocrite, and Pharisee!"*
A Convocation of the Episcopal church was held during the
same reign, one specific object of which was to condemn the
Baptists for maintaining that infants could be saved without
baptism. They set forth, for that purpose, several articles
"to be diligently preach'd for keeping the people steady,"
among which we notice the following†—" That the sacrament of baptism was instituted and ordained in the New
Testament, by our Saviour Jesus Christ, as a thing necessary
for attaining everlasting life, according to the saying of Christ
—Nisi quis renatus fuerit, etc.—Unless one be born again
of water, &c. 2. That it is offer'd unto all men, as well
infants, as such as have the use of reason, that by baptism
they shall have remission of sins, &c. 3. That the promise of grace and everlasting life, which promise is adjoined
unto the sacrament of baptism, pertaineth not only to such
as have the use of reason, but also to infants, &c.—they are
made thereby the very sons and children of God. Insomuch
as children dying in their infancy shall undoubtedly be saved
thereby, otherwise not. 4. Infants must needs be christen'd because they are born in original sin, which sin must
needs be remitted, which cannot be done but by the grace
of baptism, whereby they receive the Holy Ghost, which
exercises his grace and efficacy in them, and cleanses and
purifies them from sin, by his most secret virtue and operation. 6. That they ought to repute and take all the Anabaptist's and Pelagian's opinions contrary to the premises,
and every other man's opinions agreeable unto the said
Anabaptists's and Pelagian's opinions in this behalf, for
detestable heresies, and to be utterly condemned." The
publication of these articles was instantly attended with the

---

* Wall's Hist. Inf. Bap. vol. ii. p. 210.

† Fuller's Church History, Lib. 5, sect. 4. Wall, vol. ii. p. 208, 209.

most appalling consequences to our oppressed brethren. Wall, whose language in substance I adopt, affirms that it was but a short time ere "*four* Baptists, three men and one *woman*, were condemned to bear fagots at Paul's Cross, and that three days after a man and woman of their sect were *burnt* at Smithfield. *Ten* other Baptists were, in a few weeks more, put to death; and some months subsequently *fourteen* more suffered the same fate, 'for the crime of denying,' in the language of Fuller, the historian, 'that the sacraments had any (saving) effect on those that received 'em.'"*

On all occasions, when a crowd of heretics were condemned to the stake, whoever else received clemency, the Baptists were sure to suffer. Even Queen Elizabeth, pardon whom she might, had little compassion for us. As a single instance among many, illustrative of the truth of this remark, I observe that, when the little church which had been secretly collected at Aldgate, London, was, by the vigilance of the police, unfortunately discovered, the officers of "Her Majesty" succeeded in capturing twenty-seven of its unoffending members. These were all imprisoned in the severest manner, and *eleven* of them, ten of whom were *women*, were convicted of "anabaptism," and condemned therefore as guilty of capital crimes against the peace and dignity of the empire. Of these eight were banished from the country, and *two* were *burned at the stake* in Smithfield. Fox, the celebrated Martyrologist, interceded with Elizabeth to save these two victims from the flames, and to have their sentence commuted to banishment, that they might go with the others. The Queen replied, that she could not comply with his petition, because it was necessary to make

---

* Hist. &c. vol. ii. p. 220; and the same incidents are narrated in Fuller's Ch. Hist. Lib. 5, sect. 5, and Martyrology, ed. 2. p. 956.

examples of them; and added: "I wonder that such monstrous opinions"—as those professed by the Baptists—"could come into the mind of any Christian. But such is the state of human weakness, if we are left never so little a while destitute of the divine light, whither is it that we do not fall?"* Happy would it be for the memory of our American Fathers if "the Statutes at Large" of Virginia, and the musty Legal Tomes of the staid Puritans of New England contained the only evidence of Pedobaptist intolerance towards us even in this country. Baptist blood has stained the soil of the New as well as the Old world. But I forbear. I have digressed too far.

Am I asked, whether I intend to charge the Pedobaptists of the present day, with the guilt of all these monstrous and sanguinary proceedings of former ages? I reply that such a thought is far, very far, from my heart. Our brethren of other denominations are now peculiarly friendly, and affectionate, but, I presume, not the less, on that account, desirous that we should abandon our odious anabaptism. I design only to contrast the difference of spirit with which in various ages they have approached us. In former days of darkness, how bitterly would Protestants have scouted an invitation to sit down with us at the Lord's table, and had a Baptist, without a total and public abandonment of his principles, have dared to venture among the crowd to their communion, they would have spurned and driven him hence, with the deepest indignation. We endured the spirit of the storm while it prevailed; the tempest at last exhausted the rage of many a slow moving century, and we came forth still brighter, from the conflict. A change has come. Our brethren, of the several denominations, have discovered that we are really not demons, and that it is possible that Baptist doctrines and

* Fuller's Church Hist. Book 9, sect. 3, pp. 42, 43.

obedience may claim affinity to Christianity. They, indeed, now believe that, excepting our bigotry in pertinaciously adhering to those antiquated and obsolete forms of religion, established by Jesus Christ, and believed and practised by the primitive disciples, we are excellent brethren. They accord us the honour of being " a *branch* of the Church of Christ." They expect to "commune with us in heaven," and they propose to antedate our celestial unity by an earthly amalgamation. While prisons, and fires, and chains, were their instruments, we stood firm and unmoved amidst them all. Shall we at last be seduced from our allegiance by the syren voice of flattery? Of the two this is immeasurably the stronger weapon. The danger that we shall now make shipwreck of faith is greater than ever before.

> " Praise from the rival'd lips of toothless bald
> Decrepitude, and in the looks of lean
> And craving poverty, and in the bow
> Respectful of the smutched artificer,
> Is oft too welcome, and may much disturb
> The bias of the purpose; how much more
> Poured forth by beauty, splendid and polite,
> In language soft as adoration breathes."

" Violence is no more heard in our land; wasting nor destruction within our borders." The sunshine of prosperity casts about us a halo of brightness. Our brethren approach us, not with fetters and fagots, but with smiles and kindness. They say to us in effect—Do give up your principles as Baptists, and then we shall have no more difficulty. We love you as brethren, but your doctrines and practices are most unfortunate. They are indescribably odious; and while they can be of no consequence to genuine religion, they serve only to make you "*unpopular*." Pray let us blot out the Baptist church. It is such a stubborn, bigoted, illiberal church, and, withal, in this country, so flourishing, numbering, with its adherents, one fourth of the population. Let us blot it out, and the result will be so glorious. Then there will be no impediment, and we shall all unite in one delightful fellowship of love and communion!

Having bravely fought the battle, and, during eighteen hundred years, maintained the faith once delivered to the saints, shall we, so near the goal of all our hopes, ignobly put off our armor, and ingloriously perish in the affectionate embraces of fraternal *liberalism?* But I am told that all this is mere fancy, a dream of the imagination, that our promiscuous communion could not, and would not have any such effect. We have already seen that it could not take place without either an abandonment of our principles, or a practical falsification of them. Of this fact it is impossible to doubt. After having been thus despoiled of our integrity, would the desire be worth even a thought still to continue in separate existence? What motive could remain to prompt the inclination of being? And even if cherished, with whatever anxiety, it would be hopeless. The strongest advocate open communion ever had, and all its most discerning friends concur with him, candidly confesses that its universal prevalence would certainly, and resistlessly, annihilate the Baptist church. On this subject Mr. Hall remarks—" Of the tendency of mixed communion to promote a more candid inquiry into our principles it is scarcely possible to doubt; whether it would have the effect of rapidly extending the Baptist church as such, is less certain. For were that practice universally to prevail, the mixture of Baptists and Pedobaptists in Christian societies would, probably, ere long be such that the appellation of Baptists might be found, not so properly applicable to churches, as to individuals, while some more comprehensive term might possibly be employed to discriminate the views of collective bodies. But what then? Are we contending for names, or for things? If the effect of a more liberal system shall be found to increase the number of those who return to the primitive practice of baptism, and thus follow the Lamb whithersoever he goeth, he must be possessed of a deplorable imbecility, and narrowness of mind, who will lament the disappearance of a name, especially when it is remembered that whenever just views on the subject shall become universal, the name by which we are at present distinguished will necessarily cease. An honest solicitude for the restoration of a divine ordinance to its primitive simplicity and purity is not merely innocent but meritorious; but if the ultimate consequence of such an improvement should be to merge the appellation of a party into that which is derived from the divine founder of our religion, it is an event that none but a bigot will regret."*

It is not my design to make any comment upon this passage, introduced so much at length. The proof which it affords of the truth of our proposition now in question is conclusive. Having renounced the *faith* of the Gospel as a *concession* to Christian union, we next give up our existence as a church, and distribute our members among the surrounding sects, and for what? In the vain hope that as a compensation for our voluntary destruction, they will receive baptism, which to bequeath to them is the only motive for our death. And what, should they condescendingly fulfil our hopes, will they do with it? They will add it to their *pedoism*, and engraft it upon their Arminianism and Calvinism, their Presbyterianism, Lutheranism, and Episcopacy. and what would their religion be the better of it? To say the least it would be not less heterogeneous in its composition, or inconsistent in its form, than it is at present. What

* Works, vol. ii. pp. 228, 229.

Baptist is sufficiently free from "imbecility, bigotry, and narrowness of mind," to feel prepared for this "meritorious" act of "improvement." Which of her sons will raise his voice or his hand, rudely to extinguish the only church which, like the sun in mid heaven, has poured the pure light of truth upon the world. Such a religious *felo de se* would be equally displeasing to God, and fatal to the interests of piety among men. That close communion will ere long cease to exist, we too are fully assured. The event, however, will not be induced by an abandonment of the truth, on the part of its advocates, nor by the destruction of the church of the Redeemer, but by the conscientious and full obedience of all the people of God. Thus we have seen that, to adopt the popular system of free communion, we must renounce our cherished principles, confess that the sprinkling of infants is true and lawful baptism, and that we are re-baptizers; or otherwise practically falsify, and dishonor all our professions, rob the church of her honors, and abandon her to darkness, and non-existence. We are not prepared to meet these results. No peculiar affection towards us, or promises, by other denominations, of love, sympathy, or obedience, can lay us under obligations to prove thus recreant to all that is sacred and holy. The word of God is our only standard, and to the duties it imposes we must conform at all times, and in every particular. The consequences of our obedience we leave to Jehovah. These considerations constitute our first reason for declining to unite with our Pedobaptist brethren in Sacramental Communion.

CHAPTER IX.

WE CANNOT ENGAGE IN CONMUNION WITH OUR PEDOBAPTIST BRETHREN, BECAUSE THEY ARE NOT BAPTIZED, HAVING RECEIVED THE RITE IN THEIR INFANCY.

There is no law for infant baptism—The commission does not authorize it—The teachings of the Apostles—Their practice—The object for which baptism is received—The actions of those baptized by the Apostles—Infant baptism is an evil—It is prohibited in the word of God.

A SECOND reason exists prohibiting our sacramental intercourse with Pedobaptists. The law of Christ requires baptism as a preliminary measure, and they have not been baptized. To this fact we have already very frequently referred, and we now proceed more fully to explain ourselves in the premises.

"Baptism is an ordinance of Christ," says Dr. Gale; "it must, of necessity, be celebrated exactly as he appointed. And since, to the very being of baptism, a subject to whom it must be administered is necessary, and a mode of administering, without which it would only be a notion in the brain, these things are as necessary as baptism itself."* In another place he remarks:—"That only is baptism which Christ appointed; and, therefore, that which differs from what he appointed, differs from baptism; and to bring in alterations, is to change the thing, and make it not the same, but another."

On Wall, Lond. ed. 1828, p. 66.

These propositions are most clearly so many axioms, and in view of them I proceed to remark that Pedobaptists are not baptized, because they received the rite in their infancy. In religion, or in any of its ordinances, we admit of no authority but the Bible. Who, according to this standard, are we to regard as entitled to receive baptism? I answer, believers, and believers only. Of this fact we are assured by the law of baptism; by the teachings of the apostles on the subject; by the practice they pursued in its administration; by the objects had in view in receiving the rite; and by the actions performed by the baptized. A very brief notice of each of these points will be sufficient for my present purpose.

That believers, and believers only, are entitled to receive this ordinance is proved, by the law of baptism.

This is the same law with that of the Lord's supper,— the apostolic commission, in which it is proper to for us to observe, that several distinct and dissimilar duties are enjoined. "Go ye, and teach all nations." Such is the first obligation imposed. The word — $\mu\alpha\theta\varepsilon\tau\varepsilon\upsilon\sigma\alpha\tau\varepsilon$ — translated *teach*, is, as every scholar knows, properly rendered to *disciple*. "It is used," says the Christian Review, "in no single instance, either in sacred or classic writers, in which the idea of instruction is not involved. To become a disciple of Christ is to believe in him, and obey him. To disciple all nations, therefore, is to bring them by faith into the school of Christ in which they are to learn his will. When this is accomplished, and not in any instance before, a second duty becomes imperative. They are to be baptized, in the name of the Father, and of the Son, and of the Holy Ghost. How this is to be done, is an inquiry which belongs to a discussion of the action of baptism. When this is accomplished, the disciples are, lastly, to be instructed to observe all other things enjoined by the word of revelation: 'Teach ing *them* to observe all things whatsoever I have commanded you.' "*

To every one, who reflects a moment on the subject, it is as obvious as that these commands have any authority at all, that, to the acceptableness of our obedience, they must be observed, as we have before fully seen, in the order in which they were delivered. On this point, it cannot be necessary for me now to add many remarks. This order is not accidental, nor can it be violated without a breach of the law itself. As long as it is the duty of ministers to preach, and of sinners to believe, so long it will be the duty of every believer, when he becomes such, to be baptized. For the correctness of this exposition of the commission, we have the highest authority which the Pedobaptist world can produce —the attestation of their own best, and most cherished writers, some of which we will adduce.

Jerome, a celebrated Latin Father of the fourth century, acknowledged the most learned writer of the age in which he lived, in commenting on the commission, alludes to the point before us in the following language:—" They—the apostles and their successors in the ministry—*first* teach all nations; then, when they are taught, they baptize them in water; for it cannot be that the body should receive the sacrament of baptism, unless the soul has received *before* the true faith."†

John Calvin, of Geneva, the great Reformer, and father of the Presbyterian church, in his Harmony of the Evangelists, remarks: — " Because Christ requires *teaching before* baptizing, and will have *believers only* admitted to baptism, baptism does not seem to be rightly administered, except *faith* precedes."‡

* Vol. iii. p. 205.   † Gale on Wall, p. 319.
‡ Comm. in loco.

To the famed Richard Baxter we have before had reference; I will be permitted to quote again from his work respecting the "Rights to the Sacraments," in which he introduces the following passage:—"As for those that say they are discipled *by baptizing*, and not *before baptizing*, they speak not the sense of the text, nor that which is true or rational. Else why should one be baptized more than another? This is not like some occasional historical mention of baptism, but *is the very command of Christ, and purposely expresseth their several works in their several places and order.* The first task is, by *teaching*, to make *disciples*—which Mark calls *believers*. The second work is to *baptize* them. The third work is to *teach them all other things* which are afterwards to be learned in the school of Christ. To contemn this order is to renounce all rules of order; for where can we expect to find it if not here? My conscience is fully satisfied from this text, that it is one kind of *faith*, even *saving*, that *must go before baptism*, and the profession whereof the minister must expect."*

We could readily quote numerous other writers who maintain the same doctrine, whose piety and learning have adorned every age of the church, but these are sufficient to prove that our Baptist exposition of the commission, as respects the persons lawfully entitled to receive the ordinance, is no novelty in the science of hermeneutics.

The Scriptures, in the hands of a man familiar with all their parts, on most topics satisfactorily interpret themselves. This remark is especially true in regard to the subject now under consideration. The law of baptism, as recorded by Mark,† affords a striking explanation of the same law as recorded by Matthew.‡ According to Mark, it has the following reading: "Go ye into all the world, and preach the

---

* Pp. 91, 149, 150.   † Chap. xvi. 15, 16.   ‡ Chap. xxviii. 19, 20.

Gospel to every creature; he that believeth and is baptized shall be saved; and he that believeth not shall be damned." Matthew's version is: " Go ye, therefore, and teach all nations, baptizing them in the name of the Father, and of the Son, and of the Holy Ghost; teaching them to observe all things whatsoever I have commanded you; and, lo, I am with you alway, even unto the end of the world." A moment's comparison of this law, as recorded by the two sacred writers named, must convince every man that the persons called by one *the taught*, are, as Jerom, Calvin, Baxter, and many more, justly maintain, by the other called *believers*. It is therefore true, beyond a reasonable doubt, that if the law of Jesus Christ, and the only law on that subject he ever enacted, or announced to the world, is to govern us, believers *alone* are to be baptized, and every believer, as soon as he becomes such, is required to submit to the ordinance.

These facts, it will be seen, leave no room for infant baptism. If such a rite has been administered, it was unlawful, and we are not permitted to recognize it. The law requires every man, *when he becomes a believer*, to be baptized. The order of the commission is peremptory. No reservations or exceptions are admitted. The baptism of every *believer*, when he is a believer, is essential to a compliance with the divine requisition. It is, therefore, true, that if even an inspired command exists, in any other part of the word of God, directing the baptism of unbelievers, or of infants, or of any other classes of persons than those described in the statute, it is *another baptism*, and does not, and cannot affect, in the slightest degree, the validity and force of this order, to baptize every man when and as soon as he becomes a believer. The law, I again remark, makes no exceptions. None are intimated. The description of the person to be baptized, as obviously excludes all others, as it requires him to obey. The baptism of infants, contended for by our brethren of other churches, if it has a legal existence, is *another baptism*. There is, however, but *one baptism*. Paul asserts, that as there is but *one* Lord, and *one* faith, so there is but *one baptism*.* There is, therefore, no baptism for infants, or for any other class of persons but those who believe, evangelically, in our Lord Jesus Christ.

That believers, and believers only, are lawfully entitled to receive the ordinance of baptism, is still further manifest by the teachings of the apostles and evangelists on the subject.

They well knew the extent of the authority confided to them by the great Head of the church in this matter. To them, personally, the law was delivered; they were endowed with wisdom from on high to understand its true interpretation; and they were preserved from error in their instructions and administrations by the presence and inspiration of the Holy Spirit. What did they teach on the subject before us? A correct reply to this inquiry is derived most easily from an examination of their instructions.

A few days after the ascension of our Lord, the apostolic company were all together in the city of Jerusalem, when they addressed a vast assembly with the most astonishing effect. The speech of Peter, on this occasion, has been preserved and transmitted to us. In that speech,† we find a reference to baptism in the following language: "Repent, and be baptized, every one of you."

On the memorable occasion when the Gospel was given to the Gentiles, another instance occurs of the teaching of the apostle of the circumcision. The word had been fully proposed to the assembly in the house of Cornelius. They had been *taught*, and had embraced the truth of the religion of

---

* Eph. iv. 5. † Acts ii. 38.

Christ. The Holy Ghost had descended upon them, regenerating and filling their souls with joy and peace in believing. Then said the apostle, "Who can forbid water, that these should not be baptized who have received the Holy Ghost as well as we? And he commanded them to be baptized."*

The teachings of the evangelists conform strictly to those of the apostles. Philip, when the church was scattered, and its members driven from Jerusalem, by the violence of the persecution which followed the martyrdom of Stephen, "went down to Samaria, and preached Christ to them." It is added,† "When they believed Philip preaching the things of the kingdom of God, and the name of Jesus Christ, they were baptized, both *men* and *women*." So scrupulous was this evangelist in his determination to conform to the commission by baptizing believers, and believers only, that on another memorable occasion, although previously divinely instructed as to his character, when the treasurer of Candace, queen of the Ethiopians, had been taught by him, had avowed himself a convert, and had made application for baptism, he paused to question him on his religious experience, and replied to his request,‡ by saying, "If thou believest with all thine heart, thou mayest" be baptized.

When Saul of Tarsus had repented of his sins, had believed in the Lord Jesus Christ, and, to employ the scripture terms which express his regeneration, "the scales had fallen from his eyes," Ananias, of Damascus, said to him, "*Now* why tarriest thou? Arise, and be baptized, and wash away thy sins, calling on the name of the Lord."§

Such are the instances of the teachings on this subject, of the apostles and apostolic ministers; and they conform, with-

* Acts x. 47.
† Acts viii. 12.
‡ Acts viii. 38.
§ Acts xxii. 16.

out an exception, to the interpretation of the commission which we have submitted.

Let it not be presumed that Baptists are alone in the firm opinion that, in no instance, does an apostle, or apostolic minister teach that any but believers should be baptized. I will offer for consideration the opinions of two or three of the great German critics, of the present century, all of whom are Pedobaptists, and acknowledged to be among the most profound Biblical scholars the world ever produced.*

The great Schleirmacher, in his Christian Theology, remarks:—"All traces of infant baptism which one will find in the New Testament, must first be put into it."† Professor Hahn, in his Theology, says:—" Baptism, according to its *original* design, can be given only to adults, who are capable of true knowledge, repentance, and faith. Neither in the Scriptures nor during the first hundred and fifty years, is a sure example of infant baptism to be found; and we must concede that the numerous opposers of it cannot be contradicted on Gospel grounds."‡

Professor Lange, on Infant Baptism,§ observes:—"All attempts to make out infant baptism from the New Testament fail. It is totally opposed to the spirit of the apostolic age, and the fundamental principles of the New Testament."

We need not extend our observations on this head. It is now, I trust, sufficiently evident, so far as the teachings of the apostles, and apostolic ministers are concerned, that believers only are entitled to receive the sacrament of baptism.

The doctrine we now defend is still further established by the recorded practice of the apostles, and their associates, who never, in a single instance, administered baptism to any but

---

* I quote the translation of the Christian Review, vol. iii. 197, 198.
† P. 383.   ‡ P. 556.   § P. 101.

those who had previously professed their faith in our Lord Jesus Christ.

The first baptism administered after the ascension of Christ, took place, as we have already intimated, in Jerusalem. On this occasion those who were admitted to the ordinance are particularly described*—"*They* that gladly received the word were baptized." The pronoun *they*, as here employed, as necessarily excludes all others from the ordinance then administered, as it attests the fact that "they that gladly received the word" were admitted.

Paul and his companions preached the Gospel in Corinth. —It is added†—"Many of the Corinthians, *hearing, believed*, and were baptized."

When the Eunuch‡ had solemnly professed his faith in the Lord Jesus Christ, "they both went down into the water, and Philip baptized him."

The Samaritans, both *men* and *women*,§ "when they *believed*, were baptized."

Crispus, the chief ruler of the synagogue in Philippi, and every member of his family, through the instrumentality of Paul, who boarded in the house, *believed*, and were all baptized, by the hands of the apostle himself.

Such are the instances of the apostles' practice. Those who received the Holy Ghost, and spake with tongues, as in the house of Cornelius; and those who believed in the Lord Jesus Christ, and rejoiced in hope; were baptized "both men, and women;" but not the slightest intimation is given that children, in a single instance, were admitted to this sacred rite. On the contrary no case can be found on record in the Sacred Scriptures, in which it is not either

* Acts ii. 41. ‡ Acts viii. 38.
† Acts xviii. 8. § Acts viii. 12.

expressly stated, or plainly implied, that the person baptized was, previously, a believer in our Lord Jesus Christ.

Lest, however, any one may presume that I have selected the instances adduced to suit our own views, and that, although none of *these* favor infant baptism, there are *others* that do, I beg leave to refer again to some of the most learned and candid Pedobaptist divines, who, in their works, deliberately arranged, written, and published to the world, have explicitly admitted the truth of all the facts I have now stated.

Dr. Goodwin, a member of the Assembly of Divines at Westminster, holds this language :—" Baptism supposeth regeneration sure in itself first. Sacraments are never administered to begin, or work grace." He adds—" Read all the Acts of the Apostles, still it is said—They *believed*, and were baptized."*

Professor Limborch says—" No instance can be produced from which it may be indisputably inferred that any child was baptized by the apostles."†

To these testimonies we will only add that of a man of our own age, whose name, and literary character, are known to every scholar. I refer to Bretschneider. He says :‡— " Rheinard, Morus, and Döderlein, say—Infant baptism is not to be found in the Bible." The Christian Review quotes this passage and adds§—" We need say nothing of the literary character of these three great men."

We are now, I think, authorized to say, that the practice of the apostles justifies the conclusion that believers and believers only are entitled to receive the ordinance of baptism.

I further observe that the objects designed to be effected

---

* Works, vol. i. part 1, p. 200. ‡ Theology, vol. ii. p. 758.
† Com. Sys. Div. Lib. 5, cap. 22. § Vol. iii. p. 200.

by baptism can possibly be accomplished only when believers are the subjects of the ordinance.

Baptism is the appointed form in which, in part at least, we make a profession of the religion of Christ. Such a profession is not, and cannot be, complete without it. This truth is so obvious that I suppose it will be cheerfully admitted by the well informed Christians of every denomination. If, in the apostolic day, a man was baptized, he was regarded by all as having made a profession of religion. So it is now, and so it has been in all ages and countries.

Paul teaches this doctrine in the plainest, and most unequivocal terms. He says to the Galatians—"Ye are all the children of God in Christ Jesus."* But how could this be true, on the Pedobaptist principle? If some members of that church were baptized infants, then either Paul's statement of them was not true,—they were not all the children of God in Christ Jesus; or else he taught the doctrine that *baptism alone*, irrespective of belief in Christ, or any work of the Spirit of God—of either of which infants are incapable—did constitute the babes who received it, as fully as the regeneration of the souls of the believers, the children of God in Christ Jesus. This would have been contradictory, and manifestly absurd. He taught no such doctrine. The apostle himself tells us why he assumed this predicate of the Galatians:—"Ye are all the children of God, in Christ Jesus, for"—or because—"as many of you as have been baptized into Christ, have put on Christ" —have professed yourselves Christians. Not that baptizing them made them Christians. This absurdity Paul never countenanced. They were made Christians by faith in Christ Jesus, upon a profession of which, he assumes it as a matter of course, they had been baptized, and united

* Ch. iii. 26, 27.

with the church. He, therefore, naturally concludes they were all regenerated persons—in other words, " the children of God in Christ Jesus." Archbishop Tillotson, with whom, on this subject we entirely agree, expressly says*—" In baptism we put on Christ"—or make a public profession of religion.

Baptism, therefore being the appointed form in which we profess the religion of Christ, how can he who has no religion make a profession of it, without hypocrisy? And when baptism is applied to infants, incapable of any volition whatever, and much more of professions of any kind, can it be supposed, without the abandonment of reason, that the object of the ordinance is accomplished? Unquestionably it cannot. The practice, sometimes adopted, of appointing sponsors, who profess as the proxies of the child, and in its name; and bind themselves that at maturity, it " shall renounce the devil and all his works, the pomps and vanities of this wicked world," while it is an indirect confession, in theory, of the truth of the Baptist doctrine, but adds, in its practice,—besides the sin of religiously promising what no one pretends to think he can perform,—another item to the absurdity of Pedobaptism, by presuming that the faith of one man can be appropriated to the justification of another.

Neander, known in our country as the author of the latest and best Ecclesiastical History that has been written; who is a converted Jew and Professor of Theology in the most eminent University in Prussia; a member of the Lutheran Church, and of course a Pedobaptist, refers to the matter now under consideration in the following terms:—" As baptism was closely connected with a conscious entrance into Christian fellowship, and as faith and baptism

---

* Works, vol. v. Serm. 7, p. 179.

were always joined together, it is altogether probable that it was administered only when these two things were united."* How else, I ask, could the object of baptism have been attained? An involuntary confession of Christ, and which is true of baptism in every case, except in that of a believer, is of no force or value, at the tribunal of either God or man.

Augustine, the Bishop of Hippo, fourteen hundred years ago, defined baptism: " The outward and visible sign, of the inward and spiritual grace." Most of the prevailing denominations have adopted this ancient definition. But what does it mean? Its sense must be that in the regeneration of the soul by the Holy Ghost, our sins are forgiven, and the grace imparted which dwells within, of which baptism is at the same time a figure and a profession. On this account, baptism is metaphorically said to be the washing away of sins. But what " inward and spiritual grace" is there in the child, of which " baptism is the outward and visible sign?" Surely regeneration is necessary to impart " the inward and spiritual grace," or none can exist. Does any one pretend that infants are regenerated before they are baptized? *"The Standards"* maintain, as we shall have occasion hereafter to show, that baptism *imparts* regeneration; but what Pedobaptist now confesses his belief in this dogma? Is baptism necessary to salvation? Will the opinion that it is, be, in this enlightened age, publicly avowed! That the word of God *directly* enjoins their baptism, no well read man will, I presume, risk his reputation by asserting. What benefit can it impart? It is impossible—physically and morally impossible—for the unconscious babe to make a profession of religion.—Their baptism, therefore, is without signification. It is of no

---

* Hist. of Apostolic Age, vol. i. p. 140.

benefit to them in this world, nor in the world to come. It is not an act, whether on the parts of the parents or the child, of obedience to Christ, because *he* has not commanded it. Why, then, subject them to the rite, appointed as the form in which Christians are to profess the religion of Christ, and of which infants can at best be only the involuntary and passive objects? The design, therefore, proposed to be effected by baptism, can be secured only when believers are the subjects, and consequently the ordinance is to be administered alone to believers.

The actions said to have been performed by those who received it, complete the proof that, in the days of the apostles, believers and believers only were regarded as entitled to baptism.

Those who were baptized on the day of Pentecost "gladly received the word," and "continued, steadfastly, in the apostles' doctrine and fellowship, and in breaking of bread, and in prayers." The Corinthians "heard," and "believed." The guests of the Centurion "received the Holy Ghost," and "spake with tongues." The household of Lydia were "comforted" by the promises of the Gospel. The household of the jailer of Philippi, *believed* in God, and *rejoiced*. And so of all the others. Their feelings and acts were such as were dictated by enlightened and ardent piety. They were natural to *believers*. They were, in the aggregate, such as among Baptist churches, generally, we constantly witness. But they were, without exception, all impossible to infants, and as necessarily exclude them from the ordinance, as if it had been expressly affirmed, that those only were baptized, who were members of the national council, soldiers in the army, or merchants in business. The actions of the baptized are particularly described in the New Testament; they are those of which infants are incapable; therefore it is impossible that infants could have been baptized in the days, or by the authority of the apostles.

In these plain and obvious conclusions, it gives us great pleasure to have the concurrence of the best and most learned writers among Pedobaptists themselves, the testimony of some of whom I will be permitted to transcribe.

Dr. Wall, the great champion of infant baptism, has in his history made an admission in these words:—"Among all the persons that are recorded as baptized by the apostles, there is no express mention of any infant."*

Martin Luther, also, the incomparable Reformer, a much greater man than Wall, has said:—" It cannot be proved by the sacred Scriptures, that infant baptism was instituted by Christ, or begun by the first Christians after the apostles."†

In the facts and considerations now adduced we have shown as we have proposed, from the plain sense of the law of baptism enacted by Christ; from the teachings and practice of the apostles ; from the objects designated to be effected by baptism ; from the actions performed by those who received the ordinance ; and from the concessions of the greatest and most learned men of the Pedobaptist world, fathers, reformers, and moderns, that believers, and believers only, are lawfully entitled to receive the ordinance of baptism. We have also seen that infant baptism is not enjoined in the Bible, was not practised by the apostles, nor commenced during the first, and purest ages of the church. How then, when an infant is sprinkled, can we recognize this as true Gospel baptism ?

But we go further than this. We propose to prove that infant baptism is an *evil*, and that it is *positively prohibited* in the word of God.

* Introduction, pp. 1
† Inst. R's, apud Van. of Inf. Bap. part 2, p. 8.

Before I proceed, however, in the argument, I will briefly reply to an inquiry which has, I doubt not, before this time, suggested itself to the mind of my reader. The explanation will also prevent the necessity of referring to the same topic on collateral subjects in future. The numerous Pedobaptist writers quoted in this and other chapters, certainly believed the baptism of infants lawful and obligatory, otherwise they would not have practised it. How, it may be asked, could they cherish such a belief, and still make the concessions which have been recited? I answer, they certainly did both, and seemed not to be at all conscious that any inconsistency could be charged against them. There are men of little reading and humbler abilities, who believe it is enjoined in the New Testament; but the great and learned men I have quoted, received and practised infant baptism, not because they presumed it to be directly taught in the divine law,— this, they maintain, is not the case,—but because they found it in the " Standards ;" it was the *practice* of the church ; and they imagined they could not *conveniently* dispense with it ! It has been defended by some on the ground of "*Christian feeling.*" This seems to be a favorite idea with the German critics. Some advocate it because they say it will do the child no harm, and probably render the parents more sensible of their obligations to rear it in the nurture and admonition of the Lord. Some derive it, by analogy, from the circumcision of the Mosaic dispensation, others from proselyte baptism, and others plead for it on the ground that all men are born sinful and heathen, and baptism must be administered to wash away their sins, reclaim them from heathenism, and initiate them into covenant with God. Others still place it, like Calvin, upon the ground that the church has the right to change the form of the sacrament; and still others, with the fathers of Protestant Episcopacy, claim that "the Church has power to decree rites and ceremonies." It is a remarkable fact, that although all the Pedobaptist churches concur in baptizing their children, yet no two of them can agree as to the reasons why they do so, or what children they shall baptize. These facts explain the whole mystery how the admissions we have quoted could be made, and yet their authors believe in infant baptism, and practice the ceremony. Great men are not always great in every thing. I shall not here attempt a refutation of their arguments. For this purpose I refer my reader to the admirable History of Baptism, by the Rev. Isaac T. Hinton; the excellent little work of the Rev. Milo P. Jewett, with such other books as Judd's Review of Stewart; Carson on Baptism, and many more of high character. How can such Pedobaptists as I have quoted read and applaud, as so many of them do, the immortal maxim of Chillingworth, and yet be Pedobaptists? "The Bible—the Bible alone, is the religion of Protestants." How could Chillingworth himself mingle so great a truth with his own Pedobaptism? But I proceed with my argument.

My postulate is, that the baptism of infants is an evil.

This proposition may, at the first annunciation, startle the reader. He may even be tempted to pronounce it unpardonably bold. I beg indulgence, however, and attention, for but a moment, and my reasons for the sentiment will have been submitted. They will not be likely to pass for more than they are worth.

The admission of infants to baptism destroys one of the main designs had in view in the institution of baptism. All denominations and all ages agree in regarding baptism as constituting a principal part of the visible line which distinguishes the church from the world. No one can be recognized as a member of any church who is not baptized; and, on the other hand, all, both infants and adults, who have been baptized, are considered, in some sort, members of the church. Infant baptism, however, as far as it prevails, destroys this distinction, and, by confounding them together, ruins the church, without benefiting the world. We will imagine, for illustration, that from this moment, Pedobaptist principles are fully adopted and practised by all people, upon the face of the whole earth. Every child, as soon as born, would be initiated into the church, and, as a consequence, in one generation, every man, woman, and child in the whole world, would be in the church. As baptism in infancy renders no one, in any respect, more moral or religious than he would have been without it, or increases in any case the likelihood of conversion, the church would exhibit, with perhaps a few holy men, as at present, a horde of infidels, drunkards, murderers, thieves, and robbers, all church members! The visibility of the church would be lost; nor could it ever be regained until, by a return to Baptist principles, believers, and believers only, were admitted to baptism.

Infant baptism is an evil on another account. It prevents those who have received it from being, when they become believers, baptized, as the law of Christ commands. This law requires the baptism of believers: "He that believeth and is baptized." To the believer is the promise made, and to those who do not believe and yet are baptized, there is made, on that account, no promise. Any ceremony, therefore, which prevents obedience is an evil.

Infant baptism is an evil because the practice serves to perpetuate the error that originated it—the supposition that all repudiate, that all still feel, and to which, in moments of excitement, they instinctively bow, that baptism is mysteriously connected with the salvation of the child, or in some way materially affects its condition and prospects in another state of being. If this be not so, how can we account for the trembling solicitude manifested by the mass of otherwise even intelligent people, when they imagine their little ones in danger of death? If the skies pour down floods, and the earth is rocked in storms, if the living thunders are leaping every moment from their tempestuous home, and darkness like a mantle covers the world, not a moment must be lost, the minister must come, and the child must be baptized at midnight, lest it die! I reverence parental affection; but why should it suggest a resort to baptism? Disguise it as we may, the deception is fixed in the soul.

Numerous other proofs of the same fact suggest themselves, but these are sufficient. Infant baptism, therefore, is an evil because it confounds the church with the world; and because by it both parents and children are betrayed into radical error, and deceived in relation to vital articles of the Christian faith.

I have said that the baptism of infants is peremptorily and explicitly prohibited.

It is prohibited on the ground that it is useless, that it is unreasonable, and that it is an evil. All these facts we have fully proved, and the arguments need not be repeated.

The apostolic commission prohibits the baptism of infants. We have seen that this holy statute describes particularly the person to be baptized. They are believers. It is impossible that a command to baptize believers can include infants. No explanation can bring them into it. Even if there was a command, in some other part of the word of God, authorizing or requiring the baptism of infants, which we have seen is not true, it would not, unless some exception could be discovered, in which the law of the commission, requiring every one to be baptized when he becomes a believer, may be suspended, interfere with its regular administration. The law of God, therefore, prohibits the baptism of infants.

But we have still more direct authority on the point in question.

Baptism, as we have seen, is enacted by positive law. The obligation to obey a positive law arises solely from the authority of the Lawgiver. Therefore the law of the institution is the only rule of obedience. If, then, there is no plain command there is no law. We have seen that all the great Pedobaptist writers confess there is in the Bible no direct command for infant baptism. But the matter does not rest here. With regard to all the commandments enacted as positive laws, Jehovah has promulgated a special edict in these words:—" Ye shall not add unto the word which I command you, neither shall ye diminish aught from it, that ye may keep the commandments of the Lord your God which I command you."* So important does God regard it to preserve his institution pure from all change and contamination, that he twice repeats this solemn law, and adds at last a most fearful penalty. He says: " What thing soever I command you, observe to do it. Thou shalt not add thereto, nor diminish from it."† And, " If any man shall add unto these things, God shall add unto him the plagues that are written in this book ; and if any man shall take away from the words of the book of this prophecy, God shall take away his part out of the book of life, and out of the holy city, and from the things that are written in this book."‡ Is infant baptism directly commanded? Its advocates themselves confess that it is not. It is, then, directly, explicitly, peremptorily *prohibited*, and he who dares to introduce it, or carry it into practice, does so at his peril.

With all these facts before us, and with our common

* Deut. iv. 2. † Deut. xii. 32. ‡ Rev. xxii. 18, 19.

Baptist reverence for the word of God, and the teachings of his holy apostles, it is not surprising that we should feel shocked at the attempt of any body of men, professing to be *Christians*, to bring into the church, not only without authority to do so, but in direct opposition to the express statute of the divine word which forbids it, the ceremony of infant baptism, and plead for it as useful and obligatory. To such a loose and licentious theology we cannot subscribe. On the contrary, against it, in all its parts, we feel ourselves bound to enter our most earnest and solemn protest.

These, briefly, are our reasons, and we believe they are good and sufficient reasons, for refusing to recognize the rite as legitimate when administered in infancy. Pedobaptists have received no other baptism but this, which is a nullity. They are not baptized, and, therefore, we dare **not**, **until** they are, admit them to the Lord's table.

CHAPTER X.

WE CANNOT COMMUNE WITH PEDOBAPTISTS BECAUSE, NOT HAVING BEEN IMMERSED, THEY ARE NOT BAPTIZED.

Immersion only is baptism, proved by the sense of the word—its philology—Its sense confessed by critics—By theologians—Ancient Confessions of Faith—The English Liturgy—Use of the word in our common translation—Ancient version of the New Testament—reasons why it received its present rendering—Translations into Hebrew—Conclusions.

PEDOBAPTISTS are not baptized for other reasons than that we have now considered, and especially because, although the subject might have been an adult, and a believer, yet the ordinance was administered by sprinkling, or pouring, which is not, and cannot be baptism, therefore, they have not complied with the preliminary law, the observance of which is expressly required to qualify them to partake of the Lord's supper.

Because a profession of religion is a declaration of our faith in the death, burial, and resurrection of Christ, and a determination, by his grace, to live a new and holy life, and baptism is the divinely appointed form in which such profession is required to be made, therefore, "we are buried with Christ by baptism into death, that like as Christ was raised up from the dead, by the glory of the Father, even so we also, should walk in newness of life." To be buried with Christ in baptism is to be immersed; and after mature, protracted, and anxious examination, we have arrived at the settled, and unalterable conclusion, that immersion in water, by an authorized administrator, of a properly qualified candidate, in the name of the Father, and of the Son, and of the Holy Ghost, and this alone, is Christian baptism. In proof of the correctness of this opinion I shall offer a few brief considerations.

This proposition is sustained by the meaning of the word employed in the New Testament to, describe the action of baptism.

The word invariably is Βαπτιζω, in some one or other of its forms. This word is derived from " Βαπτω, which signifies primarily to *dip*, and as a secondary meaning obviously derived from the primary, it denotes to *dye*. Every occurrence of the word may be reduced to one or the other of these acceptations. It has been said that it signifies to *wash*. This meaning has been given by Lexicographers, and is admitted by Baptists, but it is not warranted by a single decisive example either in the Scriptures, or in classical authors." It has also been said that it is a generic word, and without respect to mode, or exclusive of all modes, denotes any application of water. This idea is wholly fanciful. Except when the word signifies to dye, it denotes *mode* and nothing else.

The root βαπτω, and its derivative βαπτιζω, are often considered as synonymous. There is, however, "a very obvious difference," says Carson, "in the use of the words; and a difference that materially and naturally affects the point now at issue." It is this—"*βαπτω is never used to denote the ordinance of baptism*, and βαπτιζω," used for this purpose, "*never signifies to dye*. The primary word βαπτω has two significations, the first to *dip*, and the second to *dye*. But the derivative is formed only to modify the primary; and in all the Greek language, I assert, that an instance cannot be found in which it has the secondary meaning of the primitive word. If this assertion is not correct it will be easy for learned men to produce an example in contradiction. That βαπτω is never applied to the ordinance of baptism any one can verify who is able to look into the passages of the Greek Testament, which refer to the ordinance. The derivative βαπτιζω is alone used to describe the sacred ordinance; and in the whole history of the Greek language, it has but one meaning; it not only means to dip or immerse, but it never has any other meaning."* If any scholar disputes this statement, let him bring forward the passages that sustain him, from the Septuagint or from the New Testament; from any of the Greek classics, such as Elian's Varia Historia, the Idyls of Theocritus, the works of Aristotle, of Aristophanes, Sophocles, Herodotus, Homer, Hypocrates, or any others; or from any of the Greek Fathers. Let the passages be produced. But the utmost efforts of *ages* have been exerted, and it *has not* been done, it *cannot* be done. If, therefore, any respect is due to the meaning of words used to describe actions, Christian baptism is confined exclusively to immersion.

In these conclusions, regarding the meaning of the word, we have the concurrence, strange as it may appear, of the *great* and the *learned*, even of the Pedobaptists themselves; and given, too, with more or less cheerfulness, by men of all the leading denominations of Christians. This fact is as true as it is interesting and important, of which I shall at once proceed to give satisfactory testimony.

Our first witness shall be that great man, before several times quoted, whose name is synonymous with the Reformation. Martin Luther,† remarks:—" The term baptism is a Greek word. It may be rendered a *dipping*, as when we dip something in water, that it may be entirely covered with water. And though that custom be utterly abolished among the generality, for neither do they dip * * * * * but only

---

* Carson, p. 19.   † Apud Du Veil, on Acts viii. 3.

sprinkle with a little water, nevertheless they ought to be wholly immersed, and presently drawn out again. For the etymology of the word seems to require it. The signification of baptism is, that the old man of our nativity, which is full of sins, which is entirely of flesh and blood, may be overwhelmed by divine grace. The manner of baptism, therefore, should correspond with the signification of baptism, that it may show a certain and plain sign of it."*

No Baptist could have expressed his own sentiments more lucidly than they are here declared by this distinguished man. The German critics, though all Lutherans, still maintain the same doctrines. The necessity of consulting the utmost brevity will permit me to present but a single instance. Storr, who is distinguished alike by his learning and candor, in a late profound work on Biblical Theology, emphatically says :—†

" The disciples of our Lord could understand his command in no other manner than as enjoining immersion." He then proceeds to prove that, in the fourth century, only immersion was considered valid baptism, and to establish this position he refers to a case narrated in the sixty-ninth epistle of Cyprian—Ed. Bremo. p. 188—and mentions the instance of Novatian, contained in the letter of Cornelius, the Roman bishop, recorded in Eusebius—Eccl. Hist. Lib. vi. cap. 43. Speaking of the modern practice of sprinkling for baptism,

* "Luther De Sacramento Baptismi"—Vide works, Genoe 1556, Vol. i. p. 336, "Primo nomen Baptismus Græcum est, Latine potest verti, mersio, cum immergimus aliquid in aquam, ut totum tegatur aqua, et quamvis ille mos jam absoluerit apud plærosque (neque enim totos demergunt pueros, sed tantum pancula aqua perfundunt) debebant tamen prorsus immergi, et statim retrahi. Id enim etymologia nominis postulare videtur. Et Germani quoque baptismum *tauff* vocant, a profunditate, quam *tieff*, ille sua lingua vocant quod profunde demergi conveniat eos qui baptiscuntur."

† Andover ed. 1826, pp. 290, 291.

Storr adds:—"The ancient immersion ought not to have been changed;" asserts that Luther himself was of that opinion, and wished to restore the primitive practice. His words are:—"It is certainly to be lamented that Luther was not able to accomplish his wish with regard to the introduction of immersion in baptism, as he had done in the restoration of wine in the eucharist."

Our second witness shall be the renowned Reformer—John Calvin.

In his Institutes of Religion, as translated by Allen, he says:—"The word baptize, signifies to immerse, and it is certain that immersion was the practice of the ancient church."* In several other instances this great man maintained the same important truth. For example, in his Commentary on John iii. 23, and also on Acts viii. 38—he has this remark:—"From these words we perceive how baptism was administered by the ancients, for they immersed the whole body in water."

Our third witness shall be the famous Episcopalian writer—Dr. Wall. In his History of Infant Baptism, he observes:—"This is so plain and clear [the necessity of immersion to baptism] by an infinite number of passages, that, as we cannot but pity the weak endeavors of such Pedobaptists as would maintain the negative of it, so we ought to disown, and show a dislike to the profane scoffs which some people give to the Antipedobaptists [Baptists] merely for their use of dipping, when it was, in all probability, the way in which our blessed Saviour was baptized, and, for certain, was the most usual way by which the ancient Christians did receive their baptism."† And in another place Dr. Wall adds:—"The ordinary and general

---

* Vol. iv. cap. 15, p. 343.
† Hist. Inf. Bap. vol. ii. p. 351.

practice of John, the apostles, and the primitive church, was to baptize by putting the person into the water."*

Take, as a fourth witness, the learned body of divines who composed the book called " The Assembly's Catechism." In their Annotations on Colossians ii. 12—" Buried with him in baptism"—they say: " In this phrase the apostle seemeth to allude to the ancient manner of baptism, which was to dip the parties baptized, and, as it were, to bury them under the water."

The venerable John Wesley shall bear testimony as our fifth witness. He, with the others, admits that baptism was primarily so administered.† In a sermon on Rom. vi. 3, 4, using the language of Doddridge, he observes : " It seems the part of candor to *confess* that here is an allusion to the manner of baptizing by immersion."‡ Dr. Adam Clark, in his note on the same passage, says: " It is probable that the apostle here alludes to the mode of administering baptism by immersion, the whole body being put under the water."

The most ancient Confessions of Faith and Directories speak on this subject in perfect accordance with what we have now seen to be the sense of the word, and the understanding of the most learned even of Pedobaptists, as to the form of baptism. In illustration of this remark, we submit two or three instances.

The Helvetic Confession of Faith, drawn up by Bucer, in 1536, for the use of the Protestant churches in Switzerland, ten years before the death of Luther, and republished by the Pastors of Zurich, has this passage : " Baptism was instituted and consecrated by God, and the first that baptized was John, who *dipped* Christ in the water in Jordan."

---

* Defence of Inf. Bap. p. 129.

† I do not intend to intimate that any of these witnesses thought nothing baptism but immersion.

‡ Family Expositor. Note in loco.

In the Confession of Faith, written by Melancthon, in 1551, and adopted by the Saxon churches, he says: "Baptism is an entire action, to wit, a *dipping*, and a pronouncing these words—I baptize you," &c.

The first Liturgy of the English—Episcopal—church was drawn up in 1547, in which Augusti says: "Trine immersion was enjoined."* At the commencement of the reign of James II. the Liturgy was revised, and the rubric thrown into its present form, which runs thus—" Then the priest shall take the child into his hands, and ask the name, and naming the child, shall dip it in the water, so it be discreetly and warily done, saying—N., I baptize thee," &c.†

We may now be permitted to observe, that not only is the word employed perfectly and confessedly definite, but such is the rich variety of the Greek language, in which the New Testament is written, that a different term is used for every possible application of water, whether for sacred or any other purposes, such as ραινω, ραντιζω, εχχεω, νιπτω, λουω, πλυνω, βαπτω, βαπτιζω, αγνιζω, καθαιρω, and a few others. Some of these words express different actions, and others the same action with regard to different objects, but all describe the application of water for different purposes. It is inconsistent with our conceptions of the wisdom and benevolence of God, as taught by his holy word, to presume for a moment that in his blessed revelation, respecting the instructions of which it is so necessary for us to have correct ideas, that the Holy Spirit did not use words with the utmost precision of import. Among so many words, in the richest and most copious language which ever existed, is there not one so definite to describe the action of baptism, that we may certainly know precisely what that action is? Let us take up our common

---

* Dunkeward, p. 229.   † Prayer Book, Lond. ed. 1639.

translation, and compare it with the Greek original, and we shall find the following interesting results. In the original we shall see that the word to sprinkle occurs sixty-two times; the word to pour, and its derivatives, a hundred and fifty-two times; to wash, and its derivatives, a hundred and thirty-nine times; to dip, with its derivatives, twenty-two times; and to plunge, once. Let this inquiry be now answered—Did the translators, in a single instance, render the word which means to immerse, to sprinkle? Not an example can be found. Did they ever translate the same word to pour and to immerse? Never. Did they, in any case, translate βαπτιζω to sprinkle or to pour? Never. And not an instance occurs in which ραινω, or ραντιζω, is translated to baptize, to dip, or to plunge. Are not these instructive facts? In the judgment of our translators, these words are so definitely expressive of certain and fixed actions, that they never could be rendered into our language by one and the same word, and if not, the actions they describe cannot be one and the same action. How then can baptism be performed indifferently by sprinkling, pouring, or immersion? It is impossible. To sprinkle, therefore, is one action, and to baptize is another and a very different action. To pour is one action, and to baptize is another and a very different action. To sprinkle and to pour so nearly resemble each other, and in effect are so much the same, that ραινω, and the compounds of εχχεω, are both rendered to sprinkle, but so impassable is the gulf between pouring and sprinkling, and baptism, that never once is either ραινω, λουω, or εχχεω, or νιπτω, or πλυνω, translated to baptize—to dip, or immerse. How, therefore, can sprinkling or pouring be baptism? It cannot be,—it is impossible.

Had the Holy Spirit, in dictating his revelation, designed to leave upon our mind an indefinite impression, which doubtless would have been the case, had he, as our Pedobaptist brethren are wont to tell us, intended to confine baptism to no particular mode, he would not have adopted $\beta \alpha \pi \tau \iota \zeta \omega$ as the word to describe it, lest immersion should be understood; nor $\varepsilon \chi \chi \varepsilon \omega$, lest pouring should have been supposed to be the action prescribed; nor would he have chosen $\varrho \alpha \iota \nu \omega$, lest sprinkling should have been considered as enjoined; but he would have selected some word, not, as is true of that used, denoting mode and nothing else, but having reference to the effect rather than the action. Was any such word at command? Instantly upon the suggestion of the inquiry, are presented to our mind, $\alpha \gamma \nu \iota \zeta \omega$, to purify, and $\varkappa \alpha \theta \alpha \iota \varrho \omega$, to cleanse, in any convenient method of applying water. But the Holy Spirit did not adopt an indefinite term. He did not, therefore, command an indefinite action to be performed. The word used cannot, in any possible case, mean to sprinkle or to pour; therefore it is impossible that baptism ever can be performed by sprinkling or pouring. The term selected by the Saviour conveys always the definite idea of immersion, therefore God will regard only immersion as Christian baptism.

Having now seen that the word which describes this ordinance means immersion and nothing else, and that to this definition the learned world, ancient and modern, substantially give their full sanction; and that in the Bible it is so employed as never, in any instance, to be capable of expressing the idea of pouring or sprinkling, we shall probably be asked, why, then, our translators of the Bible did not honestly render it to *immerse*, and save all the ill will and confusion which have grown out of the controversy? The history of this matter is singular, and deserves in this place, a moment's attention.

In all the best ancient translations, and those also of more

PEDOBAPTISTS ARE NOT BAPTIZED. 161

modern date, in which the example of England has not been followed, the word Βαπτιζω has been rendered by terms in the several languages which mean to immerse, and, as all learned men are fully aware, immersion is, at this moment, and ever has been, the practice of the greater part of the Christian world. The amplest evidence of the following facts in relation to the several translations of the Scriptures, is accessible, in some form, to almost every reader.* In the translation of the Scriptures into the old *Syriac*, or *Peshito*, which was made in *the beginning of the second century*, the word Βαπτιζω is rendered by AMAD—to immerse. The *Coptic*, or *Egyptian*, made in the *second century*, has TOMAS—to immerse. The *Sahidic*, the language spoken in Upper Egypt, made in the same century, has it, to immerse. In *Ethiopic*, or *Abyssinian*, made in the fourth century, the word is rendered by TAMAK—to immerse. The *Amharac*, a language descended from the Ethiopic, has the same word. The ancient *Armenian* version, made in the fourth century, has MUGURDEL—to immerse. The modern *Armenian* has the same word. The *Georgian*, made in the eighth century, has NATHLISTEMAD—to immerse. The *Arabic* version, made in the eighth century, has AMAD—to immerse. The same facts are true of the Persian, Turkish, Tartar, and many other Eastern languages. In regard to the Western versions, I remark that the *Gothic* of Ulphilus, made in the fourth century, has DAUPYAN—to dip. The *German* translation by Luther, has TAUFEN—to dip. The same word is used in both the *Swiss* and *Saxon* translations. The *Belgian* version, made by order of the Synod of Dort, has DOOPEN—to dip. The *Danish* has DOBE—to dip. The *Swedish* has DOPA—to dip. The *Welch* has *bedyddio*—to dip; and so of several others. Even the English dared

* Judd's Review of Stewart, p. 163, et seq.

not to translate the term by any other word than to immerse or dip, and as they would not give either of these, for reasons we shall presently show, they refused any translation whatever.

When the English Church emerged from Popery, which had bound the Western nations for so many centuries in her heavy chains, she made, in several particulars, commendable, though somewhat tardy, advances towards more purity both of doctrine and practice: yet she retained, and does still retain, many things which had found both their origin and support alone in that corrupt hierarchy. Edward VI., the son and successor of Henry VIII., appointed a committee of Bishops to reform still further than his father had done, the offices of the church. "In the prosecution of this work," says Neal, in his History of the Puritans, "the committee examined and compared the *Romish Missals* of Sarum, York, Hereford, Bangor, and Lincoln, and out of them composed the Morning and Evening service, almost in the same form as it now stands. From the same materials they compiled a Litany—the same with that now used." This was not all the English church retained from popery; she also adopted all her Ecclesiastical orders and vestments, infant church membership, and, in some instances, sprinkling for baptism. All these had been received into the English church before the present version of the Scriptures was made. It is necessary to remember this in order to understand the policy of the parties concerned, and the reasons why they refused to allow any translation to go forth, which should expose to the public mind the unscriptural character of these emanations of popery. They constituted the basis upon which stood the very offices that had made them great, and given them honor, dignity, and emolument. The Bishops, with the consent of King James, prohibited, therefore, the translation of all "the old ecclesiastical words," among which with others *baptism* was found. They required that the original Greek words should be transferred, only changing them so much as to give them an English termination. Thus the word *baptism* obtained admission into the version, and immersion, the true rendering, was excluded from our Bible. In testimony of these facts, I refer to—" A complete History of the several translations of the Holy Bible and New Testament into English," by John Lewis, A. M., &c., London ed. 1813. At p. 317, &c., we have a copy " of his Majesty's instructions"— also contained in Fuller's Church History, book x. pp. 46, 47—the third article of which is in these terms :—" The old ecclesiastical words to be kept, as the word *church*, &c." In giving the preface of the translators, Mr. Lewis represents them as saying*—" They had, they said, on the one side, avoided the scrupulosity of the Puritans, who left the old ecclesiastical words, and betook them to others, (*i. e.* translated them) as when they put *washing* for *baptism*, and, on the other hand, had shunned the obscuritie of the Papists in their *azymes, tunike, rational, holocaust, prepuce, pasche*, and a number such like." Of this course on the part of the translators, there was much complaint at the time, and several books written, among the best of which was one by John Canne—1664—in which he insists upon yet another and more faithful version, and among many other deficiencies to be remedied—p. 343—says, referring to these terms— " Some words which are in the original tongues left untranslated, should be translated, and their signification opened." But when the temporal interests of men come in conflict with any portion of divine truth, how prone is poor human nature to sacrifice the latter to advance the former!

A scene similar to this has been acted over again, in our

* P. 326.

own day. "When the London Society for promoting Christianity among the Jews," says Mr. Frey, an eminent Hebrew scholar, who was then a Pedobaptist, and, at the time President of the Society*—"commenced the translation of the New Testament into pure Hebrew, they soon met with the word under consideration, and which occasioned not a little difficulty. Not with respect to the primary meaning of the word, nor to find out a corresponding Hebrew word, but the difficulty was to avoid giving offence. Had they adopted the word *taval*—or *tabal*—to immerse, * * * * whilst they would have done justice to the text, they would have given offence to the mass or bulk of Pedobaptists; on the other hand, had they used the word *shaphach*—to pour, or *zarak*—to sprinkle, besides doing violence to the original, they would not only have given offence to the whole large and respectable body of Baptists, but even many pious and conscientious Pedobaptists would have condemned their conduct. Policy, therefore, led them not to translate the word at all, but" [as their predecessors had done with regard to the English translation] "to metamorphose the Greek word into Hebrew, for the use of the text, and in the margin they put the words *taval*, to immerse, and *rachatz*, to wash; but nowhere did they use the words *shaphach*, to pour, or *zarak*, to sprinkle." A more recent attempt, by the British and Foreign, and the American Bible Societies, to engraft upon the Foreign Translations now in process, and heretofore made by Missionaries, these Pedobaptist corruptions, has severed them both, and they will ultimately meet the fate which will, sooner or later, involve every effort to falsify, or conceal, the teachings of the word of God. The Jewish Society, in their late translation of the New Testament into the Polish Hebrew dialect, have, as I am informed, pursued a

* Essays on Bap. 1st ed. pp. 74, 75.

different course. Here the word *taval* is, in the text, invariably adopted.

The arguments of our Pedobaptist brethren, founded on the use of the preposition with which the verb is connected, and by which they seek to turn aside the force of the word βαπτιζω, might now be noticed, but I do not consider them of sufficient importance to merit more than a passing remark. Every one knows, who has thought or read at all on the use of prepositions, that their meaning is subordinate to the principal words in the sentence in which they occur. If it is only said that a man went *to* the river, we should have no evidence that he went *into* it. But if it is said he went *to* the river and *bathed*, we at once know he went *into* the water. So in relation to the prepositions *from*, and *out of*. Were you informed that your friend, having been *immersed*, came up *from* the water, you could not resist the conviction that he had bathed in the stream. Whatever, therefore, may be the sense of εν, and εις, εx, and απο, it cannot weaken, in the slightest degree, the force of the word employed by the inspired writers to describe the form of baptism.

We have now demonstrated, from the philology of the word used to describe it, that immersion is essential to the rite, and that without it there can be no baptism. Our Pedobaptist brethren have not been immersed, therefore they nave not been baptized, and consequently cannot approach the Lord's table without a violation of the divine law.

CHAPTER XI.

WE CANNOT COMMUNE WITH PEDOBAPTISTS, BECAUSE, NOT HAVING BEEN IMMERSED, THEY ARE NOT BAPTIZED.

Objections to our conclusions founded on the New Testament refuted—Facts considered—Passages of Scripture—Metaphorical allusions to baptism—The design of baptism requires immersion—The places where baptism was administered—Concurrence in our views by scholars—Reasons of their agreement with us in sentiment, and different practice—Conclusion.

SEVERAL facts recorded in the New Testament, as well as various passages, which relate to the ordinance, it is confidently maintained by many persons, forbid the belief that baptism was invariably, in the days of the apostles, administered by immersion. These, before I dismiss this part of our subject, I consider myself obliged briefly to examine.

It is alleged that the *three thousand* baptized on the day of Pentecost could not have been immersed. For this opinion two principal reasons have been assigned. The first is, that there was not a sufficient number of administrators to have performed the work in one day; and the second is, that water for the purpose could not have been found in sufficient quantity.

In regard to the supposed difficulty of baptizing so many, I observe, that three thousand candidates would have given to each one of the twelve apostles two hundred and fifty. I find by my own experience, that, proceeding with the utmost deliberation, I usually baptize three in a minute. But suppose the apostles only baptized two in a minute. They would baptize the whole in a hundred and twenty-five minutes—that is, in two hours and five minutes. Or if they baptized three in a minute, the twelve apostles alone baptized the whole three thousand in one hour and twenty minutes.

But besides the twelve apostles, there were seventy disciples, authorized to baptize, making in all eighty-two administrators, present on the occasion. Now divide three thousand candidates between eighty-two administrators, and you give to each one about *thirty-six*, all of whom could have been baptized, with perfect deliberation, in less than fifteen minutes. The case, therefore, presents not the least difficulty. And if it did, the objection lies rather against the truth of the statement of Luke, that so many were baptized, than that immersion could have been the mode. This will be seen the moment the fact is recollected, which every one knows who has witnessed or administered the ordinance, that, in a given space of time, as many, and with the same ease, can be immersed as can be poured upon, or sprinkled.

The supposition that water, in sufficient quantity, could not have been obtained in or about the city of Jerusalem, to baptize so many, is scarcely worthy of attention. What! A city, with probably more than a million of inhabitants, whose religion required of every one daily ablutions, in the midst of which were several large reservoirs for these very purposes, as the pools of Siloam and Bethesda; with a considerable stream—the Gihon, running through it—another, a branch of the Gihon—surrounding the end of it; and the Cedron laving its walls through the whole extent of one side; that such a city should not contain water enough to immerse a few hundred people is surely a dream, that never could have found admittance into any but a distempered imagination. The school geography of a child will teach any one that for such a purpose there could, in the holy city, have been no want of an abundance of water.

It is a little remarkable, however, after all the arguments on this subject, that when we turn to the inspired writers we find that they do not say that three thousand were baptized on the day of Pentecost! They that gladly received the word were baptized; but how many there were of these we are not informed; and that day there were added unto them about three thousand; many of whom might previously have been baptized by John, and the disciples, and on that occasion have been collected together, emboldened by the pouring out of the Spirit, and recognized as forming a part of the church, that they might the more distinctly be known to each other, and to the world, as the followers of Christ. But that this number was baptized on that day we have no evidence whatever.

It is again objected that baptism could not always have been administered by immersion, because the Philippian jailer must have been baptized in the house, where this form of the ordinance could not have been observed.

Why should it be supposed that the jailer was baptized in the house? Do the Scriptures say so? Examine the passage—"Then he called for a light, and sprang in, and came trembling, and fell down before Paul and Silas, and *brought them out*, and said—Sirs: what must I do to be saved? And they said—Believe in the Lord Jesus Christ, and thou shalt be saved, and thy house. And they spake unto him the word of the Lord, and *to all that were in his house*. And he took them the same hour of the night, and washed their stripes, and was *baptized*, he, and all his house, straightway; and when he had *brought them into his house*, he sat meat before them, and rejoiced, believing in God, with all his house."*

Several particulars in this narrative deserve attention.

* Acts xvi. 29-34.

BAPTISM OF THE JAILER. 169

the first place, the jailer brought Paul and Silas out of the prison, before they began their discourse. He brought them out. Where did he carry them? Undoubtedly into his own house where his family resided. In proof of this fact it will be observed it is expressly said—They spake unto *him* the word of the Lord, and *to all that were in his house.* They were now, therefore, in the *jailer's house.* Immediately on their profession, it is added:—"He was baptized, and all his house straightway; and when he had *brought them into his house,* he rejoiced." This is now the second time *he had brought them into his house.* They had previously come out of the prison, and they went out of the house to be baptized, and after the baptism returned. All this the passage declares. This event took place at midnight. If sprinkling or pouring was ever used, this, certainly, was a proper occasion for it. But it was most convenient to have done this in the house. Why then, under such circumstances, and at such an hour, should they have gone out of doors to administer this baptism, if immersion had not been essential to the ordinance? The whole narrative is inconsistent with the idea that any form but immersion was employed.

But we are told that washing and sprinkling must be baptism, because that the—διαφοροις βαπτισμοις—divers *baptisms,* translated, in our version, divers *washings,* of which Paul speaks*—"Which stood only in meats and drinks, and *divers washings,* and carnal ordinances, imposed on them until the time of reformation"—included the washing of various vessels, and other utensils, and the sprinkling of the priests for their consecration, as described in Numbers†— "Thus—saith the Lord—thou shalt do unto them to cleanse them, sprinkle water of purifying upon them."

In reply, I observe, that divers *immersions* were certainly

---

* Heb. ix. 10. † Numbers viii. 6, 7.

used by the Jews, and that Paul in this passage included the idea of laving cups, and sprinkling priests with baptism, is all imaginary, and destitute of reason or authority. The most learned Pedobaptists themselves translate these very words—διαφοροις βαπτισμοις—not "divers washings," but "divers *immersions*," among whom I would name Grotius, Whitby, and Macknight—"Divers immersions, and ordinances concerning the flesh." This whole matter is easily made plain. The reader has but to notice that, in the text, three distinct classes of injunctions are inculcated. In the first, the Jews were to worship God in meats and drinks; in the second they were to worship him in *various immersions;* and in the third by carnal ordinances, imposed on them until the coming of Christ. All that it concerns us to know is in what these divers immersions consisted, and this Moses himself explains.* "And upon whatsoever a dead weasel, mouse, tortoise, ferret, lizard, chameleon, snail, or mole, doth fall, it shall be unclean; whether any vessel of wood, or raiment, or skin, or sack; whatsoever vessel it be wherein any work is done, it shall be *put into water*, and it shall be unclean until the even; so it shall be cleansed"—by immersion. Here then are divers immersions, and frequent occasions for them. The general rule by which these immersions were conducted is recorded in Numbers:†—"Every thing that may abide the fire, ye shall make to go through the fire, and it shall be cleansed; yet it must be purified by the water of separation; and all that abideth not the fire ye shall make *go through the water.*"

The sense of the apostle, however, is definitely settled by the apostle himself, in the same chapter in which the passage occurs. The moment you take up the original you see that Paul contradistinguishes between the divers baptisms, and

* Levit. xi. 32, &c. † Numbers xxxi. 23.

the divers sprinklings of which he treats. When he speaks of the immersions he uses the word βαπτισμοις; but he immediately after has occasion to speak of sprinkling, and he drops this word and employs ῥαντιζω, the proper word denoting that action. "For if the blood of bulls, and of goats, and the ashes of an heifer, *sprinkling*—ραντιζουσα—the unclean, &c."* Verse 19—Moses "sprinkled—ἐρραντισε—both the book, and all the people." And again, in verse 21—He "sprinkled—ἐρραντισε—likewise with blood both the tabernacle, and all the vessels of the ministry." Thus we prove that in the opinion of Paul baptism does not mean to wash or to sprinkle. If he did not think so, or intended by the word *baptism* in the 10th verse to convey the idea of sprinkling, why does he drop that word and use another in three successive instances in the same chapter when he speaks of sprinkling? We must be blind, indeed, if we do not see that Paul makes a difference between the purifying of the cups, and other utensils, which was by immersing them, and the sprinkling of the priests, which he calls a carnal commandment. He says †—The Jewish priests were made after the law of a carnal commandment—they were, if you please, sprinkled; but our great High Priest, the Lord Jesus, was made a priest, not after such a law—he was not sprinkled. In his opinion, therefore, the baptisms are immersions, and the sprinklings are carnal ordinances.

Some metaphorical allusions found in the Scriptures to the sacrament of baptism, are supposed to have an important bearing in deciding in what manner the ordinance is to be administered.

"The long suffering of God," says Peter, "waited in the days of Noah, while the ark was a preparing, wherein few, that is eight souls, were saved by water. The like figure

---

* Heb. ix. 13. † Heb. viii. 16.

whereunto baptism doth even now save us, not the putting away of the filth of the flesh, but the answer of a good conscience towards God, by the resurrection of Jesus Christ."*

On this passage I make three remarks. In the first place, it is a figure. A figure, to render it such, must, necessarily, differ from the thing which it represents. Secondly, the preservation of Noah and his family, in the ark, from the consequences of the deluge, is as nearly like an immersion as any figure need be to the thing illustrated by it. They were enclosed in the ark. In this consisted the metaphor, and not, as some have supposed, in the sprinkling of the rain upon the ark. If the sprinkling of the rain upon the ark was the baptism, it was the ark which was baptized, and not the people in the ark. Thirdly, as Noah and his family obtained a temporal salvation in the ark, so we obtain a spiritual salvation by Jesus Christ, of whose death, burial, and resurrection from the dead, our baptism is a figure. This undoubtedly is a true exposition of the passage before us. It is admitted to be such by Pedobaptists themselves. If so, it forbids, as far as it has any influence on the subject, the idea that any thing is baptism but such an immersion as encloses the candidate in water as thoroughly as Noah and his family were enclosed in the ark. Such is the opinion of Sir N. Knatchbull, who says, in his Animadversions —" The proper end of baptism is the sign of a resurrection, by faith in the resurrection of Christ, of which baptism is a very lively and expressive figure; also as the ark of Noah, out of which he returned, as it were, out of a sepulchre to a new life."†

Another passage of similar character is found in 2 Cor. x. 1 :—" Moreover, brethren, I would not that ye should be ignorant how that all our fathers were under the cloud, and

* 1 Pet. iii. 20, 21.   † In Lib. N. T. ad loco.

all passed through the sea, and were all baptized unto Moses in the cloud and in the sea."

The argument from this text is, that the Hebrew fathers were all baptized, but they were not immersed, and therefore immersion is not essential to baptism. A moment's reflection will, I am sure, convince any one that the contrary of this conclusion is true. In what were they baptized? In the cloud, and in the sea. How? By passing *through* the sea, and *under* the cloud. Is not the likeness this figure bears to immersion about as near as it could well be, and still remain a figure? Dr. Whitby on this passage remarks: " 'They,' the Israelites, " were covered with the sea on both sides, Exod. xiv. 22, so that both the cloud and the sea had some resemblance to our being covered with water in baptism. Their going into the sea resembled the ancient manner of going into the water, and their coming out of it their rising up out of the water."*

The only other figurative allusion requiring our attention is the baptism of the Holy Spirit. The Spirit is said to have been poured out upon the people, and its reception baptism, it is therefore concluded that pouring is baptism.

I remark, in reply, that the pouring out of the Spirit is never, in the Scriptures, called the baptism of the Spirit: nor indeed does it bear any more relation to it than the pouring out of water into the baptistry does to the baptism of water. It is not the mere sending forth of the Spirit that is the baptism, but its reception as at Pentecost. When the disciples were assembled, they heard a rushing sound, it came down and filled the house. It was the sound which is described. At the same time the disciples were *filled with the Spirit*. If these events are to determine the mode, then baptism is not pouring, sprinkling, or immersion, but

---

* Booth's Pæd Exam. vol. i. p. 187.

filling the candidate with water. The baptism of the Spirit is the putting men under his influence; and the baptism of water is the act of putting men under that element.

It cannot, I think, be questioned by any really intelligent man, that, independent of the fact that figures never change the literal meaning of plain texts, nor is their exposition determined by them, all the metaphorical allusions in the word of God to the action of baptism, so far from casting any doubt upon the subject, actually strengthens the force of our conclusions that immersion is essential to Christian baptism.

The design for which baptism was instituted, to represent the death, burial, and resurrection of Jesus Christ, cannot be effected unless the mode is immersion.

"How shall we that are dead to sin," asks the apostle,* "live any longer therein? Know ye not that so many of us as were baptized into Jesus Christ were baptized into his death?" Christ died for our sins. We, by faith in Christ, are dead to sin. "Therefore we are *buried* with him by baptism into death; that like as Christ was raised up from the dead by the glory of the Father, even so we also should walk in newness of life. For, if we have been planted together in the likeness of his death, we shall be also in the likeness of his resurrection." In other words, as Christ was buried in the grave, so we are buried in the water of baptism; and as Christ arose and came out of the grave, so we arise and come out of the water. Our representing his burial necessarily brings us to represent his resurrection. For if we are planted together, or are buried as he was, we shall also rise in baptism, in the likeness of his resurrection. "Knowing this, that our old man," sinful nature, "is crucified with him," in the person of Christ, who bore our sins in his own **body on the tree,** "that the body of sin might be destroyed,

* Rom. vi. &c.

that henceforth we should not serve sin. For he that is dead," as by our religious profession we have declared ourselves to be, to sin, and buried to the world, " is freed from sin. Now, if we be dead with Christ, we believe that we shall also live with him ; knowing that Christ, being raised from the dead, dieth no more." We, if we be dead indeed with him to sin, and alive with him to righteousness, die no more, and therefore live to the glory of him who died for us and rose again.

Such are the great truths for the representation of which baptism, according to apostolic teaching, received its specific form, and from which two conclusions cannot be avoided. One is, that worthily to receive baptism we must have a living faith in the efficacy of the atonement of Jesus Christ, and satisfactory testimony that its saving power has been applied to us, by the Holy Spirit; and the second is, that, as a man when he dies, leaves all the scenes and pursuits of his former life, and enters upon a new state of being, so having died to sin, and been buried in baptism, we leave all our former folly, and live a new life of holiness, by faith in the Son of God. The same doctrine is taught, and nearly in the same words, in the epistle to the Colossians, and in other portions of the word of God.

Particularly with regard to the representation by baptism of the resurrection, as this point is more disputed than any other, Paul asks*—" Else what shall they do who are baptized for the dead ? If the dead rise not at all, why are they then baptized for the dead ?" The apostle in this chapter proves the doctrine of the resurrection of all flesh from the dead, by the resurrection of Christ. Among others he uses the baptism of the Corinthians as an argument. The substance of his reasoning is this—You have been taught that your baptism is a representation of the burial and resurrec-

* 1 Cor. xv. 29.

tion of Christ; but if there is no resurrection of the dead, as the Sadducees contend, then is not Christ risen, and the ordinance has no significancy, one half of it being based upon an event which never occurred. "If the dead rise not, why are ye then baptized for the dead?" "But now is Christ risen from the dead, and become the first fruits of them that slept," and it was no dream of the imagination which you represented when you were buried in baptism, and rose again from the emblematic grave.

If the object of baptism be to represent the death, burial, and resurrection of Christ, and I think the proof I have now submitted will convince the most incredulous that it is, I need not ask whether this can be accomplished by pouring or sprinkling. The importance of the mode of baptism, therefore, is apparent—"It marks, in a figure, the way in which we become partakers in the benefit of Christ's death. This is by our being, by a divine constitution, one with him. His death is a proper atonement for us, because we die with him, so that, in reality, his death is ours. This is not necessary in all cases of substitution. To have a debt discharged by another, there is no necessity to become one with him. But it is not so in crime. Justice is not satisfied unless the criminal himself suffers. And, by the divine constitution, that makes believers one with Christ, they are all considered as having died with him. The criminals have suffered, since he who suffered is one with them."* In the same sense they have triumphed over death, and arisen conquerors. These are the glorious facts marked by baptism. It shows, in a figure, that union with Christ, in his death, burial, and resurrection, which we have by faith. The only baptism which will do this, and, therefore, that only which God approves, is immersion.

* Carson, p. 254.

If in these sentiments we have not the concurrence of some whose minds are imprisoned in the dark cells of sectarianism, I have the satisfaction of standing side by side with such men as the great Locke, who in his Paraphrase says—" We are baptized into a similitude of his death. We did own some kind of death by being buried under water, which being buried with him, *i. e.*, in conformity with his burial, as a confession of our being dead, was to signify that, as Christ was raised up from the dead into a new life with his Father, even so we, being raised from our typical death and burial in baptism, should lead a new sort of life, wholly different from the former."* When we read this, and similar expositions, and compare them with the cautious admissions, the tortuous labyrinths of special pleading, and the evasive arguments of the diminutive polemics of the present time, we cannot but feel that they are worthy the scholar, the philosopher, and the Christian, who conceived the Essays on the Human Understanding

All the considerations we have now adduced in this and the preceding chapter, taken together with the constant declaration that, in the days of the apostles, baptism was performed in rivers, and in places affording much water, and the assurance that in its administration, they went down into the water, and came up out of the water, none of which is necessary or ever observed in pouring or sprinkling, render the fact so unquestionable that immersion is the only scriptural mode of baptism, that we shall here rest the case, and, with one remark on a collateral subject, close the present, argument.

The remark to which I allude, is in answer to the inquiry, which probably will be made in reference to the action as we have already noticed in relation to the subjects of the

* On Rom. vi., &c.

ordinance; if the first and most respectable of all classes of divines agree with the Baptists in opinion, that immersion only is taught in the Bible, as would seem to be true from our numerous quotations of their works, how does it come to pass that they all practise pouring and sprinkling for baptism? Two of their greatest men shall reply in behalf of the whole. John Calvin says—"*The Church did grant liberty to herself since the beginning to change the rite somewhat, excepting the substance;*"*—and Bishop Stillingfleet says—"*Rites, and customs, apostolical are altered, as dipping in baptism.*"† Upon these statements I need make no commentary. Their daring and sacrilegious presumption will meet a rebuke in every honest heart. Dr. Cox most truly observes —"It is, in the highest degree, hazardous to tamper with the positive institutions of God. As they are supported exclusively by the expressed will of the founder, we, although the act prescribed, in respect of moral attributes may, in itself, be altogether indifferent, are under moral obligation to obey."‡ The very essence of obedience, also, consists in a rigid adherence to the authoritative prescription, and, therefore, any alteration in its forms of observance, or any substitution of one thing for another, abrogates, wholly, the institution itself, and adopts for the law of God, the commandments of men. Pedobaptists have done this very thing. They have taken the unconscious babe instead of the believer, and they have sprinkled or poured water upon the candidate instead of baptizing him; therefore, Pedobaptists have never been baptized, and the essential preliminaries being disregarded, they cannot approach the table of the Lord.

* Comm. on Acts viii. 38.
† Apud Booth's Pæd. Exam. p. **215.**
‡ Baptists in America, p. 327.

We have now examined the word used in the Scriptures to describe the action of baptism, and find that it means immersion, and nothing else; that in all the ancient versions of the Scriptures it is actually so rendered, that where sprinkling or pouring is mentioned, words are employed entirely different from baptism, and never used convertibly with that term; and that it is unaffected in its sense by the prepositions with which it is associated; we have examined all the facts, passages, and metaphorical allusions in the New Testament, supposed to forbid the idea that baptism was invariably administered by immersion, and we find them utterly destitute of force; and we have seen that the design for which baptism was instituted, and the circumstances attendant upon its administration, prove that it could have been alone by immersion; we have seen the principles upon which the Confession of Faith and Pedobaptist writers and divines have made the concessions we have quoted, and proved that their substitutions and alterations have wholly abrogated the ordinance, and that they have no such thing as Christian baptism among them.

Thus we have submitted the second reason why **we cannot commune with Pedobaptists.**

CHAPTER XII.

BAPTISTS CANNOT COMMUNE WITH PEDOBAPTISTS, BECAUSE THEY ADMINISTER BAPTISM FOR ILLEGAL PURPOSES, AND ATTACH TO IT AN UNREASONABLE AND UNSCRIPTURAL DEGREE OF EFFICACY AND IMPORTANCE.

Pedobaptist doctrines of baptism—Baptismal regeneration held by the fathers—This originated infant baptism, pouring and sprinkling—The Catechism and Canons of the Council of Trent—All Pedobaptist Churches believe in baptismal regeneration—Book of Common Prayer—Confession of Faith—Discipline—Disciples of Christ—Conservative influence of Baptist principles.

THE third reason why we cannot commune with pedobaptists, is, because they administer both baptism and the Lord's supper for purposes such as God has not authorized, and attach to them an unscriptural and unreasonable degree of efficacy and importance.

Independent of the inquiry, whether, as they have never received the initiatory ordinance, they can lawfully administer the rites of the church, a matter which I shall not now pause to consider, Pedobaptists of all classes regard baptism as the instrumentality of entering into the covenant of salvation, and therefore as at least synonymous with regeneration; and the Lord's supper they look upon as a "certain means and seal of grace." We must of necessity, when administered for such purposes, decline to be their recipients.

I am aware that these very tenets, in all their repulsiveness, have been so long and so industriously charged as a capital defect in our own venerable church, that the world has come to believe that we, and not our opponents, are the heterodox party. But the truth is, we are the only people who do not unduly exalt the sacraments of the Gospel. In regard, in the first place, to baptism, we shall attempt the proof of the statement now made; after which we shall adduce testimony in relation to the other ordinance.

We regard baptism as neither more nor less than a solemn and practical profession of faith in Christ by a believer in him, in the manner appointed by the King in Zion. But what do our brethren of the several Pedobaptist denominations teach on this subject? A superficial knowledge of ecclesiastical history is sufficient to convince any one that but a few centuries transpired after the apostles, before a melancholy change was effected in the opinions of the Christian world with regard to the design and efficacy of the sacraments of the Gospel. Their importance was magnified immeasurably, and they were soon believed to be so intimately connected with the vitality of religion, that they could not in any case be omitted without preventing the salvation of the soul. In the third century and onwards, the Christian fathers believed and taught that sins were only forgiven in baptism, that infants, by this ordinance, were purged from original pollution, and that all persons dying without it were lost.

This may be considerd by some a bold assertion. I shall sustain its truth by adequate proof; and for this purpose shall submit such testimony as may be deemed requisite on the subject.*

Cyprian, the Bishop of Carthage, wrote A. D. 250. On this subject he remarks as follows: " As far as lies in us, no soul, if possible, is to be lost. It is not for us to hinder any person from baptism, and the grace of God: which rule,

* Vide Baptist Manual, p. 97.

as it holds to all, so we think it more especially to be observed in reference to infants, to whom our help and the divine mercy are rather to be granted; because, by their weeping and wailing, at their first entrance into the world, they do intimate nothing so much as that they implore compassion."

Ambrose, the Bishop of Milan, flourished A. D. 390 He says: "No person comes to the kingdom of heaven, but by the sacrament of baptism. Infants that are baptized are reformed back again from wickedness to the primitive state of their nature."

Chrysostom, the Patriarch of Constantinople, wrote A. D. 390. He remarks on this subject:—" The grace of baptism gives us cure without pain, and fills us with the grace of the Spirit. Some think that the heavenly grace consists only in the forgiveness of sins, but I have reckoned up *ten* advantages of it. If sudden death seize us before we are baptized, though we have a thousand good qualities, there is nothing to be expected but hell."*

Similar testimonies, proving that, from the time we have mentioned, the church considered baptism essential to salvation, abound every where. Wall's History of Infant Baptism is full of them, and in which, Vol. i. chap. 6, 13, 14, and Vol. ii. ch. 6, will be found, and may be consulted, the originals of the passages from the Fathers I have now quoted. These proofs, from the Bishops of Carthage and Milan, and the Patriarch of Constantinople, are amply sufficient for our purpose.

This error originated two others equally egregious. The former was the administration of baptism to infants, in cases of danger of death. In this, however, they did not, during more than a thousand years, dispense with the profession of faith, so plainly and constantly required in the Gospel.

---

* Wall, Lond. ed. 1705, vol. ii. pp. 133, 139.

But this was permitted to be made by proxies, who, under the name of sponsors, or sureties, professed in behalf of the infant, to repent, to renounce the devil, and to believe the Gospel, upon which profession of the sponsor the infant was baptized. This practice was continued in the Papacy up to the time of the Reformation, and is still characteristic not only of that fallen hierarchy, but also of the Episcopal branch of Protestantism. The latter error was a substitution of a more agreeable form than immersion. Baptism was found in such cases as have been named very inconvenient, resort was therefore had as an expedient, with which they associated the priestly administrator and verbal formulary, and which they presumed would give it all necessary authority, first to pouring, and afterwards to sprinkling.

The truth of these facts will not, I presume, by any well read man, who is unprejudiced, be questioned. Still it may be proper to sustain them by adequate testimony, which I shall do by adducing the deposition of three learned and candid Pedobaptist divines, and thus place their truth beyond the reach of controversy.

Our first witness is Suicerus, Professor of Greek and Hebrew, Zurich, who says:—"This opinion of the absolute necessity of baptism, arose from a wrong understanding of our Lord's words—Except a man be born of water and of the Spirit, he cannot enter the kingdom of heaven."*

Salmasius, the learned historian and critic, is our second witness.† He remarks—"An opinion prevailed that no one could be saved without being baptized, and for that reason the custom arose of baptizing infants."

The third witness is Dr. Wall, who, in relation to the opinion which prevailed on this subject at the time of his

---

* Apud Booth's Pæd. Exam. vol. ii. p. 129.
† Booth, ut supra.

writing remarks:—"Most of the Pedobaptists go no further than St. Austin does; they hold that God, by his Spirit, does, at the time of baptism, seal and apply to the infant that is there dedicated to him, the promises of the covenant of which he is capable, viz. adoption, pardon of sins, translation from the state of nature to that of grace, &c. On which account the infant is said to be regenerate of (or by) the Spirit."*

Thus it is seen why infant baptism, and ultimately sprinkling, found their way into the world.

The facts, and considerations, now submitted, sufficiently illustrate the early prevalence, and extensive spread of the doctrine which attributes to baptism a sanctifying and saving power; and *we now assert, that the same doctrine, without*, as Dr. Wall remarks, *any material modification, is held in all the " Reformed Churches," which have admitted into them the sprinkling of infants as true and lawful baptism.* This startling proposition, if sustained, will establish the truth of the statement with which I set out, that they attribute to baptism an unscriptural and unreasonable degree of efficacy and importance. The reproach has been constantly hurled against us of making a Saviour of baptism. We shall now see who it is that entertains this absurdity. The demonstration will be attempted that ours is the only denomination who place this ordinance in its true position, where it was left by Christ, and his apostles; who refuse, on the one hand, to despoil it of its solemn and appropriate forms, and who do not, on the other, unduly exalt its importance and efficacy.

The Roman Catholic is the oldest of the Pedobaptist denominations. Let us examine on this subject, their Cate-

* Vol. i. ch. 15, p. 148, Hist. Inf. Bapt.

chism, and Canons, of the Council of Trent, and in Session 7, Canon 5, we shall find it thus written:—

"If any one shall say that baptism is not necessary to salvation, *let him be accursed.* Sin, whether contracted by birth from our first parents, or committed ourselves, is, by the admirable virtue of this sacrament, remitted and pardoned. In baptism, not only sins are remitted, but also all the punishments of sins and wickedness are graciously pardoned of God. By virtue of this sacrament we are not only delivered from these evils, but also we are enriched with the best and most excellent endowments. For our souls are filled with divine grace, whereby, being made just, and the children of God, we are trained up to be heirs of eternal salvation also. To this is added a most noble train of virtues, which, together with grace, is poured of God into the soul. By baptism we are joined and knit to Christ, as members to the head. By baptism we are signed with a character which can never be blotted out of our soul. Besides the other things which we obtain by baptism, it opens to every one of us the gate of heaven, which before, through sin, was shut."*

These are the doctrines in relation to baptism, and in their own words, of Roman Catholics. They are undisguised and definite. The inquiry is now proper—Do the several prevailing Protestant denominations of Pedobaptists embrace this feature of Popery? Do they teach that baptism is essential to regeneration, to the forgiveness of sins, to admit us into covenant with God, to confer grace, and to secure the salvation of sinners. I am fully aware of the earnestness, and I doubt not the sincerity, with which many will protest that they do not. What some *individuals* believe or teach on this subject, does not concern our present inquiry. We

* Apud Judd's Review, p. 111.

have but too much evidence to justify the conclusion that there are men who will make baptism every thing, any thing, or nothing, to suit the exigency, or popular current of the moment, or what may happen to be the fancy of the times. Not unfrequently they use the term baptism with a sort of double meaning. Consequently, when, with Professor Stewart they exclaim:—" Baptism is an outward ceremony, and, therefore, no part of real religion; the external mode of an external rite never can, with our present views of Christianity, become to us a matter of peculiar interest,"* they mean only the mode of baptism, which they are, on other occasions, accustomed to distinguish from baptism itself. The *mode*, they tell us, is of no consequence. The church, says Calvin, has changed it, and Bishop Stillingfleet says it is altered. Ask them again, what they think of baptism, and with the same mental reservation, leaving the *mode* out of sight, they will reply with Dr. Wall—" We hold that God, by his Spirit, does at the time of baptism, seal and apply * * the promises of the covenant * * adoption, pardon of sin, translation from the state of nature to that of grace,"† in a word, that it is nearly the sum of religion, and especially regeneration itself. With such equivocations, insincerities, "palterings in a double sense," constantly before me, I find it useless to ask what individuals or masses of individuals believe or profess in the premises. Words are but air. They must, to be tangible, be written, and receive the ecclesiastical signature and seal. I appeal, therefore, to the standards—confessions of faith, catechisms, &c.—of the several denominations. These all their people have solemnly subscribed, and that they contain the true exposition of the word of God, they have, in the presence of God and man,

---

* Judd's Review, p. 89.

† History, &c., vol. i. p. 148.

deliberately professed to believe. Either these standards, particularly, and their accredited writers, generally, do embody their real sentiments, or else they have acted hypocritically in publicly embracing them. The latter they will hardly confess. The former, therefore, is true. Here we find a substantial position, and shall firmly occupy it.

The doctrine, on this point, of the Lutheran church, the Reformed Dutch, and others of German origin, I shall not examine, because they do not prevail very extensively in this country. If I felt disposed to do so, I would point to the *ninth* article of the Augsburg Confession of Faith, written by Melancthon, and which is now embraced by *seventeen* of the sovereigns, and near *thirty millions* of the inhabitants of Europe. It is in these words—"They teach concerning baptism, that it is necessary to salvation, because by baptism the grace of God is offered. Infants are to be baptized, who, being brought to God by baptism, are received into his favor. They condemn the Anabaptists, who disallow the baptism of infants, and affirm that they may be saved without it."* I proceed to consider the views of those Protestant churches that more generally prevail here.

For an exposition of the doctrine of our Episcopal brethren we take up the Book of Common Prayer, and turn to the "Directory for the Administration of the Sacraments." Previous to administering baptism, the officiating priest, by a prescribed form, is instructed to pray thus :—"Almighty and immortal God, the aid of all that need, the helper of all that flee to thee for succor, the life of them that believe, and the resurrection of the dead; we call upon thee for this infant, that he, coming to thy holy *baptism*, may receive *remission of his sins by spiritual regeneration.*"

This prayer teaches us what they suppose the baptism

* Cox's Life of Melancthon, p. 162.

will effect. And that infants *are* regenerated by it in their opinion, is shown by the fact that immediately after the baptism in which they have prayed that this spiritual change may take place, the clergyman is thus required to address the church :—" Seeing, dearly beloved, that *this child* is *regenerate,* and grafted into the body of Christ, let us give thanks to Almighty God for these benefits." The prayer too, now directed to be said, gives additional evidence that they consider that the work is done. It begins thus:—"We yield thee hearty thanks, most merciful Father, that it hath pleased thee to *regenerate* this infant with thy Holy Spirit." Thus much is taught in the Ritual.

The Catechism—" that is to say, an instruction to be learned by every person before he is brought to be confirmed by the Bishop"—begins with the following questions and answers.

"*Quest.* What is your name?

"*Ans.* N. or M.

"*Quest.* Who gave you this name?

"*Ans.* My sponsors in baptism, wherein I was made a member of Christ, the child of God, and an inheritor of the kingdom of heaven."

The second question and answer, after repeating the Lord's prayer, are these:—

"*Quest.* How many sacraments hath Christ ordained in his church?

"*Ans.* Two only, as generally *necessary to salvation,* that is to say, baptism, and the Supper of the Lord."

Such are the teachings of the Catechism.

" The Directory" orders:—As soon as the children " can say the Creed, the Lord's Prayer, and the Ten Commandments, and can also answer such other questions as in the short catechism are contained," they shall be brought to the

Bishop to be confirmed. In the progress of the service, and immediately before, and at the time, this prelate lays his hands upon the candidates for confirmation, he recognizes, in his solemn prayer to God, and his assurance to the individuals, the *regeneration* conferred in their baptism in infancy, thus:—"Almighty and everlasting God, who hast vouchsafed to *regenerate* these thy servants, *by water*, and by the Holy Ghost, and hast given unto them *forgiveness of all their sins*"—And to the candidates and audience, he says:—" We do *certify* them, by this *sign*, of God's *favor*, and gracious goodness towards them."

We have no need to carry this examination further. Their Ritual, Catechism, and Directory, sufficiently develope the doctrine of that church as to the objects for which they administer baptism. An infant, if the Book of Common Prayer teaches us correctly, receives in baptism *forgiveness of sins*, is *regenerated*, is *grafted into the body of Christ*, is made *a member of Christ, the child of God, and an inheritor of the kingdom of heaven.* All this is done in *baptism*, which, with the Lord's Supper, is expressly declared to be "necessary to salvation." Such are the doctrines on this subject of the Episcopal church. No remarks are necessary to prove that they are identical with those of the Council of Trent.

We will now examine the baptismal doctrines of our brethren of all classes and sects of the Presbyterian church. What do their standard and accredited writers teach?

To determine this inquiry we will take up the " CONFESSION OF FAITH," and we shall find a declaration in these words :—

" IV. Not only those that do actually profess faith in, and obedience unto Christ, but also the infants of one or both believing parents are to be baptized."

" V. Although it be a great sin to contemn or neglect this ordinance, yet *grace* and *salvation* are not so *inseparably* annexed unto it, that *no* person *can* be *regenerated* or *saved* without it, or that *all* that are *baptized* are *undoubtedly* regenerated."*

Much guarded caution characterizes the language of this passage, indeed it appears to be almost a jumble of nonsense—but the doctrine of baptismal regeneration is nevertheless fully embodied, and maintained. Our brethren profess to believe that *grace* and *salvation* are not *so inseparably* annexed unto baptism as that they are conferred by that ordinance in *every case* in which it is administered; or to make it in *every case,* absolutely essential to *regeneration* and *salvation.* What then are its position and influence? That I suppose, maintained in the Book of Common Prayer—it is " *generally* necessary to salvation ;" and, in most cases, those who receive the rite are by it regenerated. When the Confession says—it is not *positively certain* that *all* who are baptized are by this ordinance *undoubtedly* regenerated, the idea is as unquestionably implied that *some* who are baptized are thereby undoubtedly regenerated, as that when I assert that *all* who were at the battle of New Orleans were not soldiers, I mean to maintain that *some* were soldiers, and that others were citizens. My reader may possibly be curious to inquire, if any infants be regenerated by baptism, why it should be doubted whether all that receive it are not equally benefited. Our brethren who subscribe the Confession of Faith in question explain themselves. It is known that they are Calvinists. They believe in eternal, personal, and unconditional election and predestination. Hear their Confession upon this point—" By the decree of God, for the manifestation of his glory, some men, and angels, are

---

* Phila. ed., 1828, pp. 121, 122, 123.

predestinated unto everlasting life, and others foreordained to everlasting death. These angels and men, thus predestinated and foreordained, are particularly and unchangeably designed; and their number is so certain and definite, that it cannot be either increased or diminished."* This being the case, they doubt whether all the infants they baptize are of the elect. But the Confession is still more in point—

"VI. The efficacy of baptism is not tied to that moment of time wherein it is administered; yet notwithstanding, by the right use of this ordinance, the grace promised is not only *offered*, but really *exhibited*, and CONFERRED, by the Holy Ghost, to such (whether of age or infants) *as that grace belongeth unto, according to the counsel of God's own will*, in his appointed time."†

Here we have the necessary explanations. The efficacy of baptism is such that *grace*, either at the time of the administration or afterwards, is really *offered, exhibited,* and *conferred*, in this ordinance, by the Holy Ghost; *provided always*, that the child so baptized is embraced in the counsels of God's mercy—is one of the definite elect unto life—and therefore one of those "that grace belongeth unto." If he is one of the eternally chosen, the grace that is only *exhibited* and *offered* to others, is upon him actually *conferred*, and he is undoubtedly regenerated in baptism.

In the "Directory for the worship of God" of this church, Article—"Of the administration of baptism"—the minister reads to his people the reasons why an infant is to be baptized. The form prescribed requires him to use this language:—This infant is to be baptized not only because some children are federally *holy*, but also because "we are (all) by nature, *sinful, guilty,* and *polluted,* and have need of cleansing by the blood of Christ, and by the sanctifying

* Pp. 16, 17. † P. 123.

influences of the Spirit of God."* By federal holiness of children they mean, I presume, only that their parents are religious. My design, however, is to call attention specially to the fact that this Directory teaches us that the object secured by baptism is thereby to obtain an application of the blood of Christ; and the sanctifying influence of the Spirit of God, to cleanse the recipients from pollution. I ask whether the baptism of a child has this effect? If so, and they profess to believe it has, truly is it a capital article in religion, and essential both to regeneration and to salvation.

The Cumberland branch of the Presbyterian church have adopted substantially the same Confession of Faith, Catechism, and Directory, with their mother church, repudiating only the doctrine of election and predestination, and some things in relation to the ministry. On baptism they teach precisely the same doctrines, and in the same words with their progenitor, as any one may see who will be at the trouble of comparing their standards. The same remarks are true of the Hopkinsians, the Old School, the New School, and all the other sects of that denomination.

In the Articles now examined, we have again exhibited before us the doctrines of the Council of Trent, which are indeed still more fully, and with less disguise, taught by the wisest and most eminent divines of their faith, to two of whom, as a specimen of all the others, I shall briefly refer. The former is the late learned President of Yale College, Dr. Timothy Dwight, whose System of Theology, in many respects so excellent, is adopted as a standard work by the several branches of the church, of which he was a distinguished member; and the latter is the pious and eminent commentator, Matthew Henry.

Dr. Dwight remarks—" When children die in infancy, and

* P. 431.

are scripturally dedicated to God in baptism, there is much and very consoling reason furnished to believe that they are accepted beyond the grave."*

This is a very pretty, and apparently a very pious passage. But it is expressed with the cautiousness of a man who is conscious that he is on dangerous ground. It is the statement of a positive, and we only are concerned to know what the negative is which it contains. When Dr. Dwight singles out the baptized children who die in infancy, and tells us " there is much and very consoling reason furnished to believe that *they* are *accepted* beyond the grave," are we not to understand him as maintaining negatively of unbaptized children who die in infancy, that there is *little reason* furnished, and *none* that *is consoling*, to believe that *they* are accepted beyond the grave?

Mr. Henry, in his " Treatise on Baptism," uses on the subject under consideration, the following language : " The Gospel contains not only a doctrine, but a covenant; and by baptism we are brought into that covenant. Baptism wrests the keys of the heart out of the hand of the strong man armed, that the possession may be surrendered to him whose right it is. The water of baptism is designed for our cleansing from the spots and defilements of the flesh. In baptism our names are engraved upon the breastplate of the High Priest. This, then, is the efficacy of baptism; it is putting the child's name in the Gospel grant. We are baptized into Christ's death, that is, God doth, in that ordinance, seal, confirm, and make over to us all the benefits of the death of Christ."

If, as Mr. Henry here maintains, we are brought by baptism into " the covenant of grace," cleansed from the spots and defilements of the flesh, have our names put into the

---

* System of Theol., first Serm. on Bapt.

Gospel grant, and secured to us all the benefits of the death of Christ, which in that ordinance are sealed, confirmed, and made over to us, it must be regeneration, sanctification, salvation—indeed nearly the whole sum and essence of the religion of Christ.

We are now prepared to decide what the standards and accredited writers of the Presbyterian church teach in relation to the efficacy of baptism. They hold that, provided the child is one of the elect, grace and salvation are annexed unto baptism, and that in this ordinance, whether the recipient is adult or infant, such grace and salvation are absolutely offered, exhibited, and conferred by the Holy Ghost; that in it are applied to our cleansing from sin, the blood of Christ, and the sanctifying influence of the Spirit of God; that it brings the child into covenant with God, and seals, confirms, and makes over to it all the benefits of the death of Christ; and that it prepares it for acceptance with God beyond the grave! These undisputed and indisputable facts show that the Presbyterian comes behind no other church in the tenacity with which she upholds and supports the doctrine of baptismal regeneration and salvation.

The only remaining Pedobaptist denomination prevailing extensively among us, is the Methodist. Do our brethren of that church hold and teach the same doctrines on the subject in hand which we have seen are maintained by Roman Catholics, Episcopalians, and all the branches of Presbyterians? To this inquiry it is not difficult to furnish, from authoritative sources, a full and satisfactory reply.

Let us examine the book of "Discipline." We find in the order entitled "The ministration of baptism to infants," that the minister is required to commence this service by reading to his people an address, copied almost verbatim from the Book of Common Prayer, as follows:

"Dearly beloved, forasmuch as all men are conceived and born in sin, and that our Saviour, Christ, saith, none can enter into the kingdom of God except he be regenerate and born anew, of water and of the Holy Ghost; I beseech you to call upon God the Father, through our Lord Jesus Christ, that, of his bounteous mercy, he will grant unto this child *that thing* which by nature he cannot have; that he may be baptized with water and with the Holy Ghost, and be received into Christ's Holy Church, and be made a lively member of the same."*

I have, in this passage, emphasized the words *that thing* —that God would grant unto this child *that thing*, which by nature he cannot have. What thing? To be *regenerate*, and *born anew* of *water* and of the Holy Ghost. When? Now, in his baptism! It is in this short quotation twice repeated—by baptism, born anew of water and of the Holy Ghost; and it is added—Our Saviour Christ saith, without this none can enter into the kingdom of God. Without what? Without being regenerated, and born anew of *water* and of the Holy Ghost! We have here embodied the doctrine of this church regarding the advantages and efficacy of baptism. All its members solemnly profess to believe, and to take for their guide a book which teaches that, in their baptism, infants are regenerated and born anew of water and of the Holy Ghost, and that without this none can be saved! It is in perfect coincidence with this sentiment that the Discipline dictates to the minister a prayer for the child, in which he is directed to beseech Almighty God. that, in his baptism, he would "wash him, and sanctify him with the Holy Ghost;" and what is it to be washed, and sanctified with the Holy Ghost, but to be regenerated, which

New York cd. 1829, p. 100.

the Discipline teaches us is done in baptism, and that without which none can be saved!

Let no one imagine that I have either mistaken or misrepresented the doctrine of the Discipline upon this subject. Lest some one should be inclined to indulge such an opinion, I shall prove my exposition of it to be correct by testimony that cannot be questioned. Mr. Wesley wrote, or copied from the Book of Common Prayer this Discipline—certainly this part of it. Whoever else may be mistaken, he himself knew what he intended to teach in the premises. His opinions in other works in which he has discussed the same subject will illustrate and define his meaning in the book before us. In his "Treatise on Baptism," Mr. Wesley says: "By baptism, we who are by nature the children of wrath, are made the children of God. And this *regeneration*, which *our Church* in so many places ascribes to *baptism*, is more than barely being admitted into the Church, though commonly connected therewith. Being grafted into the body of Christ's church, we are made the children of God by adoption and grace. John iii. 5. By water, then, as a means, *the water of baptism*, we are *regenerated and born again*, whence it is called by the apostle, 'the washing of regeneration.' In all ages the *outward* baptism is a means of the *inward*. Herein we receive a title to, and an earnest of, a kingdom which cannot be moved. In the ordinary way, there is no other way of entering into the *Church*, or into *heaven*. If infants are guilty of original sin, then they are proper subjects of baptism, seeing, in the ordinary way, they cannot be saved unless this be washed away in baptism."[*]

Who, that reads this passage, can doubt that the Discip-

---

[*] Works, vol. vi. pp. 15, 16. New York ed. issued by the Book Concern of that church.

line designs to teach baptismal regeneration and salvation, in the broad sense of Austin, Jerom, and others of the fathers, who figured so largely in the Pelagian controversy of the fourth century. I am not unapprised of the objection that Mr. Wesley wrote the book I have quoted while yet an Episcopalian, and before he escaped from the mists of that age. I reply, it was long after he had organized his society, and written his Discipline. I will not inquire whether he ever left the Episcopal church, but will simply remark, that among the last, if not the very last book he ever wrote, was his "Notes on the New Testament." In relation to the baptism of Paul, on these words—"Arise, and be baptized, and wash away thy sins, calling on the name of the Lord," he observes; "Baptism is both the *means* and the *seal* of pardon, and God did not ordinarily, in the primitive church, bestow his grace upon any, save through this means."

Such are the doctrines of the Discipline and of its great author. They are too unequivocal to admit of any misapprehension. They make regeneration and salvation dependent on baptism. We are baptized, says the Discipline, because we are conceived and born in sin, and our Saviour Christ saith, none can enter into the kingdom of God except he be regenerate and born anew of water and of the Holy Ghost; and because in baptism we are washed and sanctified with the Holy Ghost; and we are baptized, says Mr. Wesley, because by it we are made the children of God, are connected with the church, are regenerated and born again, receive a title and earnest to heaven, and because without it infants, if they are partakers of original sin, cannot be saved!

With all these facts before us, I appeal to the intelligence of my readers, whether I have not, as I proposed, satisfactorily proved that all the prevailing reformed churches which have admitted into them the sprinkling of infants as true and lawful baptism, attribute, as the Papists have ever done to this ordinance, a sanctifying and saving power. Do they or we, then, magnify most its importance and efficacy? The exact difference between our Pedobaptist brethren and ourselves on this subject may now readily be determined. They baptize to give a preparation and title to heaven; and we teach that it is alone the experience and grace of salvation that can give a title to baptism.

The inquiry will probably be suggested whether sects practising only adult immersion as baptism, have not sometimes appeared, who also maintain and teach that this ordinance is essential to regeneration, and intimately affects salvation? I reply in the affirmative. Instances have occurred in the Old World, and an example recently in our own country. It is, however, a remarkable fact, that such sects seldom arise, and when they do are of short continuance. The doctrine soon leads, as it did in the third century, to Pedobaptism, or its absurdity becomes so apparent, that, in a few generations, it finds no advocates, and is abandoned.

The party maintaining the principles in question at present in our country, has acquired all its importance within the last twenty years. The " Encyclopedia of Religious Knowledge," a work lately published,* contains an article written by Mr. Alexander Campbell, their founder, somewhat in the form, and which serves the purpose of a declaration of faith, expressly for this volume, by which it will be seen that he has named them " *Disciples of Christ*"—they are known to the public by the name of *Campbellites*. The specific views on this point of the sect are set forth authoritatively in the article in question in these words : " They consider immersion into the name of the Father, Son, and Holy Spirit, after a public, sincere, and intelligent confession of faith in

* P. 462, 463.

Jesus, as necessary to admission to the privileges of the kingdom of Messiah, and as a solemn pledge on the part of Heaven of the actual remission of all past sins, and of adoption into the family of God. The Holy Spirit is promised only to those who believe and obey the Saviour"—are immersed. "No one is taught to expect the reception of that heavenly Monitor and Comforter, as a resident in his heart, till he obeys the Gospel"—is baptized. "They proclaim faith and repentance—as preparatory to immersion, remission, and the Holy Spirit." We have here reiterated the same old doctrine of the Council of Trent, characteristic of Popery, that baptism is essential to the remission of sins, to the bestowment of the Holy Ghost, and that of these, and of our adoption, it is the pledge of Heaven!

These sentiments are more diffusely and perspicuously expressed in their several relations, in the accredited organ of the "Disciples of Christ." This work, edited by their originator and leader, was commenced in 1823, and at that time bore the name of "Christian Baptist." In one of its articles Mr. Campbell says: "If a man can have any evidence of the forgiveness of his sins without baptism, I would advise him not to be baptized." Subsequently the name of the periodical was changed to that which it now bears, "The Millennial Harbinger." In Mill. Harb. Extra, No. 1, on Regeneration, Mr. Campbell remarks: "On this side and on that of baptism"—or before and after it—"mankind are in quite different states. On this side they are in a state of condemnation; on the other they are pardoned, justified, reconciled, adopted, and saved." In Mill. Harb. Extra, No. 1, p. 30, we have this assertion: "If any of them wilfully neglect or disdain immersion, we cannot hope for his salvation." And in Mill. Harb. Extra, No. 1, p. 29, it is added: "Nothing is personal regeneration but the act of immersion."

In his recent work, entitled "Christianity Restored," Mr. Campbell says :—" But one thing we do know, that *none* can *rationally*, and with certainty, enjoy the peace of God and the hope of heaven, but they who, intelligently and in full faith, are born of water—or are immersed for the remission of sins."

We cannot, with all these testimonies before us, and we could add to their number indefinitely, mistake the doctrines of the Disciples on the subject in hand. They embody all the objectionable features of the several Pedobaptist sects, with this exception in their favor; they immerse only in baptism, and administer the ordinance to none but "confessing" adults. In all other respects, and particularly in holding baptism to be essential to regeneration and salvation, they advocate the same doctrines with the Book of Common Prayer, the Confession of Faith, the Discipline, and the Catechism and Canons of the Council of Trent. "By baptism," says the Roman Catholic, "our sins are remitted and pardoned, and we are joined and knit to Christ, as members to the head." "By baptism," says the Episcopalian, "we are regenerated and made members of Christ, the children of God, and heirs of the kingdom of heaven." "By baptism," says the Presbyterian, "we are brought into covenant with God, cleansed from the defilements of the flesh, and God doth seal, confirm, and make over to us, all the benefits of the death of Christ." "By baptism," says the Methodist, "we, who are by nature, the children of wrath, are made the children of God, are regenerated and born again." And "by baptism," says the Disciple, "we are regenerated, pardoned, justified, reconciled, adopted, and saved."

Such are the conclusions to which we are conducted by a brief review of the several leading denominations of the South West. The evangelical portion of them will, I doubt not, earnestly protest that, whatever their books of faith, and their great writers may teach, they do not believe that baptism has any regenerating or saving influence whatever; that spirituality, and not a mere rite, is the sum of religion. I question not their sincerity. I respect it. I am gratified to concede to them that their knowledge of the Bible, and of experimental religion, has taught them the errors of their creed-makers, and their schoolmen, and that in their preaching, and other religious exercises, they forget them all, and practise upon better principles. Yet there are two or three matters connected with their conduct which to me are unaccountable. One is, that notwithstanding their oft repeated protests against them, still they solemnly subscribe these very standards, publicly profess their belief that they do contain the true exposition of the word of God, teach them to their children, and publish them to the world as their articles of faith. Another is, that they should inveigh so unceasingly against the importance of baptism, with mental reservation, wishing to make, on the public mind, an impression that they mean baptism, when, in fact, they have reference only to a particular mode of its administration. And the third is, the excitement they manifest on this subject, when their unbaptized children are in danger of death. The fact may be disguised with all possible carefulness, yet the impression is in the heart, latent indeed, but easily elicited, that baptism does, in some way or other, affect the happiness, and is a very essential preparation for another world. I cannot repel the opinion, and I hesitate not to express it, that nothing prevents all the extravagant practices, formerly connected with this sacrament, from being carried here to the same corrupt extremes that they have reached in Catholic countries, but the antagonist influence of Baptist principles.

CHAPTER XIII.

BAPTISTS CANNOT UNITE WITH PEDOBAPTISTS IN SACRAMENTAL COMMUNION, BECAUSE THEY ATTACH TO THE LORD'S SUPPER AN UNREASONABLE AND UNSCRIPTURAL IMPORTANCE AND EFFICACY.

Early superstition—Roman Catholics—Infant communion—Came into the church with infant baptism and accompanied it for a thousand years—Its abrogation—When and why—Opinions of the Episcopal church—Of the Presbyterian—Of the Methodist—Communion with them is an assent to their doctrines on communion which we cannot give—Open communion is impracticable—It is subversive of all discipline—The law of God the only safe rule—Close of this part of the argument.

THE same unreasonable and unscriptural efficacy and importance, with which, as we have, in the last chapter, seen our Pedobaptist brethren of all sects, invest baptism, they also attach to the sacrament of the Lord's supper. The proof of this statement,—for I ask no man to give it credit without the amplest confirmation,—will occupy our present attention. The Roman Catholics dispense it under the name of the mass, as an expiatory sacrifice, and all the other denominations refuse, on that account, and would continue to do so had they no other reason, to receive it at their hands. But the Protestants, with certainly no better authority, administer it professedly, as " an *effectual* means of grace ;" to " *seal* and *exhibit* the benefits of the mediation of Christ ;" and as " necessary to salvation." When such objects are avowed, is it possible Baptists can be among the recipients ? Such an expectation ought not to be entertained. We can approach the holy table only when the design is legitimately scriptural,—to "show the Lord's death till he come," to express our faith in the vicariousness of his great sacrifice, and to exhibit an emblem of that fellowship in spirit, which we have "with the Father, and with his Son Jesus Christ our Lord." The Protestant, though, perhaps, more modest than the Popish dogmas, are to us, not less objectionable.

These propositions, however, we may be possibly told, are extravagant and ridiculous. We appeal to the History of the Church, the standards of the several denominations, their writers of authority, and their public conduct and professions.

Their greater antiquity entitles the Roman Catholics to priority in our attention. On the decline of religion, about the third century, when the transition in the minds of men began to take place from its substance to its forms, baptism and the Lord's supper arose together in public estimation. They soon became the two leaves which compose the golden gate of the New Jerusalem. If the former was an indispensable preliminary to the latter, both were alike necessary to salvation. These facts we shall presently see fully established. The motives, therefore, that prompted the baptism of infants, very naturally led to the administration to them, without distinction, of the supper of the Lord. A fact so singular as INFANT COMMUNION will doubtless appear to many who may peruse these pages, I will not venture to state, without at the same time, giving such testimonies of its truth as may seem to be requisite. Preposterous as infant communion may appear, it is not more so than infant baptism, with the whole system of which it is perfectly consistent. History is exuberant upon this point. Dr. Wall asserts that "the baptized person was, quickly after his baptism, admitted to partake of the Lord's supper. This was always, and in all places, used in the case of adult persons, and in some ages and places in the case of infants."*

Mr. Daillé, in his work on "The right use of the Fathers," collates the testimony of Cyprian, Austin, and Pope Innocent I., all of whom he proves to have been warm advocates and supporters of infant communion, and adds:— "All the rest of the Doctors, in a manner, of the first ages, maintained that the eucharist was necessary for infants; if at least you take Maldonatus' word, who affirms that—'This opinion was in great request in the church, during the first six hundred years after our Saviour Christ.' Down as far as the end of the sixth century," continues Mr. Daillé, the Fathers held that *the eucharist is as necessary to salvation as baptism*,—and consequently to be administered to infants; and concludes from that, as from one of his two chief instances, how little heed—now that infant communion is abandoned—"is given to the practice of primitive times." But Maldonatus' meaning, we are assured, by the prosing Vicar of Shoreham, was mistaken by Mr. Daillé. He maintains that—" This opinion [of the necessity to their salvation of infant communion] began to be entertained in the year four hundred, and continued from that period, six hundred years." But Wall, himself, supplies the materials by which the opinions he advocates are most readily refuted. He exhibits, on the matter now before us, one of the numerous instances which occur in his works, of his singular blindness, when he does not wish to see the facts that lie before him. We will, for ourselves, consult the Fathers, whose names have been mentioned, with others who record the same history, and maturely determine the nature of the lessons they teach us.

* Hist. Inf. Bap., vol. ii. ch. 9, from section 15, p. 353, to the end of the chapter, where will be found all the statements and authorities here introduced.

Cyprian, in his book De Lapsis, narrates numerous incidents attending the administration, by himself, at Carthage, of the Lord's supper to infants, who were not yet old enough to speak. The story is too prolix, fanatical, and visionary, to be repeated. It may be seen by consulting the Magdeburgenses, Salmasius, Suicerus, Wall, ut supra, and Hinton's History of Baptism."* It is sufficient for my purpose that Cyprian refers to infant communion, and to the propriety of it as undoubted.

" Innocent I., Bishop of Rome," says Wall, " does, indeed, anno 417, plainly, and positively, say that infants cannot be saved without receiving the eucharist, and that too in a Synodical Epistle, written to the Milevitan Council."† This grave and reverend conclave had, in a formal address, represented to Innocent, the master of the triple throne, and the infallible arbiter of all truth, that the Pelagians had dared to embrace and even to defend the sentiment that, possibly, infants might be saved without baptism. The Pontiff immediately, and indignantly, replied in these words:—" That which your brotherhood says that they teach—that infants may, without the grace of baptism, have eternal life, is very absurd, since—'Except they eat the flesh of the Son of Man, and drink his blood, they have no life in them ;'—they can have no eternal life without receiving the communion ; and they cannot do that until they are baptized." The character, and stations, of the parties concerned in this correspondence, evince the extent to which the Christian world had, in that early age, adopted the principles, and practised the ceremony of infant communion.

Austin writes in the following emphatic terms:—" 'The Christians in Africa do well to call baptism itself one's sal-

* P. 326.
† Vide also Innoc. Epist. 93, inter Epist. to Augustine.

vation; and the sacrament of Christ's body one's life. From whence is this but, as I suppose, from that ancient and apostolical tradition, by which the churches of Christ do naturally hold that, without baptism and partaking of the Lord's table, none can come either to the kingdom of God, or to salvation and eternal life. Neither salvation, nor eternal life, is to be hoped for, by any, without baptism, and the body and blood of our Lord; it is in vain promised to infants without them."*

We need not multiply testimony in the premises. All that I proposed to establish is sufficiently apparent. Infant baptism, and infant communion, beyond question, came into existence at the same time, were sustained by the same arguments, and flourished together for a thousand years. Both were believed to be necessary equally to the salvation, whether of an adult or an infant, and they are certainly reserved, when the church shall return to her primitive purity and holiness, to share the same destiny. It is worthy of remark, en passant, that modern advocates of infant baptism, dwell with great emphasis on the statement of Austin, that this practice had come down to them as an apostolic tradition. But the same Father, and others also, assert, as we have just seen, precisely the same thing in favor of infant communion. That too was a tradition received from the apostles. If the argument is conclusive in the former case, it cannot be defective in the latter. But here they reject its authority, and have abandoned the practice. Few Pedobaptists have the candor of Bossuet, who says—"The church has always believed, and still believes, that infants are capable of receiving the eucharist as well as baptism, and *find no more obstacle* to their communion in the words of St. Paul—'Let a man *examine himself*, and so let him eat,' than they find

* De Pecatorum, Meritis, lib. i. cap. 27.

to baptism in these words of our Lord—'*Teach*. and baptize.' "*

In regard to the age at which the child was expected to approach the Lord's table, and the manner in which they communicated, we have the most explicit information. Respecting the former I observe, that the age of the communicants is indicated by the several ordinals of the times, which have come down to us. Gregory in his Sacramentarium, has an order, in these words —" Infants should be allowed to suck the breast before the holy communion, if necessity so requires."† The lenity of this enactment was not always permitted. The old Ordo Romanus, of the ninth century, directs thus :—" Infants, after they are baptized, should *not* eat any food, nor suck the breast, without great necessity, till they have communicated in the sacrament of the body of Christ." Salmasius observes on this subject—" It was the invariable practice to give to catechumens the eucharist immediately after they were baptized. Afterwards the opinion prevailed that no one could be saved unless he were baptized, so the custom of baptizing infants was introduced. And because to adult catechumens, as soon as they were baptized, no space of time intervening, the eucharist was given, so after Pedobaptism was introduced, this was also done in the case of infants."‡ As touching the latter, the manner of administering the Lord's supper to infants, Hugo de Sancto Victora, who lived about A. D. 1000, with other writers, gives us full information.§ The priest, he very gravely tells us, dipped his finger into the chalice, and put it into the

* Bossueti Traite de Communion sous les deux Espèces, part i. p. 3, apud Hinton's History of Baptism, p. 329.

† In Offic. Sabt. Sanct.

‡ In Libro De Consubstantione, contra H. Grotium, Hinton's Hist. p. 329.

§ Wall's History, &c., vol. ii. ch. 9.

child's mouth, for him to suck. This was the Latin custom. With the Greeks, who we are told still cling to the practice, the method was different. The wafer was mixed with the wine, and given in minute quantities, in the manner of giving medicine, not to preserve the body from disease, but to restore the soul to holiness, and confer everlasting life.

The Papists, and all the Protestants who are or have been under this influence, have, as we have already intimated, long since abolished infant communion. On this subject Dr. Wall remarks:—" The Roman church, about the year one thousand, embraced the doctrine of transubstantiation, and an excessive superstition prevailing in relation to the elements of the eucharist, they let fall the custom of giving the holy elements to infants. And the other Western churches, mostly following their example, did the like. But the Greeks—who received this custom from the Latins—not having the said doctrine [of transubstantiation] continued, and do still continue, the custom of communicating infants." The "custom," it is true, " was fallen in the west," still it was not formally abrogated, until by a decree of the Council of Trent. That council *repealed* what former councils, popes, and fathers, time almost immemorable, had taught as a *law of God*, and the practice it involved as inculcated by apostolical authority. The reasons for its suppression will be found among their proceedings thus stated :—" It [the Lord's supper] is not at all necessary for them [infants] since, being regenerated by the laver of baptism, and incorporated into Christ, they cannot, in that age, lose the grace of being the children of God, which they have now obtained."

Such are the origin, the doctrines, the forms, and present condition of infant communion. " For ten centuries," says Mr. Hinton,* the idea of withholding one sacrament from

* Hist. Bap. pp. 323, 324.

those who had partaken of the other, even in the case of infants, had certainly never been conceived. This was reserved for the most corrupt age of the church of Rome, when the doctrine of transubstantiation 'was come to the full;' so that the *Reformers* have followed the corruptions of the ancient church in giving baptism to infants, and the corruptions of modern Romanism in withholding from them the Lord's supper; and then, in the adoption of this compound error, with the facts of history staring them full in the face, they ask the Baptists to follow them." When we refuse to do so they courteously pronounce us for our squeamishness, exclusive, sectarian, self-righteous bigots. "But none of these things move us." Kindly, but firmly, we must decline; and soon, we trust, there will be no occasion for further contention. Infant communion has already been nearly destroyed by the influence of a like error, and infant baptism must ultimately fall by the power of omnipotent truth.

I have occupied more time than was necessary to show the importance attached by the Papists to the eucharist. I offer as an apology my desire to illustrate, somewhat, the collateral subject introduced, from the supposition that many of our people are without the means of its satisfactory investigation. I will study more brevity in deciding the inquiry whether the other Pedobaptist denominations attribute to this sacrament the same unscriptural efficacy with which it is regarded by the Romanists.

What the Episcopal church teaches her catechumens on this subject we had occasion to notice in the last chapter. When asked :—" How many sacraments hath Christ ordained in his church?" they are instructed to answer, and to believe they answer truly—" Two only, as generally *necessary to salvation*, baptism, and *the supper of the Lord*." After what we have before seen with reference to this sect, nothing,

I apprehend, need be added to prove that they attach to the ordinance in question, an unreasonable and unscriptural efficacy and importance.

The doctrine of all classes of Presbyterians may be learned by the following passage from their standards—"Question 161. How do *the sacraments* become effectual *means of* SALVATION? Answer. The sacraments become effectual means of salvation, not by any power in themselves, or any virtue derived from the piety or intention of him by whom they are administered, but only by the working of the Holy Ghost, and the blessing of Christ by whom they are instituted."* The manner in which the working of the Holy Ghost, and the blessing of Christ are received in the eucharist, in the next question and answer, is explained:—"Question 162. What is a sacrament? Answer. A sacrament is a holy ordinance, instituted by Christ, in his church, to signify, *seal*, and exhibit, unto those *who are within the Covenant of Grace*, the benefits of his mediation." We are here most certainly taught that the sacraments are *effectual means of salvation*, and that they *seal* to those who are within the covenant of grace the benefits of Christ's mediation. All this must surely render them of unspeakable moment in the work of salvation.

The service of the Methodist is nearly a transcript from the Episcopal church, from which it originated. In the matter before us only some portions among the most absurd are omitted, such as sponsors, and some other accompaniments. The idea, however, that the Lord's supper is "a means and seal of grace," is professedly retained and carried out in all their ministrations. Dr. Adam Clark, it is presumed, speaks the sentiments of his brethren when he says: "Every man who believes in Christ as his atoning sacrifice, should, as

* Confession of Faith, pp. 284, 285.

frequently as he can, receive the sacrament of the Lord's supper. And every minister of Christ is bound to administer it to *every man who is seeking the salvation of his soul*, as well as to all believers. Let no man dare to oppose this ordinance; and let every man receive it according to the institution of Christ."* That the practice of this denomination very generally corresponds with the vague and unscriptural notion just quoted, I presume, is unquestioned. As an illustration of this remark, I will introduce a statement of one of my correspondents, not long since published in several newspapers, on both sides of the Alleghanies:

"During the present summer, I attended a Methodist camp meeting, was in the crowd when the Lord's supper was administered, and persons were invited to unite themselves with the church. Two presiding elders were present. One of them solicited those who were professedly unregenerate to join the church as a means of regeneration, and urged that serious unconverted persons were more favorably situated to be born again who were church members, than those who were not. He narrated several cases of individuals who joined the church as seekers, who were afterwards brought to trust in Christ, and who had since declared their conviction that had they not done so, they never would have been converted. Among the cases he mentioned, one was that of a man who had connected himself with the church, was baptized, and partook of the Lord's supper, and who ascribed his spiritual change to the instrumentality of this latter sacrament. He, therefore, invited all who intended to join them to come to the sacred table with them. That evening *seven* persons came forward, their names were registered, an invitation was given to the unregenerate, who desired conversion, to go into the 'altar' to receive instruction, and to unite in

* Comm. on 1 Cor. xi. &c.

prayer, when, to my surprise, *six* of the seven went forward and kneeled. I was asked by a Methodist why I did not partake of the Lord's supper with them. I replied, that if I had no other reason, the consideration would be insuperable, that the ordinance had that evening been administered professedly as a means of *grace, regeneration,* and *salvation,* and that I considered myself obliged to withhold my assent from doctrines so unscriptural and injurious, and which I thought proper to evince by declining a participation."

This, doubtless, is a practical illustration of what they suppose to be taught by the *Discipline,* and accords with the canons of Episcopacy, which order that this sacrament shall be offered to all men. Clark* most strenuously contends, that "There is not a Popish priest under heaven, who denies the cup to the people, (and they all do this) that can be said to celebrate the Lord's supper at all; nor is there one of their votaries that ever received the holy sacrament. All pretensions to this is an absolute farce, so long as the *cup,* the emblem of the atoning blood, is denied." We agree with him here, most heartily. But let me ask, whether a dismemberment of the eucharist in reference to its object and design, is not equally fatal with a similar disseverance of its elements? If so, and I think its truth is obvious, the doctor's conclusion is legitimate against himself, and he and his brethren fail, after all, to receive the sacrament to which they attribute such miraculous power and virtue.

What, now, is the sum of the argument submitted? The Romanists tell us there is no eternal life without the sacrament of the body of Christ; the Episcopalians, that it is "necessary to salvation;" the Presbyterian, that it is an "effectual means of salvation," and "*seals*" to the recipient "the benefits of Christ's mediation;" and the Methodist, that it is

* Ut supra.

a means of grace and regeneration, and as such to be administered to every man who is seeking the salvation of his soul. Can all this be true? It is impossible. Is not the proof, therefore, perfectly conclusive, that all the Pedobaptist denominations attach to the Lord's supper an unscriptural and unreasonable degree of efficacy and importance? If we partake with them, we, by that act, publicly profess that we recognize their doctrine as correct, and in substance declare that we expect by it, not merely to perform an act of obedience, indicative of our love and submission to Christ, and to show his death till he come, but also to receive the grace and salvation of which they hold it to be productive, and have *sealed* to us all the benefits of his mediation. That we can, after an understanding of the subject, do this, is impracticable, without insincerity, hypocrisy, and sin.

Thus we have given our third and last principal reason why we cannot commune with our brethren of the several Pedobaptist denominations.

I might, indeed, add numerous others of minor import; such as that open communion is incapable of being carried into existence, and is, as we shall hereafter see, not practised even by those who claim so much credit on the score of their liberality. There is no principle upon which it can be conducted. Who are we to receive? If it is replied, all Christians, the difficulty is not removed. How are we to know who are Christians? We cannot, at such a time, stop to examine candidates. The same remarks are applicable with regard to our intercourse with the several sects around us. If we receive the members of two, or three, or four denominations, and reject others, we are still on close communion grounds, and yet subject to all the reproach which has hitherto been heaped upon us. Shall we admit all who have taken upon them the Christian name? This, I presume, will be considered out of the question. Open communion is also wholly subversive of all ecclesiastical discipline. The church which adopts it must immediately renounce the hope of preserving any order among her members. Exclude whom she will from her fellowship, he has only to go and join some other denomination, a course constantly adopted, and for which every facility is held out, and the next Lord's day he returns and communes with the church, no longer expelled. But I will not multiply considerations.

Let us recapitulate this part of our subject. We have seen that we cannot commune with our Pedobaptist brethren because, in the first place, to do so we must either actually renounce, or practically falsify, all our principles in relation to both baptism and the Lord's supper; because, in the second place, they have not been baptized; and because, in the third place, they attach to each of the sacraments an unscriptural and unreasonable efficacy and importance. We have determined, therefore, as individuals, and as churches, and, I believe, have determined wisely, to be guided, in this, as well as every other duty, alone by the law of Christ, and are prepared cheerfully to meet all the consequences attendant upon undeviating fidelity.

CHAPTER XIV.

THE POLICY OF FREE COMMUNION CONSIDERED, AND SHOWN TO BE DISASTROUS TO THE CHURCH.

Close communion is odious—the Church would be more prosperous were it abandoned—Argument from reason—from facts—Principles of free communion Baptists—Results of the practice—Bunyan's church—Foster's—Hall's—Giles' instances—Open communion abandoned by its advocates—Close communion most consistent with prosperity and harmony.

THE opinion has been entertained, and often expressed, by Baptists and others, that, notwithstanding all we have said, if the church would adopt the policy of open communion, she would be more prosperous and happy. This impression, together with the disposition to shrink from the odium attached to our present practice, has, in some places, prevailed so extensively that whole congregations have been strongly inclined to overturn the barriers that surround us, and adopt the liberal system so much eulogized. "The first effect," says Mr. Hall, appealing to the denomination in advocacy of the course suggested, "necessarily resulting from restricted communion, is a popular prejudice against the party which adopts it." He adds:—"From him who is truly solicitous to extend the triumphs of truth, we should expect nothing would be more abhorrent than such a system"——"It answers no other purpose than to make ourselves unpopular."

That the practice of restricted communion has been, with many persons, rendered extremely odious, and that in various quarters it is most unpopular, is readily conceded. The strongest prejudices of the human heart have been called forth, and set in an array against it. All the ministers, and people, without exception, whatever they may have yielded in private, or through the press, of every denomination around us, have industriously employed their whole energies during the last fifty years, to create and fix this odium, this prejudice, this unpopularity, and they have been but too successful. But does any one on this account think for a moment of faltering in his course? If so I must confess, and I do not regret it, that with him I have no sympathy. I ask not, I never will ask, whether any doctrine or practice of mine is odious or unpopular. All I wish to know is, whether it embodies that truth and righteousness which God has revealed. If I find it to be so, no earthly consideration shall deter me from a strict and hearty obedience. Had the apostles, the primitive Christians, and early martyrs, shrunk from the odium of the Christian profession, then so unpopular and withering, where would now have been the religion of Christ? Is the close communion that we practise, which by the way we intend presently to show is the most open and liberal communion existing, *odious?* Why should it be so? Is it on account of the principles which govern us, or the consequences to which these principles lead us? They are both the same in many respects which are professed by all other Christians. They too require faith and baptism as the terms of communion! What more do we? What then can it be that is so repugnant? It is our baptism. To destroy this is, after all, the great object for which they labor. Is any Baptist prepared to barter an ordinance of Christ for a miserable popularity? Do we not in all these respects act in accordance with the law of the Redeemer? To avoid the odium of obedience, must we become transgressors? Must we fear and honor men more than God, and that too, not to advance truth, but to screen ourselves from the opprobrium of perverted minds? While the odium of the cross is remembered, which Jesus Christ bore to redeem us, let me never be told of the unpopularity which may attach to that obedience requisite to preserve the purity of his sacraments.

Does the reason of the case lead us to the conclusion that were the church to adopt the open communion policy she would be more prosperous and happy? I presume not. Is it lawful to commune with any but baptized persons? Certainly it is not. Is the immersion in water, of a believer, by a properly authorized minister, in the name of the Father, and of the Son, and of the Holy Ghost, the only baptism? All Baptists reply in the affirmative. Then Pedobaptists are not baptized. To commune with them, therefore, is to violate the law of Christ If promiscuous communion is in contravention of the law of God, how can it be productive of an increased degree of prosperity and happiness? Did not Christ know what is best for us, and for his cause, and did he frame the rules of his word in conflict with the interests of his people? Shall we consult the advancement of his church by violating the laws which he has enacted for her government? It is impossible. On the principles of reason, therefore, open communion cannot be good policy.

Unfortunately for the happiness of the church, and for the advocates of "the liberal policy," we are not left to be guided in this matter alone by the doubtful light of reason. We are furnished by authentic history with the means of settling, definitely, the question whether the practice we debate is favorable to the prosperity of the church. The experiment has been tried, and it has most signally failed. In England there is, and has been ever since the days of John Bunyan, Toombs, and others equally popular, a considerable number of "Free Communion Baptists." Have they prospered or declined? The answer to this inquiry will solve the problem now under consideration.

It is proper here to remark that these ministers and churches have been immeasurably applauded, as great, learned, and liberal. Their works, especially those of Bunyan and Hall, have been industriously circulated by Pedobaptists, and profusely quoted against us. That they deserved all the reputation that has been accorded them I doubt not. But we would remind our Pedobaptist brethren, that open communion Baptists differ much more widely from them in principle than we do, and, therefore, ought to be regarded with less favor. They, as sincerely as ourselves, believe Pedobaptists to be unbaptized. "We are compelled," says Mr. Hall, and Bunyan and others concur in the same sentiment, "We are compelled to look upon the mass of our fellow Christians as unbaptized."* They justify their practice on one of two grounds, or on both, either that baptism is not a prerequisite to communion, or that Pedobaptists are weak and deluded, but sincere, and to be admitted in compassion for their simplicity. Says Mr. Hall,† "The apostles admitted the weak and erroneous, providing their errors were not subversive of Christianity. We do precisely the same." And ‡ "The only method of arriving at a satisfactory conclusion is to consider how the apostles conducted themselves towards sincere though erring Christians, together with the temper they recommend us to cultivate towards such as labor under mistakes and misconceptions not inconsistent with piety." In the former case—the supposition that baptism is not one of the terms of communion—if what in a former chapter we have seen to be the faith of all nations and ages is to be respected, they have embraced an error, and Pedobaptists ought to continue, as they have done heretofore, to

---

* Works, vol. ii. p. 212.   † Ibid. p. 216.   ‡ Ibid. p. 217.

bear their testimony against it. In the latter, I should think their position much more repugnant than ours. Are our brethren of other churches so ready to confess themselves weak, deluded, and imbecile? And even if it is so, the argument is nothing more than the absurdity, that if a man sincerely believes a thing to be right to him it is right, thus substituting sincerity for obedience, and fostering a deception hurtful to truth and righteousness. Will Pedobaptists accept communion on either of these grounds? They may, nevertheless, find it convenient, on account of certain advantages they imagine to be held out by open communion arguments, to give their verdict in their favor, and extol the liberality and wisdom of their authors, while they take good care not to adopt the principles upon which they are based.

But we return to the inquiry, whether open communion Baptist churches have been particularly prosperous. To those familiar with Baptist history, the fact is well known that, notwithstanding all the advantages of popular prejudices in their favor—if these can be considered advantages—and the advocacy of the most learned and eloquent men the world ever saw, these churches have, to say to least, gained nothing by the practice, either in numbers, respectability, piety or influence.* This fact may be demonstrated by an examination of **Ivimy**, Kinghorn, the younger Fuller, and other writers on the subject. Even Mr. Hall himself has unwittingly borne testimony in favor of this statement. Referring to the progress of Baptist principles in England, as open communion gained ground, he remarks—" It may be doubted whether, since the recent revival of religion, our progress is in a fair proportion with that of other denominations. It may be possible to assign the second causes of this remarkable

---

* This fact is elaborately, and incontrovertibly, sustained in the late English edition of this work, by the learned editors.

event, but as second causes are always subservient to the intentions of the first, it deserves our serious consideration whether we are not laboring under the frown of the great Head of the church; and 'is there not a cause?' A visible inferiority to other Christians in zeal and piety will hardly be imputed; nor have we been left destitute of that competent measure of learning and talent requisite to the support of our doctrines. The cause of the failure then is not to be looked for from that quarter."* The learned writer wished to make the impression that the denomination was suffering because so few had embraced his favorite doctrines, but the evil is now seen evidently to have had its origin in the extent to which they had been acted upon by the churches, and the consequent agitation and disorganization with which they were attended.

Let us, however, descend to somewhat more of particularity. The father, I suppose we may so call him, of open communion, was the justly celebrated John Bunyan, author of the Pilgrim's Progress, and numerous other reputable works. He was pastor of the Baptist church in Bedford, England. This venerable church admitted Pedobaptists, and as they were allowed all other privileges they could not be denied membership, or what was the same thing, the right of suffrage in the church-meetings, for it would be preposterous habitually to commune with a man and then not permit him to vote in ordinary matters, relating to the order and instruction of the congregation. The Bedford church was not so *illiberal*. But the consequences were fatal. The Pedobaptist party soon became the most numerous. On the discovery of this fact, they immediately took effectual measures, routed the Baptists, took possession of the meeting-house, called a Pedobaptist pastor, and from that time have

* Works, vol. i. p. 339.

generally held possession. "Such was the state of the church," says Mr. Kinghorn, "with which he was long connected, that on his death they chose a Pedobaptist; and from the year 1688, in which he died, to the year 1788, when Mr. Joshua Symonds died (one hundred years), the ministers who succeeded him were *Pedobaptists*, except the last, who, some years after his settlement with the church, changed his sentiments and became a Baptist. This took place in 1772, and though Mr. Symonds continued at Bedford, it was on condition that he should not introduce the controversy [on baptism] into the pulpit, nor into conversation, unless it was first mentioned by others. We have also been informed that one instance occurred in 1700, and another in 1724, in which the church refused to grant a dismission to members who desired to unite with Baptist churches in London, because they were strict communion churches."* Mr. Symonds was succeeded by Pedobaptist ministers. Here is a practical illustration of the advantages of open communion. Take another.

The Rev. James Foster, D. D., was, during more than twenty years, pastor of the Baptist church in Barbicon Place, London. "In his day," says Mr. Kinghorn,† "he advocated the cause of mixed communion." The consequence was, "he left the Baptists, and (without changing his principles—still a Baptist minister) accepted the pastoral charge of the Independent Church at Pinner's Hall." What were the practical advantages? The Barbicon church could have received no benefit by his withdrawal; Mr. Grantham Chillingworth assures us not one member of the Pinner's Hall church ever was baptized; and thus the services of Foster were wholly lost to the Baptist denomination. Yet Mr. Hall says: "Of the tendency of mixed communion to

* Defence, Preface, p. 15. † Ut supra.

promote a more candid inquiry into our principles, it is scarcely possible to doubt."

The church in Leicester, of which Mr. Hall was pastor, and afterwards that in Bristol, to which he removed, notwithstanding their free communion, and the unrivalled eloquence, amazing learning, unaffected piety, and unprecedented popularity of their minister, who wrote on the subject the most elaborate works which have ever been published, were no more numerous or flourishing than many other churches of fewer advantages, and who practised close communion. I have the best authority for the remark—that of a clerical eye-witness, the Rev. Jonathan Davis, author of the History of the Welsh Baptists—that in this church not a single Pedobaptist habitually communed, nor was it to have been expected, unless, as in the case of Bunyan, they were assured they could take possession of the church, and succeed its Baptist pastor with a minister of their own.

"Mr. Giles," says Fuller, in his Conversations,* "in his very interesting Letters to Rev. Robert Hall,† presents us with some striking exemplifications of the tendency of both mixed and strict communion. The following," he says, "have come under my own observation:

"'In a town in the south of our island, a most serious division took place in our Independent congregation. Sixty or more of its members separated from their brethren, attended the Baptist meeting-house, and expressed their desire to join in communion with the church. The Baptists, from a wish to evince their brotherly affection, and from a confident persuasion that such an act of liberality would not fail to be followed with conviction, at least among some of these mistaken brethren, agreed to alter their terms of communion, and receive them. Some of their members, and some of their neighbour-

* Pp. 250, 251. † Pp. 63-65.

ing ministers and brethren remonstrated with them, and assured them the result would prove to be the opposite to what they expected. But these remonstrances were disregarded, and the liberal plan adopted, with a confident persuasion of its success. This mixed fellowship continued for, I believe, a year and a half, or more; but not one of the Pedobaptists could see baptism to be of sufficient importance to submit to it! At last some Independent minister, from the kindest motives, no doubt, attempted, and really effected, a reconciliation between the remaining members of the church and the brethren that had seceded, the result of which was, that every one of them returned to his own fold, leaving the Baptists without the accession of a single member from them! There is no one but would rejoice in such a reconciliation; but it assuredly proves that your doctrine of expediency is not so certain in its results as you would have us believe. I think I might venture to affirm, from what I have experienced, that had this church stood firm to its own previous system, some of those Pedobaptists would have been induced so to examine the subject of baptism, that conviction would have followed, and that they would have been baptized.

"'I am acquainted with another church at ―――――. This church, for the purpose of receiving a few unbaptized persons, altered its constitution. The consequence was, that as soon as the alteration was made, as many baptized brethren withdrew as unbaptized persons joined. This church has tried your plan for some years, and, strange as it may appear, though it retains these Pedobaptists in communion, it has resolved never to receive another unbaptized person into fellowship. The reason for this extraordinary resolution, given both by the minister and some of its members, was, that they had tried and proved the inexpediency of mixed communion, and on that inexpediency alone had resolved in future to prevent it. This, sir, is another matter of fact against the expediency of your theory.

"'The last that I shall mention, and which I had related to me very recently by the pastor of the church, forms the opposite of the two cases already stated. At ———— an unhappy division took place in an Independent congregation, which resulted in the ultimate removal of its pastor. Many of this congregation united in worship with the Baptists. The Baptists retained their accustomed terms of strict communion; and several of these Pedobaptists have been baptized, have joined the church, and now rank among its most pious, active, and useful members. These cases, sir, confirm the truth of the adage, 'honesty is the best policy,' and of the maxim that 'what is morally wrong can never be politically right.'"

Such is a fair example, drawn from experiments and facts, connected with their history, of the benefits derived from open communion by the churches who have adopted it. I am assured by a reverend brother, formerly of London, now of Virginia, himself a disciple of the liberal school, that so well convinced are many of the churches in that metropolis and other parts of Britain, that free communion is bad policy, that they have alone on this ground abandoned it. And is the opinion still entertained by any man that there are many persons who, but for our close communion, would cordially unite with us, and who on that account join other denominations? We are, it is true, often approached by individuals in language like the following: I agree with you in all your great and essential doctrines. I am pleased with your admirable and Scriptural form of ecclesiastical government; your truly primitive, solemn and impressive baptism; your piety, your zeal, and your principles and practice generally. I am a Baptist in sentiment. But your *close communion*—

I cannot bear that. O, it is horrible, horrible. I would join you but for this feature in your discipline; but as it is I cannot. I must unite with some other church! Now this man, perhaps, is sincere. He probably really thinks that but for this obstacle he would be a Baptist. I for one, however, do not believe it. The persons who talk thus generally want some excuse to offer to their consciences for not obeying the truth, and here they imagine they have found it. They are not accustomed to analyze the feelings of their own hearts. They would, could they be persuaded to scrutinize their motives, soon perceive that they are influenced by other considerations, and this is presented only, and probably involuntarily, for the double purpose of making a show of friendship, and of concealing, almost if not quite, even from themselves, the real considerations which impel them from us. But some good, simple-hearted brother listens attentively to the story, and gives it entire credence. His soul is sad. He regrets to lose, on any account, from his church, a man who, in his opinion, would make so good a member; and, forgetting that appearances are deceptive, is strongly moved to regard our practice as impolitic and injurious. The facts, however, now before us, teach us another and a wiser lesson. They prove conclusively that when Pedobaptists are invited and even urged to come to the sacred table with us, they refuse to comply, unless as a matter of self-advantage, and that scarcely an individual would join us as open communionists who would not and does not, under existing circumstances.

Of the great Baptist family in the United States, some small fractions, the Free Will churches for example, practise unrestricted communion. They are pious, intelligent, and zealous, but are they more popular, prosperous, or happy, than we are? It will not be considered invidious, every one knows it to be true, if I reply that they are not. The opposite, indeed, is the fact. Little churches have sprung up in several states, at different times, upon the free communion principle. They have had talented and laborious ministers, and pious and efficient members. But they have invariably dwindled, and in a few years ceased to exist. Such has been, and such I apprehend ever will be, the history of churches conducted upon this principle. Do these effects occur without an adequate cause to produce them? I presume not. Do these facts prove that to free communion is attached the quality of attracting and retaining members in the Baptist church?

These actual experiments and facts are sufficient to convince any reasonable inquirer that free communion never, on the one hand, leads to prosperity, and that, on the other, it seldom fails to detract materially from the concord and happiness of its supporters. Indeed, in Europe, as we have seen, where its efficacy has been tested on a large scale, the very brethren who still believe it to be right in principle, have, nevertheless, from the conviction that in policy it is injurious to the best interests of truth and righteousness, abandoned it in practice. But, shall I respectfully inquire how that **can be right** in principle which is wrong in policy? If the Bible is the exclusive rule for our conduct, and the immersion of a believer in the name of the Holy Trinity is the only baptism, both of which propositions all Baptists most firmly believe; and if, as is admitted by Pedobaptists of every grade and denomination, baptism is an indispensable preliminary to communion, how can it be lawful to join in this sacrament with those who have only been sprinkled, and who received even that unauthorized ceremony in unconscious infancy? That it is in conflict with the law of God I must ever believe. Can Baptists, then, reasonably expect to be prosperous and happy in a practice which sets aside divine authority, and is regulated by perverted and mistaken views of mere expediency? All experience proves, and its testimony is corroborated by reason and revelation, that the hope is vain and delusive. Are the dictates of our own prudence a better guide in religious duties than the word of God? Wisdom, benevolence, brotherly love, do they require for their full and perfect exercise a disregard of the instructions of him who said:—"If you love me keep my commandments?" What Baptist is there who can subscribe to an opinion so monstrous? How then can we account for the fact that some of our most esteemed brethren have advocated and practised open communion? Is it a violation of charity to surmise that, unconsciously, they may have been under the influence of the same motives which have led the Pedobaptist world to persevere in unending declamation against what they are pleased to call our bigotry and unchristian exclusiveness? Not so much a love for truth, as an overweening desire for popular applause!

> "O popular applause! what heart of man
> Is proof against thy sweet seducing charms?
> The wisest and the best feel urgent need
> Of all their caution in thy gentlest gales;
> But swelled into a gust, who then, alas!
> With all their canvas set, and inexpert,
> And, therefore, heedless, can withstand thy **power!**"

CHAPTER XV.

BAPTISTS, AFTER ALL, ARE MORE FREE AND LIBERAL IN THEIR COMMUNION THAN ANY CLASS OF PEDOBAPTISTS WHATEVER.

Baptists are not the only close communionists—Between Pedobaptists of different sects there is no more love or union than between them and ourselves—All Pedobaptists exclude from the Lord's Table two thirds of their own members—Episcopacy—Episcopal and Protestant Methodists—New and Old School Presbyterians—Present controversy on that subject in the Pedobaptist churches, Acts of Synods, &c.—The tone of the religious press—Inconsistency.

SACRAMENTAL communion as practised by our church has been uniformly denounced by all other denominations, generally with earnestness, often with great bitterness, as "an antichristian dogma," guided and influenced alone by "the bigoted and exclusive spirit of sectarianism"—as "the impotent and deformed spirit of proscriptive and sectarian bigotry." Such is the language which every where meets our eyes in books and periodicals, and which we are condemned to hear uttered even from the head of the holy table itself, when we are so unfortunate as to stray into a Pedobaptist assembly at the time of the administration of this ordinance. Do we, when our principles and practice are candidly compared with theirs, merit from them these unbounded denunciations? So far are we from it in fact, that it is my intention now, as I have before intimated I would do, to prove, in the face of all that has been said and believed on the subject, that we are more free and liberal in our communion than are any class of Pedobaptists whatever. If we sustain ourselves in this attempt, and the consideration is of any importance, we shall take it for granted that we are entitled to credit for a superior degree of liberality.

We had occasion to remark in the outset, that Christian communion, in its largest sense, "extends to all the modes by which believers recognize each other as members of a common head. Every expression of fraternal regard, every participation in the enjoyments of social worship, every instance of the unity of the Spirit exerted in prayer and supplication, or in acts of Christian sympathy and friendship," truly belongs to the communion of the saints. Who are more ready to acknowledge the Christian character of our brethren of other denominations than ourselves? Do we not feel as much fraternal regard for them; as ardently participate with them in social worship, and in efforts to save sinners; and give as unequivocal testimonies of sincere sympathy and friendship as any of them do towards each other? In these particulars we are certainly not inferior to any of our opponents, and are, therefore, to say the least, as free and liberal in our communion But in sacramental intercourse—in this, we are told, we do not unite. But we are ready to meet them all there also, as we do everywhere else, provided they will come according to the acknowledged laws which Christ has enacted for the government of the feast. But even at the Lord's table we are not the only close communionists; indeed, in this particular, we do not hesitate to say that we are still more free and liberal than any of the sects around us. Does any one express surprise to hear the remark now made? Does he reply, I know of no close communionists but Baptists—all the other denominations hold and practise free communion? I answer, no, sir; I presume not. At any rate the inquiry is worthy of a candid examination.

Do Episcopalians or Roman Catholics *usually* receive—do their clergy *ever* receive—the Lord's supper at the hands of Presbyterian or Methodist ministers? Every one knows that they hold and teach that such ministers are without ordination, have, therefore, no authority to officiate in sacraments, and that when they do, it is a mere lay administration. These Calvinistic and Wesleyan offices, with the sage advocates of apostolical succession and divine right, are not recognized, but endured, and that merely because public opinion sustains them. Of these facts every intelligent Christian is aware. Is there between them, therefore, any cordial communion at the Lord's table? None whatever. Of this fact no additional proof is requisite.

In reference to the several Protestant denominations, I believe they all hold that manifest corruption in doctrine and worship is a disqualification for the reception of the Lord's supper. Let that fact be remembered, and then how shall we answer the following interrogations? Do not Methodists habitually and bitterly charge both these upon the Presbyterians, on the score of their Calvinism? Are the Presbyterians less ready or adroit in hurling back upon the Methodists the same imputations on the score of their Arminianism? Each, too, has its own internal war. Old School, New School, Cumberland, Hopkinsian, and other Presbyterians; and Episcopal, Protestant, Whitfield, and other Methodists, strive on the arena of ecclesiastical combat. Do they all commune together? If they do, is it a feast of union, and the love of each other, for the truth's sake, which each denies is held by the other? If so, what means this clangor of arms, this shaking of shields, and the noise of their fierce combats which I hear? If they unite in love at the Lord's table, why do they denounce each other in derision immediately after, in the Conference, the Session, and the Pulpit? Why do they excommunicate each other to day, "snatch from God's hand the balance and the rod," and doom their competitors to a place without the pale of Christian fellowship, if they commune to-morrow with these very men who are declared at the same time to be out of their communion? Let me never mingle a want of sincerity, consistency, and candor in so solemn an act of divine worship.

For the sake of brevity, we will select some testimonies in reference to the point before us, from one of the prevailing denominations, which shall serve as an illustration of all the others.

Dr. Engles, the editor of a leading journal of the Presbyterian church,* has taken the ground that Old School Presbyterians cannot consistently commune with New School men and Methodists. In reply to some resolutions of the West Hanover Presbytery, Virginia, formally condemning this doctrine, the editor observes: " As Presbyterians we profess to receive our denominational distinction from the symbols of faith which we adopt; and we regard other denominations as having their distinctive belief and character, of which we judge by their public symbols. The opinion that Confessions or doctrinal formularies are only obligatory on the ministry, and not on the people of a church, is, in our judgment, a most dangerous one; the adoption of it must at once destroy the homogeneity of a church, and give full license to the people to embrace every form of error. On the contrary, it is presumed that a Presbyterian believes in Presbyterian doctrine, or why is he a Presbyterian? And that a Methodist believes in the doctrines of his own church, or why is he not something else? The Methodist and Presbyterian alike believe that they have very good reasons for being as they are; nay, so potent are those reasons regarded

* Vide Philad. Presbyt. Sept. 12th, 1840.

to be, that neither imagines he could ever be induced to change his position. Now all we have contended for is consistency in carrying this principle out into practice."

"As our Methodist brethren *** have taken umbrage at our language, let us ask them if they are prepared to advise their people, on all favorable occasions, to go and commune with the Presbyterians? Do they wish them to think there is no difference between the denominations? Do they regard the differences as so trivial as to invite entire oblivion of them by their flocks, when they stray into Presbyterian folds? We judge not. Why, then, should they be angry with us for following their example? Holding the faith we do, *** can we, or ought we to say to the sheep of our folds—Yonder are pastures in which we believe there are poisonous weeds growing, but still there can be little danger in feeding occasionally there? In this matter we have never found our Methodist brethren a particle more liberal than ourselves. We have never found them backward in decrying Presbyterian doctrine; and we, on the other hand, candidly tell them, as we have often told them before, that we consider their system as very erroneous. For each of us thus to think is our right, in the exercise of Christian liberty, but is it quite possible that we should forget this, and lay aside our strong feelings on the subject, while we commune together?"

Thus much Dr. Engles says in regard to our Methodist brethren. Respecting the Old School particularly, and the New School department of his church especially, he remarks:

" The West Hanover resolutions express as much solicitude to be on good terms with the New School as with the Methodists. If we understand them, they wish the whole world to know that they distinctly disavow the exclusiveness which would refuse to commune with the men whom they, as Presbyterians, *helped out* of the church. If we mistake not they took an honorable part in the exclusive measures by which the New School lost their *statues* in our church; we say, their *statues* in our church, for although the exclusion in question did not affect their ecclesiastical organization, all the world knows that the excluded party are not now, and never have been since the passage of the acts, in the *communion* of the Presbyterian church. When, therefore, this Presbytery publicly says that they wish, with all ' liberality and Christian courtesy,' to hold *communion* with *them,* what must they think? If such language does not sound like a bitter mockery in their ears, we are not well skilled in sounds. The measure by which the New School were excluded from the communion of the Presbyterian church was either righteous or unrighteous; if the former, why should we make any professions of attachment which our actions do not sustain, or if the latter, why do we not magnanimously avow it, and invite them back in a body? We believe it was righteous, and whether right or wrong in our belief, we contend that, while the causes exist which led to it, *it is utterly inexpedient to hold communion with those churches.*"

Another leading journal—The Phila. Christian Observer —under the influence of the New School, referring to the same transactions, remarks:—" Palpably inconsistent as is his—Dr. Engles'—argument with *his* denial of *this* '*premise,*' and with his professions of regard for other Christians than his own party, the inconsistency of the West Hanover brethren (in resolving to commune with other denominations with ' liberality and Christian courtesy') is still more glaringly palpable. For they not only *helped* their brethren *out* of their New Basis concern, but after they were out they would not recognize them as a church. They would not, in the fall of 1838, give Dr. Carroll a certificate of dismission, recognizing in any form the third Presbytery of Philadelphia as any part of the church of Christ, or as having any connection with it. They would not even give him such a dismission as it has been usual to give one going from the Presbyterian church to other denominations. * * * But now, forsooth, without a solitary expression of sorrow for the wrong and insult, they have become so *loving* that they would have the members of their church commune with semi Pelagians."

The Protestant and Herald, of Kentucky, referring to the writers named, and to expositions of Dr. Plummer of Virginia, resolves the whole, involuntarily no doubt, by assuming precisely the Baptist ground. His language is:—" Every *believer* in Christ, who has been *baptized* in the name of the Holy Trinity, and is in connection with an evangelic church, has complied with all the scripture requisitions in order to an approach to the Lord's table; and we dare not keep him back."

On a mature examination of all these facts, and much more to the same effect, may we not ask the question whether Baptists have not all the liberality which any of these writers or churches evince, with the advantage in addition of open sincerity, and unshrinking candor? But to make this matter still more plain, we will extend somewhat further our investigations.

A distinguished Pedobaptist writer in a neighboring state,* expresses himself in the following language:—" For the last twenty years or more, I do not recollect of having entertained a doubt that the opening of the doors of our communion to all of what are denominated evangelical churches is erroneous, that it will either be changed, or lead to errors of a still

* Vide Protestant and Herald, Jan. 12th, 1840.

more serious nature, containing in itself *essentially* an indifference to sound religious principle and practice, though slow in its development. On a subject of such extent I can say but little in a short communication, and even this, I have reason to apprehend, may, by many in the present state of feeling in the church, be considered *quite inexpedient.*"

" I object to the practice in the first place, because *I have never yet seen the man, however strenuously he might advocate it*, who could inform me *how far it was right*, AND DUTY CALLED *to extend the privilege*—a very important item in making out a line of conduct, and without which it must be unsafe, in matters of conscience, to act at all. We are told, it is true, that all who are evangelical, or who hold the essentials of religion, are to be admitted to the Lord's table; but then these essentials are undefined; some make them but two or three, at most, others, perhaps, four or five, and others still more. * * *

" I object to the practice, in the second place, because it clearly implies that our church creeds or confessions contain certain items of faith and practice THE BELIEF OF WHICH, OR CONFORMITY TO WHICH, *is not necessary to the right of church privileges*. This implies either that these things are not based on divine authority, on which supposition they are the works of men, they are schismatical too, dividing the church where there is no conscientious principle involved, and, therefore, ought to be rejected as evils; or it implies that, notwithstanding they are based on divine authority, they are indifferent—of little importance, may be practised or not as we may see proper, with impunity—which last conclusion is to me revolting. * * * I suppose a case which I think is in point. An individual applies to you for admission to baptism and the Lord's supper. After examining him to full satisfaction as to his experimental religion, you inquire of him whether he will conform to the order of God's house, in submitting to discipline, the discharge of religious duty, such as family discipline, the Baptism of his children, &c. But he replies, I do not approve of this government, and as to the baptism of children, I consider it unauthorized. You would reply, I presume, that you make subjection to this duty a condition of church membership, and of privileges connected with it. But on the supposition you practise open communion, he would reply—You admit to all the privileges I desire without such subjection, for you admit *Baptists*, and those who neither believe nor practise it. You reply—Because they submit to their own order. He takes his departure, connects himself with those who will not require this thing, and returns, and, at your invitation, enjoys with you all he asked. I see, in such a case, a predicament I should not envy. For what is your attitude now in the eyes of your own members? Most assuredly you appear inconsistent, and they must feel in consequence that they lie under a condition, their compliance with which guarantees them no privileges. You lay every distinguishing feature of your own church liable to prejudice and reproach. To me the inference would be, your conduct being right, that your church ought forthwith to relinquish its own distinctiveness, and sink into the church Catholic, and every other church practising the same ought to do likewise."

"I am fully aware that my views on this subject are esteemed very *illiberal*. This is the *argumentum ad invidiam*, which with many weighs heavier than a thousand others. I have, however, always been happy to consider them LIBERAL TO TRUTH, AND SINCERITY IN THE TRUTH. But the state of the case is misapprehended, the principle on the ground of consistency and sincerity in the truth, applies equally to all sects, who must, in charity, be supposed con scientiously attached to their own peculiarities, for where this is the case, they must needs do violence to their consciences where they dispense with such peculiarities. And I would here add that the practice is absolutely inconsistent, in my opinion, with the very idea of fellowship, which in all cases implies a community of responsibility."

We perceive, from these extracts, not only that our Pedobaptist brethren are close communionists as well as ourselves, but that some of them, at least, carry their restrictions much farther than we do. They not only require that a man shall have given them satisfactory evidences of his spiritual change, and been baptized, but he must subscribe their particular Confession of Faith, and assume with them " a community of responsibility." They would not permit *Baptists* to approach their table. Believing these doctrines, and failing to avow them, while at the same time, from a fear of *invidious* imputation, and a desire to obtain popularity, by their liberal professions, they pretend to practise *free* communion, this writer charges his brethren, in the aggregate, with a want of "*liberality to truth, and sincerity in the truth.*" I shall not question the correctness, nor vouch for the legitimacy of his conclusions, but proceed to ascertain by what means they manage to keep up a public impression that their communion is free in the ordinary sense of that term, and yet *practise* close communion. I have at hand some Synodical proceedings held in one of the Valley states which will enable us without difficulty to solve the problem.*

The Committee on Bills and Overtures, to whom was referred the question—" Is it proper that there should be

---

* Synodical Records of a Presbyterian Synod—Extracts published by order, &c.—Vide Union Evangelist, and Presbyterian Advocate, 1820, vol. ii. pp. 96-99.

intercommunication between Presbyterians and those denominations who hold Arminian sentiments?" presented the following report, which was adopted:—

"That after giving it all the attention which the importance of the subject demands, they are of the opinion that for Presbyterians to hold communion in sealing ordinances with those who deny the doctrines of grace, through the blood of Christ, &c., is highly prejudicial to the truth as it is in Jesus. Nor can such intercommunion answer any valuable purpose to those who practise it, as two cannot walk together unless they are agreed. Yet, as there are persons who have received distorted views of the doctrines of grace, who notwithstanding admit these doctrines in fact, although they are prejudiced against the terms generally used in the discussion of these subjects, your committee are of the opinion that, if any such manifest a desire to hold communion with us, that, after being conversed with, and having received satisfaction on these and other points on which their church and ours disagree, and having obtained satisfactory evidence of their piety, charity requires they should be admitted to occasional intercommunion."

Communion is not to be withheld, certainly not, this would be illiberal sectarian bigotry. Should any manifest a desire they are to be received, IF they believe in the doctrines of grace; IF, when examined—for they *must first* be examined—they shall convince their inquisitors that they have renounced their own, and embraced Presbyterian doctrine; and IF they shall give satisfactory evidences of their piety; *then* they should be admitted; not to *habitual*, but "to occasional intercommunion." This is one specimen of Pedobaptist *open* communion, as regulated, not by the false glare of pulpit declamation, but by the sober deliberations of synodical gravity. As a further illustration of our inquiry we will introduce another similar proceeding.*

"The committee on a former resolution of Synod on the subject of intercommunion reported. The report was adopted, and is as follows, viz :—

"The committee are of opinion that for Presbyterians to hold communion in sealing ordinances with those who belong to churches holding doctrines contrary to our standards, is incompatible with the purity and peace of the church, and highly prejudicial to the truth as it is in Jesus. Nor can such communions answer any valuable purpose, &c. In accordance with these views, your committee are of opinion that the practice of inviting to the communion all who are in good standing in their own churches, is calculated to do much evil, and should not be continued, while every church session is, however, left at liberty to admit to occasional communion members of other denominations, after having conversed with them, and received satisfaction of their soundness in the faith, and Christian practice."

Here again we have presented the same general views of the subject. To avow candidly close communion is not "expedient." It would give effect to the argumentum ad *invidiam.* Outward appearances must be maintained. In deep conclave, however, it is solemnly enacted that indiscriminate communion, the practice of inviting Christians— yes undoubted Christians, baptized Christians—who are in good standing in their own churches, is an evil. Communion with even such as these, unless they subscribe the standards, "is incompatible with the peace and purity of the church, and highly prejudicial to the truth as it is in Jesus."

* Extracts from Synodical Records, 1832, ut supra, vol. iii. p. 240.

Yet they are open communionists! If any of us should be so unfortunate as to wish to commune with them, what must we do to accomplish our desires? We must apply to the church session, converse with the savans, convince them that according to their standards, we are sound in the faith and Christian practice—Presbyterian faith and practice of course—and if they are satisfied, and we can succeed in getting "*a token*," then, and in that case, "Synod" is kind enough to say we may approach the holy table. We may, also, occasionally, repeat our visits afterwards, *if* we will, whenever we wish to do so, repeat the same process! And these are liberal, free communion Christians, the very men who denounce Baptists as bigoted, selfish, exclusive, close communionists!

These documents would perhaps be repudiated by many of the sect, especially in public, for effect, and this very fact, while it proves their own disunion, if sincere, serves as a full and satisfactory illustration of our present inquiry.

The synodical doctrines just noticed are fully sustained by the highest tribunal of that denomination. The General Assembly of 1839 expressly says: "Every Christian church, or association of churches, is entitled to declare the *terms* of admission into its communion." The unanimous doctrine* of their leading divines, is, that these *terms* consist in "*agreement in essentials.*" If this be regarded as too indefinite, and it is still necessary to inquire what they mean by "*essentials,*" the reports just considered afford a *definite* reply.

The views of this denomination we have presented as an example of all the others, and that it is both a fair and favorable one will not be questioned, because no man can doubt but that the Presbyterian church is as enlightened, liberal, and candid as either the Methodist or Episcopalian. I am now

---

* Vide Prot. and Herald.

ready to submit the question to the decision of any impartial tribunal, whether Baptists are not to the fullest extent *as* free and liberal in their communion as any class of Pedobaptists whatever. Indeed, the testimony I have presented will evince that we are much more so. To establish incontrovertibly this latter proposition, I shall offer one more argument.

Baptism and the Lord's supper having been associated by Christ himself, remained inseparable from the days of the apostles onward, for more than a thousand years. Whenever, in the Scriptures, or in the history of the ancient church, one of these ordinances appears, the other is invariably found in connection with it. With Baptists this sacred union is still inviolably preserved. We most cheerfully sit down at the table of the Lord with all those, if they have not forfeited their claims by heresy or immorality, whom we believe to be baptized. Do our Pedobaptist brethren act with the same liberality? Very far from it. Their public professions would lead us to conclude that this is their practice, but when brought to the point they positively refuse! Is proof of this statement needed? I ask, then, do they not believe their infants are baptized? Most certainly. Are they either heretical or **immoral**? Neither is pretended. Do they commune with them? **No,** never. Thus they at once exclude *two-thirds* of the members of their own churches from the Lord's table! But is it a fact that their baptized children are members of their churches? Turn once more to the Confession of Faith,* and it will be found thus written: "A particular *Church* consists of a number of professing Christians, *with their offspring,* voluntarily associated together for divine worship and godly living." Again†—" Children *born within the pale of the visible church,* and dedicated to God in baptism, are under the inspection and government of

* P. 273. † P. 327.

the church—and when they come to years of discretion, if they be free from scandal, sober, and steady, and have sufficient knowledge to discern the Lord's body, they ought to be informed it is their duty and privilege to come to the Lord's supper." In the Larger Catechism we find the following: "QUESTION 62. What is the visible church? ANSWER. The *visible church* is a society made up of all such as, in all ages and places of the world, do profess the true religion, *and their children.*" Porter on Christian Baptism, says: "*Baptized children are members of the visible church.*"* Dr. Dwight, in his Theology, as every one knows, maintains that children are members of " the general church."

Dr. Miller, on this subject, and the same views are maintained by both Methodists and Episcopalians in their respective formularies, distinctly remarks :—†

"Is there no advantage in solemnly dedicating our children to God by an appropriate rite of his own appointment? Is there no advantage in formally binding ourselves, by covenant engagements, to bring up our children 'in the nurture and admonition of the Lord?' Is there no advantage in publicly ratifying *the connection of our children*, as well as ourselves, *with the visible church*, and, as it were, binding them to an alliance with the God of their fathers? Is it a step of no value to our *children* themselves to be brought, by a divinely appointed ordinance, *into the bosom*, and to the notice, the maternal attentions, and the prayers *of the church*, the mother of us all?"—When our brethren are disposed to be particularly severe, they are wont to say that— " There are but two places in the universe where there are no children, one is the bottomless pit, and the other is the Baptist Church." Not to reply to them, that there is one other place where there are no infants—that is, the Pedobaptist

---

* P. 108. † On Infant Baptism, 39-42.

communion table—I ask, does not their argument imply that, in their opinion, infants are members of their churches? It is then universally conceded; and it is probable that this class make up two-thirds of their whole number, with none of whom will they sit down to the communion.

Their fathers did not, as we have seen in a former chapter, act thus inconsistently. Infant baptism was originated in the third century. From that time onward, during more than eight hundred years, they scrupulously took all their baptized children with them to the Lord's table, rightly judging that they had the same title to the one that they had to the other of these ordinances. They declared that they administered them both to their infants upon the authority of tradition from the apostles. When they discontinued, in obedience to a decree from the Council of Trent, the administration to them of the eucharist, it was because of their superstitious notions regarding transubstantiation, with which it is hoped Protestants are not infected. The standards of all their sects, as we have seen, teach that between the Lord's supper, as well as baptism, and the salvation of the soul, there is an intimate and necessary connection. Yet they totally withhold from them all this essential, this "effectual" means and seal of grace. "When Pedobaptists," says Hinton, "give their children both ordinances, they will be consistent; but while *they* withhold the Lord's supper from their children, let them not complain of others withholding baptism. Whatever arguments will sustain the one, will be equally available for the other." But they profess to believe them truly baptized, yet refuse to them the communion, thus practically excommunicating them all, a favored few only of the great mass of their own members being permitted to approach the sacred table. Of ours we receive all. None are debarred. Ours, therefore, is by far the most free and liberal communion of any denomination existing. Still these wholesale restrictionists, who have infinite reason to be silent on the subject, are perpetually decrying us for our restricted communion! Before they ever administer to us another word of reproof, they, in all good conscience, by communing with all their own members, should evince that they themselves possess some portion of that liberality they so much eulogize, and for the supposed want of which we appear to them so very obnoxious.

Let all the facts now submitted be maturely weighed, and we shall never again be told that Baptists are the only close communionists, and more exclusive and illiberal than any other Christians, the only people who exclude the members of Christ, the children of God, from the holy table. Who now can doubt that the Baptists are, to say the least, as liberal in all things as any other Christians, and that in relation to communion particularly we are more open and liberal than any class of Pedobaptists whatever.

CHAPTER XVI.

CAN THE BAPTIST CHURCH, IN MAINTAINING CLOSE COMMUNION, BE JUSTLY CHARGED WITH THE SIN OF SCHISM?

That schism exists somewhere is evident—We have not produced it, and are therefore not responsible—We have adhered to original principles—Baptists are identical with primitive Christians—When the disciples became Pedobaptists they severed themselves from us—We have maintained ever since a separate existence on original ground not connected with Papists or Protestants—Historical proofs—Confessions of Faith—Our name—Duty of Pedobaptists, having produced the schism, is obvious—they are required to heal it—It is not difficult to determine how it may be done—Its consequences.

AMONG the numerous charges preferred against us, not the least important is that, in maintaining the principles, and following out the practice, based upon them, of strict communion, we are guilty of severing the body of Christ, and thus producing agitation and schism. Pedobaptists have not been the most zealous in their denunciations on this head. I will note a few passages from a distinguished author in our own ranks.

"Are our Pedobaptist brethren," asks Mr. Hall—"a part of the mystical body of Christ? Or, in other words, do they form a part of that church which he purchased by his precious blood? You are loud in your professions of esteem for pious Pedobaptists, nor is there any thing you would more resent than a doubt of your sincerity in this particular. The persons whom you exclude from your communion are, then, by your own confession a part of the flock of Christ, a portion of his mystical body, and of that church which he has bought with his blood. The next question is, whether a formal separation from them, on the account of their imputed error, amounts to what the scripture styles *schism?* Supposing one part of the church at Corinth had formally severed themselves from the other, and established a separate communion, allowing those whom they had forsaken, at the same time, the title of sincere Christians, would this have been considered as a *schism?* That it would is demonstrable from the language of St. Paul, who accuses the Corinthians of having *schism*—σχισματα, (divisions)—among them, though they never, dreamed of forming a distinct and separate communion. If they are charged with schism on account of that spirit of contention, and that alienation of their affections from each other which merely tended to an open rupture, how much more would they have incurred that censure, had they actually proceeded to that extremity.—If there is any meaning in terms this is *schism* in its highest sense."*

In another place† he observes—" Still you plead for a visible *disunion,* nor will it avail you to reply, that you cultivate a fraternal affection towards Christians of other denominations, while you insist upon such a visible separation as must make it apparent to the world that they are *not* one."

That a schism exists in the Christian church, and that the crime of its production is referable either to Baptists or Pedobaptists, is most true. Mr. Hall insists, and the Pedobaptist world concur of course with him, that the sin is ours. The opposite I believe to be capable of the most satisfactory demonstration. If upon examination it is found that their churches are constituted and governed upon the Gospel model, and ours is not, then we are the schismatics; but if the contrary is true we cannot be liable to the charge of dividing the body of Christ. Suppose the church at Corinth had proceeded to an open rupture, who would have sustained the odium

* Works vol. i. p. 293. † P. 225.

and sin of the division? Would it have been the party who observed, or the party who abandoned the regulations prescribed by the great Legislator? It is not grateful to my feelings to fix the charge of schism, even by implication, on any one. But the question is made, and we are forced either to suffer the reproach or place it where it truly belongs. Close communion did not originate with the Baptists. It was brought into existence by Pedobaptists, and is still continued by them, and that too against our most earnest and protracted remonstrances. If I establish this proposition, and show that the barrier to universal Christian intercourse at the Lord's table was set up, and is still kept up by Pedobaptists, it will be readily acknowledged, by every candid man, that the crime of producing and perpetuating the schism, and all the odium and responsibility involved belongs exclusively to Pedobaptists.

The terms of communion, as we have fully seen, are first, repentance, secondly, faith, and thirdly, baptism. And when once the holy table is thus approached by any one, he must continue to have free access, so long as he remains orthodox, and orderly. We have before proved that infant baptism is clearly unlawful, and prohibited by the word of God. Who foisted it into the church? Its friends and advocates of course; and they did it, and persevere in the practice, against the warm and continued protestations of the adherents to primitive truth, from Tertullian down to the present time. Thus they effected one part of the schism, and sundered the body of Christ so far as it could be done by setting up that part of the barrier which dispenses with repentance and faith as a condition of baptism. It only remained after this for them to abrogate baptism also. This they ultimately did by adopting sprinkling or pouring, which is in reality to dispense with baptism altogether. Then the gulf between them and us was completely fixed. Nothing more was required. Thus they abolished all the scriptural terms of communion, refusing to comply with any of them, and still they insist that notwithstanding we shall either receive them to communion, or else deny them to be Christians. We refuse to do either. They then, by way of reprisal, attempt to fix upon us the sin of their own schism. But this cannot be done. Those who made the division must be convicted as the schismatics. We stand in this matter precisely where the apostles did. We have not made, we do not intend to make, the slightest alteration in any thing. They have made the change, and thus set up the barriers to communion. They, therefore, and they alone, are responsible, be they what they may, for the consequences. When, therefore, our Pedobaptist brethren prove that the crimes alleged are involved in close communion, and, as is often the case, grow warm and eloquently indignant in their declamations on the subject, they do but publish their own guilt, and grace with the charms of rhetoric the sentence of their own condemnation.

I have frequently in the preceding chapter spoken of the church now called Baptist, as having existed in all ages since the days of the apostles. I am aware that there are many who will regard these claims as preposterous. In maintaining the proposition that we remain unchanged and upon the true Gospel foundation, with reference to the subjects involved in the present controversy, I shall have occasion to illustrate this truth. I assert that the Baptist church has existed, in a state of comparative purity, connected with neither Papists nor Protestants, in every period since Christ, and that in this sense God has not left himself without witness. Before I proceed to the proof of this statement I will make a remark on two collateral topics.

The former has reference to apostolical succession in the

usual Episcopal sense of that phrase. I deem such a succession of no consequence. Touching the validity of the ordinances administered by our clergy, it is wholly unimportant whether we can trace a regular succession of bishops up to the apostles. It is sufficient for us to know that we are organized according to the established laws of Christ, support the true doctrines of the gospel, that our constitution and practice agree with the rule prescribed by him, and which were strictly obeyed and enjoined by his apostles, and that we keep the ordinances as they were delivered unto the saints. Such a church is Christ's representative on earth, and, according to his word, possesses all the requisite authority to create and ordain ministers, whenever the cause of Christ shall demand such a measure. If it were not so, the race of ministers would be like that of the mastodon, or some other similar class of animals. Should it by any providence become extinct, it never could be reproduced, but by a second direct exertion by Jehovah of his creative power. That an opposite opinion has prevailed in some quarters for fifteen centuries I am fully aware. But the "*divine right*" of kings and bishops stands on the same foundation, and is maintained by the same arguments. The former is beginning to be repudiated; the discovery cannot long be delayed that the latter is no less fallacious. God forbid that we should ever sanction error merely because it is venerable for its age.

The latter is the question, somewhat mooted of late, whether Baptists are Protestants. That we, like Lutherans, Episcopalians, and Presbyterians, or, as they are called in Continental Europe, the Reformed Church, ever had any connection with Papists, no one will pretend; but it is not so readily conceded that we are not a "branch of Protestantism." I remark on this part of the subject, that a protest must take place in a legislative or judicial assembly. It is, as we understand it, a solemn declaration of dissent on the part of the minority from the proceedings of the majority in such an assembly. A declaration of this description was entered by certain princes and deputies, as may be seen in Robinson's History of Charles V., and other works having reference to the events of that period, of imperial towns against the celebrated decree, dated April 19, 1550, of the Diet of Spires. The dissentients were on this account distinguished by the name of Protestants, and this appellation was subsequently extended to all those sects, both on the continent and in England, indiscriminately, which have revolted from the See of Rome. With these facts in view, it will be seen, at once, that Baptists for two reasons cannot possibly be Protestants. The former is that we do not, and never did, recognize either the legislative or judicial authority of any assembly whatever in matters of faith; and the other is, as we never had any connection with Popery, we never could have been a minority in any Roman Catholic legislative or judicial assemblies, and therefore never could have in that way protested against their decisions. No one, for example, would think of calling the Jews Protestants, or of annexing the name even to the Greek Christians. With as little reason can it ever be associated with the name of Baptist.

Many careless thinkers have classed us among Protestants, because they imagine that we sprung up among the numerous sects that divided Christendom at the time of the Reformation; and for a similar reason some have even called us dissenters; an appellation we repudiate with as much earnestness as we do the other. Luther, Calvin, and the English Fathers, adopted it is true, many of the doctrines by which we had ever been distinguished, but we must not on that account be called Lutherans, or Calvinists, or by the name of any other modern divine. Neither can we submit to be classed with those who, after casting off some of the shackles of Catholicism, denominated themselves Reformed churches. We call not our churches reformed, because we believe them no better than their predecessors, established by the primitive disciples. We are content with the name first given us at Antioch, and have allowed ourselves to be known by an appellation of more modern times, first intended as a reproach, but still expressive of the fact that we admit only believers to membership in our churches, and still adhere to the form of initiation established by Christ—their baptism in the name of the Father, of the Son, and of the Holy Ghost.

Thus it will be seen that we are not Protestants, nor Dissenters, Lutherans, Calvinists, Arminians, nor Reformers, but what we have been in all ages, the Church of our Lord Jesus Christ.

We now return to the inquiry, whether the Church at present known as Baptist has existed in all ages since the days of Christ? To answer satisfactorily the inquiry it is necessary to observe that our church is distinguished by two prominent traits—that she immerses exclusively in baptism, and admits to the ordinance none but believers. Keeping these facts in view we will, upon Pedobaptist testimony, examine the primitive Christians.

Dr. Mosheim, a distinguished Lutheran divine and historian, in describing the manner in which the Christian rites were administered during the first century, observes, " Those who amended their lives were initiated into the kingdom of the Redeemer by immersion."* In another place, " Concerning baptism during the first hundred years," the same learned writer remarks, " the sacrament of baptism was administered without the public assemblies, in places appointed

* Eccl. Hist. vol. i. cent. 1, part 1, p. 55.

and prepared for that purpose, and was performed by immersing the whole body in the baptismal font."*

In testimony of the manner in which this ordinance was administered in the second century and beginning of the third, I will, of many witnesses, for the sake of brevity, submit the evidence of but two. Tertullian—"To begin with baptism. When we are ready to enter into the water, and even before, we make our protestations before the pastor and in the church, we renounce the devil and all his pomps and ministers, afterwards we are immersed in the water."† And Mosheim adds—" The persons who, during the second century, were to be baptized, after they had repeated the creed, confessed and renounced their sins, and particularly the devil, and his pomps and allurements, were *immersed under water*, and received into Christ by a solemn invocation of Father, Son, and Holy Ghost, according to the express commandment of our blessed Lord."‡

I have now only to ask if the Christians, down as far as the beginning of the third century, were at present to be classed, with what church would they fraternize in relation to baptism? The Baptist, unquestionably.

As to the other prominent trait—whether the primitive Christians baptized infants—I will refer to a few Pedobaptist authorities.

The eminent Claudius Salmasius, in agreement with the equally learned divine of Zurich, John Gaspard Suicerus, explicitly states: "In the first two centuries, no one was baptized except being instructed in the faith, and acquainted with the doctrine of Christ, he was able to profess himself a Christian."§ Curelleus of Geneva,‖ asserts: "The baptism of infants, in the first two centuries after Christ, was wholly

---

* Vol. i. p. 108. † De Corona Militis, apud Dupin.
‡ Vol. i. cent. 2, ch. 4, sec. 13. § Booth's Pæd. Exam. ‖ Ut supra.

unknown, but in the third and fourth was allowed by some few. In the fifth and following ages, it was generally received." In the Christian Review,* we have the following testimonies on the point under consideration. Kaiser: "Infant baptism was not an original institution of Christianity."† Baumgarten—Crusius—"Infant baptism can be supported neither by a distinct apostolical command, nor apostolical tradition "‡ Neander says: "The practice of infant baptism was remote from the spirit of this age. Not only the late appearance of any express mention of infant baptism, but the long continued opposition to it, leads to the conclusion that it was not of apostolic origin."§ I will only add the statement of the learned Episcopius, as quoted by Booth.‖ He denies that even any tradition can be produced for Pedobaptism until a little before the Milevitan Council, A. D. 418, and maintains that "the baptism of infants was not practised in Asia until near the time of that council."

We will again ask, to what denomination would these apostolic Christians, who repudiated infant baptism, and baptized only by immersion, at this time be considered as belonging? To Methodists, to Presbyterians, to Episcopalians? Does not every man reply they were certainly such religionists as would now be called Baptists? When the doctrines of purgatory, infant baptism, prayers for the dead, episcopacy, the worshiping of martyrs, affusion for baptism, and others of simlar character began to be introduced, multitudes opposed and protested against them. Had we no other evidences of these facts, the two which I will mention would abundantly establish them. The former is the pressing ex-

---

* Vol. iii. No. 10, art. 4.   † Bibli. Theol. vol. ii. p. 178.
‡ History of Theology, vol. i. p. 1208.
§ In his Eccl. Hist. of the Apostolic Age, vol. i. p. 140.
‖ Pæd. Exam.

hortations addressed to professed Christians to come to baptism, with which the early Christian writings abound, and of which we have an example in Basil's Oration;* and the latter is the awful anathemas constantly hurled by the dominant party against those who denied infant baptism; allusion to which is had by Neander in the passage from his Ecclesiastical History, a moment since noticed. Of what denomination would these Christians now be considered? They were reduced to the necessity either of separating from their brethren, who were thus corrupting the gospel, or of giving their sanction to the perversions in question. They preferred the former course, and that they acted with great forbearance is manifest from numerous historical references to the events of that period. Hooker, for example,† though he speaks sneeringly, admits all that is necessary for our purpose. He remarks: "These held and practised their own opinion, yet with great protestations, often made, that they neither loved a whit the less, nor thought, in any respect, the worse of those who were of a contrary opinion."

The Athenian Society, a literary association formed in England two hundred years ago, was made up wholly of Pedobaptists. The writer of its history represents it as in every sense equal to the famed Royal Society. He says‡— "All the endeavors of all the great men of all nations and ages, from the beginning of learning to this time, have not contributed so much to the increase of knowledge as the Athenian Society. They commenced previous to 1690 a weekly periodical, called the Athenian Gazette, which name was subsequently changed to Athenian Oracle. This work was conducted by a committee of twelve of their most com-

---

* Exhort. ad Bap. Wall. part i. ch. 12, sec. 3.
† Eccl. Pol. Book 5. p. 324.
‡ Bapt. Chronicle, by Rev. Dr. Baker, vol. i.

petent men, selected from all the learned professions. Their volumes are quoted with confidence as authorities, by Hannah Adams, and other distinguished writers. In 1691, this society was thrown into a controversy with the Baptists respecting the antiquity of the church, and they affirmed* that " There never was a (separate) particular congregation of Anabaptists until above three hundred years after our Saviour." Here we have an admission that there were separate congregations of Baptists in the fourth century; and their testimony is enhanced in value by the consideration that it was given by the enemies of our principles, and with a view to our disparagement.

But this Athenian Society has introduced to us a witness whose deposition is entitled to more respect than their own— the celebrated Swiss reformer, Zuinglius, the contemporary and co-laborer with Luther. Zuingle remarks,†—" Anabaptismi institutio non nupera et nova est, etc."—" The institution of Anabaptism is not a novelty, but for *thirteen hundred years* has caused very great disturbances in the church, and has acquired such strength that the attempt in this age to contend with it, appeared futile for a time." What shall we say to this declaration? Zuingle was born in 1487, was a learned man, a doctor of the University of Basle, and enjoyed better advantages than perhaps any other individual of his day, for obtaining correct information on this subject. If his testimony is reliable, it proves that Anabaptists, as we were improperly called, existed for thirteen hundred years prior to his time, that is, from the close of the second century, prior to the period at which, as we have seen, ambitious leaders began to corrupt the ordinances of the gospel with their traditions, by substituting the commandments of men for the

---

* Supplement to the Athen. Ora., vol. iv. p. 161.

† De Pædobapt. apud Athen. Ora., vol. iv. p. 161.

precepts of heaven. There could, of course, until Pedobaptism was introduced, be no anti-Pedobaptists, and until pseudobaptism was practised, there could be no anabaptism. The testimony, however, of this great Swiss reformer further proves, not only that the Baptists had a continued denominational existence from the close of the second century—and prior to that period we have shown that all were Baptists—to the time of the Reformation, but that they existed in such great strength and numbers as to cause very serious difficulty among their opponents, and to render " futile for a time" the persevering exertions of Protestants to overcome and disperse them. To the violence and cruelty of the efforts they employed for this purpose, we have before referred. At every period the demon of persecution—

> " With delight did he snuff the smell
> Of Baptist blood on earth, and high upturn
> His nostril wide into the murky air
> Sagacious of his quarry from so far."

But we are told by many illiterate men, and even women, who have been ambitious to write our history, that they do not read of Baptists till the time of Cromwell! Indeed! And do they not know that our present name is recent? It is not the name, it is the principle which we seek. Of whom did Mosheim speak, when describing a body of Christians every where existing during the whole of the dark ages, and up to the Reformation, in the following language:—" They held that no persons whatever were to be baptized until they came to the full use of their reason."* Stennett, in his answer to Russen, speaking of the same churches, says they entertained the belief recited:—" Because to all infants, that know nothing of faith, and in whom there can be no desire

---

* Eccl. Hist. Cent. 12, ch. v. sec. 7.

for regeneration, or confession of faith, &c., the will, faith, and confession of another, seems not in the least to appertain."* Such were the avowed sentiments of a class of men prevailing always and found in every country. They were in more modern times known in Italy as the followers of Gundulphus; in France, under the name of Berengarians; of Paterenes in the Duchy of Milan; of the Petrobussians and Henricians in Languedoc and Provence; and of the followers in Brescia of Arnold.† All these are sometimes included under the general name of Waldenses, and of whom President Edwards says:—" Some of the Popish writers own that that people never submitted to the church of Rome."‡ He adds—" One of these writers says—The heresy of the Waldenses is the oldest heresy in the world." Beza affirms—" As for the Waldenses, I may be permitted to say that they are the seed of the primitive and purer church." These Waldenses were sometimes confounded with the Albigenses, and all were not unfrequently called Anabaptists or Mennonites, and of whom Mosheim remarks —" The true origin of that sect which acquired the name of Anabaptist by their administering anew the rite of baptism to those who came over to their communion, [that is, immersed when they became believers those who had been baptized in infancy,] and derived that of Mennonites from the famous man to whom they owe the greatest part of their present felicity, is hidden in the remote depths of antiquity, and is of consequence extremely difficult to be ascertained."§

The editors of the Edinburgh Encyclopedia, under the

* P. 84

† For more extensive information on this point, see Hinton's History fo Baptism, chapter vii. sec. 8.

‡ Hist. of Redemption, period 3, part 2.

§ Eccl. Hist. vol. ii. ch. 3, p. 127, Baltimore edition.

head of Baptists,* say :—"When we take a superficial view of this sect, collected, as it were, into one society, and in its present embodied form, nothing appears more easy than to write its history, and to specify the doctrines which are peculiar to it. But when we come to examine it more minutely, we find that it is composed of very different materials, and that its origin is hid in the remote darkness of antiquity." In speaking also of Anabaptists, and mistaking them for a different class of Christians from Baptists, they represent them as "a sect whose origin it is difficult to trace;" and they add:—"There can be no doubt that there were many who held these opinions before the time of the Reformation." Robertson, in his Preface to Claud's Essay, while tracing up the history of those whose followers, since the origin and establishment of the Episcopal church, have been known as Dissenters, says:—"All the Dissenters allowed Christian liberty, and all were enemies to an established Hierarchy reigning over the consciences of their brethren, and one branch uniformly in addition to all this, denied the baptism of infants."

The number of the Waldenses was, at the commencement of the Reformation, estimated by one of their own writers, at eight hundred thousand. Their opinions on the subject of baptism,† prove that in the aggregate they were Baptists. "The Book of Sentences of the Inquisition of Toulouse" describes them as holding sentiments thus delineated:—"Also that baptism by water, administered by the church, was of no use to children; because the children, so far from giving assent to it, cried at it." For this heresy they were "*sentenced*" to the cells of the Inquisition, and doomed to expiate their offence in the flames of the Auto Da Fe. They

* Amer. ed. Phila., 1812. † Jones' Ch. Hist. vol. ii. &c.

are further described by Ermengardi* in this language:—
"These heretics say, moreover, that this sacrament can be of no use to any but those who seek it with their own mouth and heart. Hence drawing this erroneous conclusion that baptism can be of no advantage to infants."

All these are testimonies drawn from the enemies and devourers of this persecuted people. What do they prove them to have been? What could they have been but Baptists? But let us examine their own declarations upon this point. Their Confession of Faith, dated A. D. 1120, that is, *seven hundred and twenty-one years ago*, and *four hundred and thirty-one years before the Reformation*, is sufficiently definite. At that time, as all learned men agree, pouring or sprinkling was scarcely ever practised, except in the cases of *clinics*. In the twelfth article of the instrument in question, they expressly confine both the ordinances of baptism and the Lord's supper to believers; and this, let it be remembered, was at a time when infant baptism and infant communion were the Jachin and Boaz of Pedobaptist Christianity. These early disciples furthermore held that "a Christian church was an assembly of believers—faithful men and women—and that of such a church, the Lord Jesus Christ, and he alone—not the pope—is the Head; that it is *governed* by his word, and guarded by his Spirit; that it behooves all Christians to walk in fellowship; that the only ordinances Christ has appointed for the use of his churches are baptism and the Lord's supper; that they are both symbolical ordinances, or *signs* of holy things—visible emblems of invisible blessings."

In another of their Confessions of Faith, written and published to abate, if possible, the vengeance of their bloody persecutors, they say—"We believe that in the **ordinance**

---

* Contra Waldensium sectam, cap. 12.

of baptism, the water is the visible and external sign, which represents to us the renovation of our minds through Christ Jesus; and by this ordinance we are received into the holy congregation of Christ's people, *previously professing and declaring our faith and change of life.*"* I further observe, that in a letter of some of the pastors of this truly primitive church to Œcolampadius, dated A. D. 1530, they say:— "We have sustained for above these *four hundred years* most severe and cruel persecutions, but not without signal marks of Christ's favor, as all the faithful can testify." Professing, in these dark ages, doctrines, so scriptural, enlightened and pure, it is an eulogy of no ordinary character upon us, which was pronounced by the learned Limborch, Professor of Divinity in the University of Amsterdam, when he said:— " To speak candidly what I think, of all the modern sects of Christians, the Dutch Baptists most resemble both the Albigenses and Waldenses."

So much I thought my former declarations required me to say in relation to the history of our church in the days of the apostles, and through the dark ages up to the time of the Reformation. From that to the present we need not trace the events by which we have been distinguished. Our history has been written in blood by the hands of our persecutors; still it is sufficiently distinct to prove beyond a reasonable doubt that we have had a prominent existence from the days of Christ in every age to the present hour.

But this is not our only line of descent. If the Christians I have described had never existed, there would not have been wanting witnesses for the truth. Among the Britons the true church existed, and the legitimate doctrines and ordinances were maintained from the time Christianity was planted in that island to the present moment.

---

* Jones' Ch. History, ed. 2, pp. 49, 50, 70.

Ivimy, in his History of the English Baptists,* and the same facts are detailed by Crosby, and others, assures us that the British Christians embraced the pure gospel in apostolic times, and until the year 596 remained undisturbed in its exercise. In that year Gregory, the Bishop of Rome, sent Austin with a train of monks to convert them to the Catholic faith. He arrived, called their ministers together, and made them three propositions, the second of which was in these words :—" That ye give Christianity to your children," *i. e.* that you *christen*, or baptize them. This they positively refused to do. I need not pause here to inquire whether these Christians were Baptists; I proceed to remark that their determination was reported at Rome, upon which Gregory decreed in these words :—" Let all young children be baptized as they ought to be, according to the traditions of the Fathers." Still they refused. Soldiers were brought upon them to enforce the order, and many were massacred. Large numbers, however, escaped to the mountains of Wales, in the fastnesses of which, by the providence of God, they were preserved from extermination, and where, at this very hour, they exist by thousands, in possession of the faith and practice of the gospel, as it was delivered to them by the apostles. But two or three centuries have passed since, according to the History of the English Dissenters by Bennet and Bogue, except a few government officers and dependants, all Wales was Baptist. On the opening of the New World, numerous whole churches were transplanted from thence, as well as from the continent of Europe, to these western shores, and the labors of whose ministers and members have been the chief instrumentality in the amazing advancement of our denomination in these United States.

These facts and considerations demonstrate that the **Bap-**

* Vol. i. pp. 42-45.

tist is the only church which can claim the apostolic origin, and that in its organization and objects it is conformed in all respects to the word of God; that the apostolic church was Baptist, and that through several channels it may be readily and surely traced in a state of comparative purity down to our times; that it struggled through the days of Popish darkness, and Protestant ignorannce and intolerance, maintaining its principles separate from both, ever bearing testimony to the truth as a witness for God. And can it be that in maintaining these principles unchanged, and adhering unwaveringly to the faith once delivered to the saints, refusing to turn aside from the laws of Christ in deference to every new fancy of modern religionists, we are guilty of producing a schism in the body of Christ? No, it cannot be credited by any intelligent man. It is too late to utter such a charge against the venerable church of which it is our honor to be members, and which, as science, literature and the arts have enlightened the minds and humanized the hearts of men, has come forth from the clouds of oppression and persecution, shining in her original brightness, and is rapidly covering the earth with the light of primitive and unadulterated truth.

We have now proved that not the Baptists, but the Pedobaptists are the schismatics. If in the present state of religious intercourse between different churches, and the several classes of the same denomination, there is a departure from the true spirit of religion, and the teachings of the word of God, those alone are responsible who, by their aberrations from the divine law have produced this state of things. Who can read the prayer of Christ for the unity of his people without feeling that it is criminal thus to resist the divine will. "For them that shall believe in me," says the blessed Redeemer, "I pray; that they *all* may be *one;* as thou Father art in me, and I in thee, that they also may be one in us; that the world may believe that thou hast sent me."* How is this union, for the blessed consummation of which, all hearts must glow with anxious desire, to be produced? It must be *a union* IN *the truth*, otherwise it would not deserve the name. It can be attained only by a return to original gospel principles. The schism in question will by this measure be instantly healed, every barrier removed to free intercourse, and thus will be secured the universal union and communion of all Christians. If such a result is desirable; if, as we have seen, all the impediments to it have been brought in, and thus far kept up by Pedobaptists; if theirs is the sin, and they alone are responsible for the consequences; it requires no great skill in casuistry to determine whose duty it is to apply the remedy. Let those who introduced now remove the barriers, and all will yet be well. This they can easily do without violating their consciences in any particular.

When Pedobaptists find their interest in it, they can, and do, as we all know, dispense with sprinkling infants. Let them discard altogether this unauthorized practice. To save a good member, or to satisfy his conscience, they can readily immerse him when he becomes a believer, although he may have been sprinkled in infancy. Such cases are of not unfrequent occurrence. Why not, then, adhere to this practice, and immerse all candidates. They are wont to tell us that all these are non-essential matters, but Christian union is not non-essential. They profess to be very anxious for universal communion. As it is their duty to produce it, and as they can so easily attain the utmost of their wishes, it is hoped they will not hesitate to sacrifice a mere *non-essential* to the union of the people of God. A believer as the candidate, and immersion as baptism, all confess to be legitimate.

* John xvii. 20, 21.

To this intelligent Pedobaptists can, with a good conscience, confine themselves. Beyond this we cannot, we dare not go. Our conscience will not permit us. Thus far all perfectly harmonize. Here let us all pause, meet, and unite, and the results will gloriously accelerate that concord to which prophecy has taught us to look forward, when " every one shall see eye to eye, and speak the same thing."

CHAPTER XVII.

RECAPITULATION AND CONCLUSION.

Contents of the several chapters—Summary of the whole—Exhortation —Union—Liberality—Prosperity—Firm adherence to original principles—Our ultimate triumph.

HAVING briefly touched in the preceding chapters the several particulars considered most vital in this controversy, and an explanation of which was regarded as essential to an intelligent decision, I hasten to close the discussion. For this purpose it may not be improper briefly to recall attention to the principal topics of argument which have passed in review before us.

In our introductory observations we have defined our object, identified the points which we have proposed to investigate, deprecated the motives which have impelled men in all ages to violate the laws of charity, and explained the reasons which have rendered on our part an examination of the principles of sacramental communion requisite. In several succeeding chapters we have explained, enumerated, illustrated, and defended the fundamental doctrines of communion, and shown that they are necessarily as immutable as that great Being of whose divine will they are at once an emanation and a transcript. They consist in the following radical truths: The terms of communion—that we are prohibited from adopting any terms, other than those ordained by our Lord Jesus Christ, and that to these we are at all times, and in all circumstances, under obligations to adhere, individually and collectively, without addition, diminution, or change.

That, in the second place, repentance towards God, faith in our Lord Jesus Christ, and baptism in the name of the Father, and of the Son, and of the Holy Ghost, are indispensable terms of approach to the Lord's table, and to which those who have observed these preliminaries cannot afterwards be debarred of access, but in consequence of a forfeiture of Christian character, by immorality or heresy. These facts we have seen are scriptural, reasonable, and that in firmly maintaining them we have the full concurrence, with the single exception of a few open communion Baptists, of all the Christian world of all nations, ages, and denominations. To all the arguments acknowledged to be of any importance against these conclusions, such, for example, as those founded on the presumed nature of the administration of John the Baptist, the inspired canons of Christian toleration, the spirituality of the Gospel, and several others, we have fully, and we trust satisfactorily replied, showing that so far from invalidating in any particular, they confirm and establish the doctrines for which we are professedly advocates. And that, in the third place, we are not at liberty to administer the Lord's supper for any purposes, however desirable they may appear to us, or however great may be the imagined advantages, other than for those designated by our Lord Jesus Christ.

Having thus traced the outlines of our faith with regard to the eucharist, we have enumerated the several reasons why we cannot engage in sacramental communion with Pedobaptists, among which we have noted especially that in so doing, we must necessarily either renounce or practically falsify all those principles which we have explained, and so fully and sincerely avowed, and which are held sacred and true equally by Baptists and Pedobaptists, and tacitly assent to others the truth or propriety of which we cannot conscientiously acknowledge. We cannot commune with them, because Jesus Christ expressly, as all of them confess, requires baptism as a preliminary, and they have not been baptized. This disqualification is apparent, not only from the fact that they received the rite, if it may be called such, in unconscious infancy, at which age the law of Christ not only does not authorize, but positively forbids its reception, but also from the consideration that sprinkling or pouring was in the administration substituted for the ordinance of Christ, which made what they received a rite of their own invention, and in no sense obedience to the command of the adorable Redeemer. As our final reason, we have shown that all the sects of Pedobaptists attach an immoderate and unscriptural importance to both baptism and the Lord's supper, representing them as the seals of divine grace, the means of entering into the covenant of mercy, and effectual instrumentalities of salvation. When administered for such purposes, or for any other than as testimonies of our love and obedience to Christ, it is very evident that we can neither receive baptism at their hands, nor mingle with them at the holy table.

The next topic we have submitted, is the tendency and effect of·open communion considered merely as a matter of policy. Under this head we have pointed out the deceptions liable to be practised upon our judgment, and our feelings; shown that, guided by the principles of reason, enlightened by the word of God, it is impossible to reach the conclusion that promiscuous communion is good policy; we have introduced its history and proved by all the facts attendant upon its progress, in both hemispheres, and during the last hundred years, that so far from exercising a salutary influence in our favor, it has proved itself as a matter of policy absolutely ruinous; and, finally, that it is ingenuously confessed by its warmest and most able advocates, that were the Baptist church universally to adopt unrestricted communion, we should soon cease to exist as such, and our members find refuge in the little communities around us, the oldest of which did not exist until our church had run a career of fifteen centuries.

We have also fully and satisfactorily shown, after all that has been said of our selfishness and bigotry on the subject of sacramental and religious intercourse, that we are palpably more free and liberal in our communion than any class of Pedobaptists whatever. This fact is demonstrated by comparing our course in reference to all our members who are confessedly baptized, with those of Pedobaptists towards theirs, two thirds of whom they themselves debar from their own table, and still complain of our want of liberality; by the exclusive claims of Episcopacy, and the intercourse, as evinced by the Acts of Conferences, Synods, General Assemblies, and the tone of the religious press, existing between the several Methodist and Presbyterian sects; and by the well known truth that the fraternal associations between them and ourselves are, to say the least, as cordial, as between the several parties into which pedobaptism is divided.

We have closed the discussion by briefly considering, and amply refuting, the charge so often, and so confidently, preferred against us, that, in maintaining a communion restricted to baptized believers, of known orthodoxy and moral character, and declining to institute any new terms of communion, or to participate in the eucharist for any purposes other than to evince our love and obedience to the Redeemer, and to show the Lord's death till he come, we are guilty of dividing the body of Christ, and obnoxious to the character of schismatics. We have demonstrated, by the word of God, that, in doctrine, in polity, and especially in sacramental practice, we are identical with the apostles; and shown by ample references to the authentic history of the times, as recorded by our opponents, that we coincide with the primitive Christians, during the first three hundred years; that when pedobaptism, sprinkling, infant communion, and the train of similar innovations, were introduced, their abettors broke off from the true church, and became a corrupt religious society, destitute of the divine favor, and despoiled themselves of ecclesiastical character and authority; their very persecutions, enjoying the favor of the Roman emperors, and therefore the stronger party, have, in part, enabled us to trace the legitimate church of Christ, which we have distinctly done, through two channels, separate, equally, from Protestants and Papists, and the perpetual prey of both, down to our times. Thus we have seen that those who have separated themselves, and not we, who have ever maintained original principles, are the schismatics. If the definition of Swift be entitled to respect, this sin consists, not so much in separating from those who profess to be followers of Christ, as in departing from the truth which he has revealed, we can, in no sense, therefore, be implicated, nor shall we ever become liable to the charge, unless we yield to the clamor of open communionists, and go over to pedobaptism. Then, indeed, shall we too be guilty, and the withering leprosy will have covered the last healthy member of the body of Christ.

The existence of schism and the criminality of its indulgence, have been fully recognized, and it has been shown that the only method by which it can be healed, is the return of all Christians to the pure and unadulterated Gospel of Messiah, to embrace it without reserve, to practise with sincerity, and to be governed by its laws in all things. When this happy disposition shall prevail, and influence the actions of men, and not until then, will the dying prayer of the Redeemer be answered, and the world be subjugated to his peaceful reign. As the whole responsibility of the existing condition of things in the religious world rests upon the Pedobaptists; as the evils that prevail are referable to them, and can only be removed by them; as they profess to feel a deep interest in the union and communion of all the people of God; and as the appropriate movement on their part, would undoubtedly accomplish all these great and glorious results; may we not hope that, laying aside all human expedients, inventions of men, and every time-serving system of policy, and submitting to the guidance of the Spirit of truth, they will, at no distant period, be found walking with us, in the path of holy and full obedience!

I have only to add my earnest and affectionate exhortation to all our brethren, in every part of our wide spread land, to stand unmoved on your original ground—

"Firm as the surge repelling rock."

On this subject I will not allow myself to entertain fears that any one will hesitate or waver. The principles and practice by which we have hitherto been characterized, so far as they accord with the word of God—and all else we repudiate—may subject us to reproach; they may, as they have done, call down upon our heads the wrath and persecution of place, ambition, and power, but they can never, in the smallest particular, be abandoned. The spirit of true religion is too exalted to stoop to the mean arts by which the demagogue courts the smiles of popular favor. The reputation of a free and generous liberality may, perhaps, be innocently desired, but it can be of little ultimate value to him who must sacrifice for its attainment the approbation of a good conscience. No Baptist can permit such considerations to occupy a place in his heart. A union with our brethren of all denominations, and a prosperity, however unbounded, which may be purchased at the expense of revealed truth and Christian fidelity, hold out no attractions for us. The bond of the one would prove a rope of sand, an association equally displeasing to God, and injurious to his people; and the brightness of the other but the glare of the *ignis fatuus*, which

"—— Leads to bewilder, and dazzles to blind."

Light is spreading. Truth is taking hold on the hearts of men. Darkness is receding. The spirit of inquiry is abroad. Revelation is assuming its rightful authority. Every religious pretension must ere long be brought to this test. Our triumph is not distant. Until it come, let every man acquit himself with a firmness and intrepidity worthy of the glorious cause it is our honor to defend.

THE END.

A
Biographical Sketch
of
Robert Boyté Crawford Howell
(1801-1868)

by
John Franklin Jones

A Biographical Sketch of Robert Boyté Crawford Howell (1801-1868)

Robert Boyté Crawford Howell–missionary, pastor, writer, editor, historian, denominational leader, helped lay the foundations of the Southern Baptist Convention--was born in Wayne County, North Carolina, on March 10, 1801. Though his heritage was Episcopal, he united with a rural Baptist church fourteen miles from his home in 1821. He enrolled at Columbian College, Washington, D.C. but left after the 1825-26 session to become a lawyer. He was awarded an honorary D.D. by Georgetown College, Kentucky, ca. 1844 (*ESB*).

Howell committed himself to become a missionary at Portsmouth, Virginia, and was ordained in January 1827. He forthwith became pastor of Cumberland Street Baptist Church, Norfolk, Virginia (*ESB*) and labored there until 1834 (Cathcart).

He accepted an appointment from the American Baptist Home Mission Society as missionary to the West and became pastor of the Nashville church January 1, 1835. The church had lost its pastor, nearly all its members, and its building to Campbellism May 24, 1828 and had ceased to exist. The church reconstituted October 10, 1830 and erected a building dedicated late in 1837 or early 1838. Howell restored respect to the Baptist name. The church excluded about 100 antimissionary members June 18, 1838 (*ESB*).

Howell began *The Baptist*, a monthly paper, in January 1835. He edited the paper most of time prior to giving it to the Tennessee Baptists in June 1848. He revived Sunday School and organized societies for education/ministerial improvement, Bible distribution, publication, and colportage. He resuscitated a missionary society organized by Luther Rice in December 1816 in Tennessee (*ESB*).

He led in establishing Union University. He also led in organizing (May 1842) the Baptist General Association of Tennessee and North Alabama to replace a convention, organized in 1833 and destroyed by antimissionary Baptists (*ESB*).

Howell championed early efforts proposed by the Southern Baptist Convention in 1849 to organize a Baptist seminary. That seminary became Southern Baptist Theological Seminary at Greenville, South Carolina. Ten years later it moved to Louisville, Kentucky (*ESB*).

He became pastor at Second, Richmond, Virginia July 5, 1850. He returned to Nashville July 1857 to find the churches controverted by Landmarkism under the influence of J. R. Graves. Opposing Landmarkism, he worked actively to free the Bible Board, Nashville, from Landmark domination (*ESB*).

He opposed creating the Southern Baptist Sunday School Union at Nashville by Graves and his followers. Howell was loyal to the Southern Baptist Publication Society, Charleston, South Carolina. The Graves-Howell controversy threatened First Baptist Church, Nashville, the third time the church's existence had been threatened in its thirty-year history (*ESB*).

Shortly after the Union army captured Nashville in February 1862, Andrew Johnson, the Union military governor, possessed for the military the building of the First Baptist Church. Howell and three or four other ministers refused to take an oath of allegiance to the Federal government, and Johnson imprisoned the refusant ministers for two months. His health failingly affected by the imprisonment, Howell resigned in July 1867 and died some ten months later (*ESB*). He died on Sunday April 5, 1868 at Nashville, Tennessee following a week of speechlessness, but consciousness (Cathcart). He was buried at Mount Olivet Cemetery, Nashville (*ESB*).

He was the second man elected to be president of the Southern Baptist Convention, presided four years (1851, 1853, 1855, 1857) over that body, and was a vice-president at the time of his death. He was elected a fifth time as president in 1859 over the "prolonged and bitter opposition of Graves," but immediately resigned to prevent that controversy further intruding into the Convention (*ESB*). He served as vice-president of the American Baptist Historical Society, a member of the Historical Society of Tennessee, and president of the trustee board of the asylum for the blind in Tennessee. He was also frequently the moderator of the Concord Association and other deliberative bodies (Cathcart).

Howell married Mary Ann Toy, in April 1829. Of ten children born to that union, two died in infancy (*ESB*).

Howell authored *Terms of Sacramental Communion* (1841), in later editions, *Terms of Communion at the Lord's Table* (1846) (*ESB*). The Tennessee Baptist Convention requested the work be published, resulting in the 456-page *Terms of Christian Communion* (1854). The book was reprinted several times in the United States and in England (Cathcart).

His *The Deaconship* (1846) (*ESB*), issued by the American Baptist Publication Society, quickly transited six editions (Cathcart). Other works included *The Way of Salvation* (1849); *The Evils of Infant Baptism* (1851); and *The Cross* (1854). *The Covenants* (1856) was later revised in ms. as "The Christology of the Pentateuch" (*ESB*);

JOHN FRANKLIN JONES

The Early Baptists of Virginia began as an address at the 1856 American Baptist Historical Society, was published in a tract; enlarged to book form in 1856, enlarged again in 1864, and was published posthumously by the American Baptist Publication Society. *A Memorial of the First Baptist Church, Nashville, Tennessee from 1820-1863* is a two-volume mss. edition of the church's history. The author's sermons exist in thirty bound mss. volumes (*ESB*).

BIBLIOGRAPHY

2000 Annual of the Southern Baptist Convention. Nashville, TN: Executive Committee, Southern Baptist Convention, 2000.

Cathcart, William, ed. *The Baptist Encyclopaedia: A Dictionary of the Doctrines, Ordinances, Usages, Confessions of Faith, Sufferings, Labors, and Successes, and of the General History of the Baptist Denomination in All Lands, with Numerous Biographical Sketches of Distinguished American and Foreign Baptist, and a Supplement.* Philadelphia, Louis H. Everts, 1881; reprint, Paris, AR: Baptist Standard Bearer, 1988.

Encyclopedia of Southern Baptists. S.v. "Howell, Robert Boyté Crawford," by Homer L. Grice.

BY JOHN FRANKLIN JONES
CORDOVA, TENNESSEE
JULY 2004

THE BAPTIST STANDARD BEARER, INC.

a non-profit, tax-exempt corporation
committed to the Publication & Preservation
of the Baptist Heritage.

CURRENT TITLES AVAILABLE IN
THE BAPTIST *DISTINCTIVES* SERIES

KIFFIN, WILLIAM	A Sober Discourse of Right to Church-Communion. Wherein is proved by Scripture, the Example of the Primitive Times, and the Practice of All that have Professed the Christian Religion: That no Unbaptized person may be Regularly admitted to the Lord's Supper. (London: George Larkin, 1681).
KINGHORN, JOSEPH	Baptism, A Term of Communion. (Norwich: Bacon, Kinnebrook, and Co., 1816)
KINGHORN, JOSEPH	A Defense of "Baptism, A Term of Communion". In Answer To Robert Hall's Reply. (Norwich: Wilkin and Youngman, 1820).
GILL, JOHN	Gospel Baptism. A Collection of Sermons, Tracts, etc., on Scriptural Authority, the Nature of the New Testament Church and the Ordinance of Baptism by John Gill. (Paris, AR: The Baptist Standard Bearer, Inc., 2006).

CARSON, ALEXANDER	Ecclesiastical Polity of the New Testament. (Dublin: William Carson, 1856).
BOOTH, ABRAHAM	A Defense of the Baptists. A Declaration and Vindication of Three Historically Distinctive Baptist Principles. Compiled and Set Forth in the Republication of Three Books. Revised edition. (Paris, AR: The Baptist Standard Bearer, Inc., 2006).
BOOTH, ABRAHAM	Paedobaptism Examined on the Principles, Concessions, and Reasonings of the Most Learned Paedobaptists. With Replies to the Arguments and Objections of Dr. Williams and Mr. Peter Edwards. 3 volumes. (London: Ebenezer Palmer, 1829).
CARROLL, B. H.	*Ecclesia* - The Church. With an Appendix. (Louisville: Baptist Book Concern, 1903).
CHRISTIAN, JOHN T.	Immersion, The Act of Christian Baptism. (Louisville: Baptist Book Concern, 1891).
FROST, J. M.	Pedobaptism: Is It From Heaven Or Of Men? (Philadelphia: American Baptist Publication Society, 1875).
FULLER, RICHARD	Baptism, and the Terms of Communion; An Argument. (Charleston, SC: Southern Baptist Publication Society, 1854).
GRAVES, J. R.	Tri-Lemma: or, Death By Three Horns. The Presbyterian General Assembly Not Able To Decide This Question: "Is Baptism In The Romish Church Valid?" 1st Edition.

(Nashville: Southwestern Publishing House, 1861).

MELL, P.H.   Baptism In Its Mode and Subjects. (Charleston, SC: Southern Baptist Publications Society, 1853).

JETER, JEREMIAH B.   Baptist Principles Reset. Consisting of Articles on Distinctive Baptist Principles by Various Authors. With an Appendix. (Richmond: The Religious Herald Co., 1902).

PENDLETON, J.M.   Distinctive Principles of Baptists. (Philadelphia: American Baptist Publication Society, 1882).

THOMAS, JESSE B.   The Church and the Kingdom. A New Testament Study. (Louisville: Baptist Book Concern, 1914).

WALLER, JOHN L.   Open Communion Shown to be Unscriptural & Deleterious. With an introductory essay by Dr. D. R. Campbell and an Appendix. (Louisville: Baptist Book Concern, 1859).

For a complete list of current authors/titles, visit our internet site at:
www.standardbearer.org
or write us at:

he Baptist Standard Bearer, Inc.
NUMBER ONE IRON OAKS DRIVE • PARIS, ARKANSAS 72855
TEL # 479-963-3831   *FAX # 479-963-8083*
EMAIL: Baptist@centurytel.net   http://www.standardbearer.org

Thou hast given a standard to them that fear thee; that it may be displayed because of the truth. — Psalm 60:4

www.ingramcontent.com/pod-product-compliance
Lightning Source LLC
Chambersburg PA
CBHW021835220426

43663CB00005B/264